THE
GREAT AMERICAN
CHRISTMAS
ALMANAC

THE
GREAT AMERICAN
CHRISTMAS
ALMANAC

IRENA CHALMERS
AND FRIENDS

GENERAL EDITOR CARLOTTA KERWIN
DESIGNED BY HELENE BERINSKY

VIKING
STUDIO
BOOKS

EDITORIAL STAFF

Text Editor:
Jean Atcheson

Senior Writers:
Richard Atcheson
Robert Ostermann

Writers/Researchers:
Laura Bross
Mary Goodbody
Andrea Israel
Nancy Kipper
Pamela Mitchell
Lisa Sorensen

Design Assistant:
Rebecca Trahan

The author and editors extend their appreciation to Michael Fragnito, Vice President and Director, Publishing Operations, and Barbara Williams, Editor, Visual Books, at Viking Penguin, Inc., and to Rachel Bolton, Marketing Media Coordinator, Hallmark Cards, Inc., for their enthusiastic encouragement, unfailing support, and many-faceted contributions throughout the making of this book.

VIKING STUDIO BOOKS
Published by the Penguin Group
Viking Penguin Inc., 40 West 23rd Street,
New York, New York 10010, U.S.A.
Penguin Books Ltd, 27 Wrights Lane,
London W8 5TZ, England
Penguin Books Australia Ltd, Ringwood,
Victoria, Australia
Penguin Books Canada Ltd, 2801 John Street,
Markham, Ontario, Canada L3R 1B4
Penguin Books (N.Z.) Ltd, 182-190 Wairau Road,
Auckland 10, New Zealand

Penguin Books Ltd, Registered Offices:
Harmondsworth, Middlesex, England

First published in 1988 by Viking Penguin Inc.
Published simultaneously in Canada

Pages 313–315 constitute an extension of this
copyright page

Chalmers, Irena.
  The great American Christmas almanac.

  1. Christmas—United States.   I. Title.
GT4986.A1C45   1988   394.2'68282'0973   87-40104

Set in ITC Clearface with ITC Benguiat Bold Condensed
by Pica Graphics, Monsey, New York

Printed in the United States of America by Arcata
Graphics, Kingsport, Tennessee

For all who give and receive the joys of Christmas

CONTENTS

O LITTLE CHILD

The famous story of the birth of Jesus Christ was first told in the Gospels of Luke and Matthew, and after that, for nearly 2,000 years, writers and musicians, painters and sculptors have told new versions of the old story.

The accounts of Luke and Matthew here are from the first edition of the King James Bible, 1611, one of the versions brought to these shores by early settlers.

Sometime in the middle of the 19th century, an Ottawa Indian in Michigan carved the figures for the Nativity scene shown here. In their simplicity, these figures of Mary and Joseph at the crib, attended by beasts, simple people, and the exultant angels holding lights on high, tell the story with the root American bluntness of the virgin continent to which the tale was brought uncelebrated.

This book tells how well we have learned to tell the story, how heartily we have kept the feast ever since, and how happily we celebrate it today.

The Gospel According to St. Luke

CHAP. II

Nd it came to passe in those dayes, that there went out a decree from Cesar Augustus, that all the world should be taxed.

2   (And this taxing was first made when Cyrenius was governor of Syria)

3   And all went to bee taxed, every one into his owne citie.

4   And Joseph also went up from Galilee, out of the citie of Nazareth, into Judea, unto the citie of David, which is called Bethlehem, (because he was of the house and linage of David,)

5   To be taxed with Mary his espoused wife, being great with child.

6   And so it was, that while they were there, the dayes were accomplished that she should be delivered.

7   And she brought foorth her first borne sonne, and wrapped him in swaddling clothes, and laid him in a manger, because there was no roome for them in the Inne.

8   And there were in the same countrey shepheards abiding in ye field, keeping watch over their flocke by night.

9   And loe, the Angel of the Lord came upon them, and the glory of the Lord shone round about them, and they were sore afraid.

10   And the Angel said unto them, Feare not: For behold, I bring you good tidings of great joy, which shall be to all people.

11   For unto you is borne this day, in the citie of David, a Saviour, which is Christ the Lord.

12   And this shall be a signe unto you; yee shall find the babe wrapped in swadling clothes lying in a manger.

13   And suddenly there was with the Angel a multitude of the heavenly hoste praising God, and saying,

14   Glory to God in the highest, and on earth peace, good wil towards men.

15   And it came to passe, as the Angels were gone away from them into heaven, the shepheards said one to another, Let us now goe even unto Bethlehem, and see this thing which is come to passe, which the Lord hath made knowen unto us.

16   And they came with haste, and found Mary and Joseph, and the babe lying in a manger.

17   And when they had seene it, they made knowen abroad the saying, which was told them, concerning this child.

18   And all they that heard it, wondered at those things, which were tolde them by the shepheards.

19   But Mary kept all these things, and pondered them in her heart.

20   And the shepheards returned, glorifying & praising God for all the things that they had heard and seene, as it was told unto them.

The Gospel According to St. Matthew

CHAP. II

 ow when Jesus was borne in Bethlehem of Judea, in the dayes of Herod the king, behold, there came Wise men from the East to Hierusalem,

2   Saying, Where is he that is borne King of the Jewes: for we have seene his Starre in the East, and are come to worship him.

3   When Herod the king had heard these things, he was troubled, and all Hierusalem with him.

4 And when he had gathered all the chiefe Priests and Scribes of the people together, hee demanded of them where Christ should be borne.

5 And they said unto him, In Bethlehem of Judea: For thus it is written by the Prophet;

6 And thou Bethlehem in the land of Juda, art not the least among the Princes of Juda: for out of thee shall come a Governour, that shall rule my people Israel.

7 Then Herod, when he had privily called the Wise men, enquired of them diligently what time the Starre appeared:

8 And he sent them to Bethlehem, and said, Goe, and search diligently for the yong child, and when ye have found him, bring me word againe, that I may come and worship him also.

9 When they had heard the King, they departed, and loe, the Starre which they saw in the East, went before them, till it came and stood over where the young childe was.

10 When they saw the Starre, they reioyced with exceeding great ioy.

11 And when they were come into the house, they saw the yong child with Mary his mother, and fell downe, and worshipped him: and when they had opened their treasures, they presented unto him gifts, gold, and frankincense, and myrrhe.

12 And being warned of God in a dreame, that they should not returne to Herode, they departed into their owne countrey another way.

INTRODUCTION

It is deliciously nostalgic to look back on all our Christmases. No two are ever the same and all of us have memories as uniquely different as our own thumbprints.

I remember a year when I was completely, and entirely happily, alone the night before Christmas, living where I am now, in a brownstone in Manhattan. It had begun to snow gently. Big, flat, lazy flakes swirled softly down from the dark sky, settling on the pavement, white beneath the street lights. I got up from my armchair by the fire a few times to draw back the curtains and watch the snow, glad to be inside in the warm, cozy room. Though it was still quite early in the evening, there was hardly anyone about and the street outside was still, in that arrested, echoless silence snow brings with it.

I heard singing without, for a moment, being consciously aware of the music. Then, jumping up from my chair, I opened the curtains. There were nine or ten young people in the deserted street, singing carols together to the night sky, not even knowing anyone could hear them. They waved up at me as I stood watching them from the window. I felt as though we were all frozen in space and time. They finished singing and called up, asking

me to choose a carol. For a second or two I was unable to think of a single one. Then I asked for "Silent Night."

I will remember those clear voices on that calm, quiet, sweet silent night for as long as I live.

For a few years, we lived in a small suburban community in Long Island. It was an interesting neighborhood, a dormitory town for New York set around a bay, and it appealed to a wonderfully diverse group of people. Some had lived there for ages and others were more recent arrivals. Many were from other countries, mostly European. The family on one side of us was Austrian and neighbors on the other side were Jewish. There were French, Swedish, and Irish families, and a lot of mixtures. I, being British, formed one of these with my American Jewish husband.

Our first year, a quite spontaneous thing happened. I remember that we, the four of us and two dogs, went next door carrying a lighted ship's lantern that I had given my husband for his birthday a year or so before. We knocked on the door and sang a carol while we were waiting for our neighbors to answer it. I can't sing at all, so this must have been quite a daring thing to do—I don't remember now who even thought of it. I do remember, though, the delight in our friends' faces and how we all decided to go to the next house together and sing another carol. And so we did, and the snowball snowballed until there were perhaps 60 or more of us. We still talk about those times, with memories of little kids happy to be up late, dogs let off the leash, and flickering candles and lanterns and pockets full of warm gingerbread cookies one of the families had just baked.

The following year we organized things a little—though not too much—and when we got cold and had had enough, everyone came back to our house. We had a big pot of onion soup and some Beaujolais Nouveau—that was the "in" drink at that time—and everyone brought the traditional treats of their own country. I remember one of the older kids had made a lute, and she sat on the floor in front of the fire and the younger kids sang with her.

And I remember farther back still, to a time when my two children were very young indeed and we had almost no money.

I love balloons, and you could, and still can, get a lot of them for not very much. That Christmas we blew up hundreds of balloons. We put armfuls of dancing balloons on the children's beds while they were still sleeping. We let great colorful mountains of balloons fall over the floor. We tied balloons to the banisters and let them cascade all the way down the stairs until they reached the lighted Christmas tree at the foot.

It was a funny idea that didn't cost more than a dollar or two and a lot of breath, but years later, we all remember the bouncing, bobbing balloons. "That was one of the *best* Christmases," we say, smiling.

This is what THE GREAT AMERICAN CHRISTMAS ALMANAC is all about. It is a cherishing of our own unique memories of Christmas, a yearning remembrance of all the nostalgia of our childhoods, and a celebration of the yearly renewal of our own individual identity through our own special family traditions.

AMERICA
CELEBRATES

PROCLAMATIONS OF CHRISTMAS

From the Prayers of Pious Pilgrims to the Music of Modern Merrymakers

BY ROBERT OSTERMANN

Mention the very word *Christmas* and it immediately conjures up an image of laughter and pleasure, of color and sound, of music and food, and giving and sharing. And so it is hard to realize that for the early settlers here, this most loving and joyous of family festivals was not even on the calendar. What immense strides we have taken as a nation since those wrenching early years!

In the Beginning

Christmas did not exist for that group of colonists we have been taught to regard as the quintessential founders of the New World, the Pilgrim Fathers. Those solid Puritans hated Christmas celebrations. They loathed them as an abomination, a human invention without basis in Holy Scripture. Like their counterparts in England, Oliver Cromwell and the Roundheads, the Puritans of the Massachusetts Bay Colony were determined to expunge joy from human life.

There was no rest or festivity for them, not even to celebrate their safe arrival in the New World; Christmas Day was just business as usual. This attitude was reflected in a reconstructed version of the original log of Thomas Jones, master of the *Mayflower*, dated December 25, 1620:

> At anchor in Plymouth harbor; Christmas Day, but not observed by these colonists, they being opposed to all saints' days, etc. . . . A large party went ashore this morning to fell timber and begin building. They began to erect the first house about twenty feet square for their common use, to receive them and their goods.

Later these colonists made certain there would be no Christmas joy by declaring it illegal

Pilgrims nix parties at Plymouth, December 25, 1620.

THUNDER FROM MATHER

Here's how it was for the Reverend Cotton Mather, Puritan *par excellence*, who felt he had command of God's thunder. On Christmas Day, 1712, he warned his congregation:

"Can you in your *Conscience* think, that our *Holy Saviour* is honoured, by *Mad Mirth*, by long *Eating*, by hard *Drinking*, by lewd *Gaming*, by rude *Revelling*; by a *Mass* fit for none but a *Saturn* or a *Bacchus*, or the Night of a *Mahometan Ramadam*? You cannot possibly think so! At the *Birth* of our Saviour, we read, *A Multitude of the Heavenly Host was heard Praising of God*. But shall it be said, That at the *Birth* of our Saviour for which we owe as high Praises to God as they can do, we take the Time to Please the *Hellish Legions*, and to do Actions that have much more of *Hell* than of *Heaven* in them?"

"Compliments of the season!"

Other Voices

Fortunately, a sturdy resistance to such institutional restraints ran deep in the American grain right from the start and the Puritans' writ did not extend as far as they—secure in their solemn righteousness—may have believed. Even though the Puritans dominated New England, as the spirit of austerity ruled Quaker Pennsylvania, their influence was steadily diluted by immigrants with different religious orientations who believed wholeheartedly in Christmas and observed it according to their denominational and ethnic traditions. And in New York, the Dutch followed the maxim "live and let live," celebrating Christmas with feasting and merriment and looking with good humor—and maybe some amazement—on their dour neighbors to the north.

But it was primarily the Southern colonists who turned their faces resolutely against the harsh, anti-Christmas spirit of doctrinaire New England, leavening it with their still-continuing traditions of grace and hospitality. In fact, the very first Christmas celebration in America, according to the records we have, predated the arrival of the Pilgrims. It occurred in 1607 in Jamestown, Virginia, where 40 survivors of the 100 original settlers tried to raise their somber, uncertain spirits by saluting the birth of Christ in their small chapel.

to celebrate this holiday that had never made the record books. In 1659 the Puritans of the American colonies—driven by dogmatic rectitude—passed this law:

> Whosoever shall be found observing any such day as Christmas and the like, either by forbearing labor, feasting, or any other way upon such account as aforesaid, every such person so offending shall pay for each offense five shillings as a fine to the country.

Southern revels, halls bedecked—and Washington won't dance. But the teenage crowd don't mind if *they* do.

And the following year, their odds of survival having improved, they feasted and rejoiced in the camp of one of the Indian chieftain Powhatan's sons. Captain John Smith wrote in his diary that his hardy group was "never more merrie, nor fedd on more plentie of good oysters, fish, flesh, wild foule and good bread; nor never had better fires in England than in the warm smokie houses."

Perhaps because their history was grounded in hardship, struggle, and uncertainty, Southerners were able to maintain a reasonable balance between observing Christmas as a sacred time and as an interval of rejoicing and relaxation. They played and worshiped without any sense of a conflict between the two.

As the 1766 *Virginia Almanack* versed it:

Now Christmas comes, 'tis fit that we
Should feast and sing, and merry be:
Keep open house, let fidlers play.

A fig for cold, sing care away;
And may they who thereat repine,
On brown bread and on small beer dine.

The radical division between those who would live Christmas up and those who would play it down continued for many years, although a movement toward a more lenient Christmas observance gradually began to emerge.

The Spice of Life

If the Puritans had been able to see beyond their several dogmatisms they might have known that their suppression of Christmas celebrations and joy was about as durable as an echo. Never mind the vast westward sweep of the continent, which they could never hope to dominate as Cromwell had dominated tiny England. There were also the diverse Christmas beliefs and customs imported and highly prized by subsequent immigrants—mostly from England, Holland, and Germany—who planted in American soil the potent seeds of the social melting pot the United States would one day become.

But we should not be surprised to learn that not all Christmas customs touched the heart with their charm, innocence, and bountiful spirits. Some were downright loony, like skits from a Marx Brothers film; others, bizarre and fanciful; still others, inspired by the hope of influencing future events. All are what we today, in our sublime enlightenment, would call superstitions.

How, for example, would you (husband or wife, equal partners in a competitive world) act on the belief that whoever first brings the Christmas holly into the house will rule the home during the following year?

Less threatening today is the assumption that if a young man saw a redheaded girl at Christmastime he should flee for his life, lest he be pursued by redheads (a terrible fate!) throughout the year ahead. And in quarters that retained a durable respect for the Celtic custom of "first-footing," steps were taken to ensure that the first person who crossed the threshold after midnight on New Year's Eve would bring a piece of coal in hand and have coal-black hair.

Deep in the hill country along the border between South and North, people filled their cats' saucers to the brim with milk to keep them pacified, because a meowing cat on Christmas Day portended bad luck. For the same reason, they carried no fire, coal or matches on Christmas. On the other hand, God help you if your fire went out on the 25th, for that would assure that evil spirits would populate your home.

And, to haunt the feminists among us, women stayed indoors on that day of days because they believed their neighbors would have ill fortune if the first person they saw was a woman, or their first visitor turned out to be such a *femme fatale*.

CHRISTMAS WITH THE SHAKERS

December 25, 1899
Christmas Day

Elder Joseph called soon after breakfast to say the Ministry Sisters would be here about 8 oclock and would attend meeting with us.

We had a very excellent meeting and then a little visit with the brethren. did not stay to dinner . . .
P.M. We commenced our entertainment about 2 oclock. G. D., Lottie and the 4 girls came from the south, all of our family except Susie and Ella were in. Every thing passed off pleasantly most everyone had something to read speak or sing. Santa (Earl) came down the chimney with pop corn etc. and we had a very enjoyable time. In the dining room we all partook of fruit and hickory nut cake and cheese, and cocoa.

A Shaker's diary, possibly from
Pittsfield, Massachusetts

"Peace on earth, the Angel sung,
and the joyful heavens rung,
Let our hearts repeat again,
Peace on earth good will to men,
For a victory has been won,
And a kingdom is begun,
Bondage sin and woe shall cease,
Hail! all hail the reign of peace."

Millennium Praises
December 25, 1862

19

Christmas Collides with History

Given the centuries that we, or others like us, have occupied this land, it is probably no more than coincidence that a number of significant events, moments, and people have come to us during the Christmas season. And yet the number is so high that one is tempted to conclude there is more at work here than mere chance.

For instance, what is to be made of the pivotal excursion George Washington made across the Delaware River on the night of December 25, 1776? The scene, depicted in giddy colors, hangs in schoolrooms all across the United States. There's the Father of Our Country, square-jawed as Kirk Douglas, leading his troops across the icy waters to attack the Hessians quartered on the Trenton side.

Why on this night, of all possible nights? Because, it is now widely believed, Washington assumed that the Germans would be enjoying their Christmas revels and therefore be careless

Christmas at Valley Forge: hard cheese, hard tack; hot soup, cold toes; slim wintry cheer, that year.

about such mundane matters as watches and perimeter patrols.

Then consider a diary entry for Thursday, December 25, 1777, recounting the experience of George Washington's troops at Valley Forge:

> Most of the Army is still in tents when it ought to be in Hutts. The poor sick suffer much in tents this cold weather. But we do treat them differently from what they used to be at home. We give them Mutton and Grogg and a Capital Medicine once in a while, to start the Disease from its foundations at once. We avoid Piddling, Pills, Powders, Bolus Linctus's Cordials & all such insignificant matters whose powders are only rendered important by causing the patient to vomit up his money instead of his disease. But very few of our sick men die.

In truth, the hardships were terrible, yet, by enduring, the sturdy soldiers of the colonies would advance yet another step toward the ultimate British surrender at Yorktown.

Almost a century later, on Christmas Day, 1864, General Sherman, he of the infamous march through Georgia, sent a telegram to Abraham Lincoln to delight his President and Commander-in-Chief. It said, in part: "I beg to present to you as a Christmas gift the city of Savannah." One wonders how Savannah felt about being so rudely dumped down the White House chimney.

Soldiers, in this regard as in so many others, seem to be less cynical than their generals. There are countless stories about U.S. fighting men striving to make Christmas real for the children in lands stricken by our wars. Their compassionate spirit was movingly commemorated on the cover of the *Saturday Evening Post* dated December 22, 1917, which showed a doughboy offering protection and largesse to a small, frightened girl crouched at his feet.

Churchill's World War II Christmas message from the White House is proof that wartime leaders can turn the season into imperishable eloquence. "Let the children have their night of fun. Let the gifts of Father Christmas delight their play. Let us grown-ups share to the full in

CHRISTMAS ON THE PLAINS

Sometimes I think our Christmas on the frontier was a greater event to us than to any one in the states. We all had to do so much to make it a success . . .

One universal custom was for all of us to spend all the time we could together. All day long the officers were running in and out of every door, the "wish you Merry Christmas" rang out over the parade ground after any man who was crossing to attend to some duty and had not shown up among us. We usually had a sleigh ride and everyone sang and laughed as we sped over the country where there were no neighbors to be disturbed by our gaiety. If it was warm enough there poured out of garrison a cavalcade vehemently talking, gesticulating, laughing or humming bars of Christmas carols . . .

The feast of the day over, we adjourned from dinner to play some games of our childhood in order to make the states and our homes seem a little nearer. Later in the evening, when the music came up from the band quarters, we all went to the house of the commanding officer to dance.

With a garrison full of perfectly healthful people with a determination to be merry, notwithstanding the isolated life and utterly dreary surroundings, the holidays were made something to look forward to the whole year round.

Elizabeth Bacon Custer
Widow of General George
    Armstrong Custer
Undated

their unstinted pleasures before we again turn to the stern task and the formidable years that lie before us. And so, in God's mercy, a Merry Christmas to you all."

And President Eisenhower, not always acclaimed for *his* eloquence, touched a deep chord by broadcasting a Christmas message to the world from the Atlas, America's first orbiting satellite, on December 19, 1958:

"This is the President of the United States speaking. Through the marvels of scientific advance my voice is coming to you from a satellite circling in outer space. My message is a simple one. Through this unique means I convey to you and to all mankind America's wish for peace on earth and good will toward men everywhere."

And, going from macro to micro, how about all those notable (or merely notorious) Americans who were born on the hallowed days of December 24 and 25? Among them: Clara Barton (1821), founder of the American Red Cross; Kid Ory (1886), key exponent of New Orleans jazz; Howard Hughes, the reclusive millionaire (1905); Humphrey Bogart (1899), the unforgettable movie "tough guy"; Robert Joffrey (1930), founder of the Joffrey Ballet. The merest sampling.

There will probably always be voices raised to protest the commercialization of Christmas. But there is as much space in this vast land for those who want to keep it as a holy day as for those who want to rejoice in the holiday. This freedom is one of the cornerstones of our nation. Let the message of Christmas enter every heart, and as Tiny Tim was heard to say, "God bless us, every one!"

Robert Ostermann is a financial writer whose avocation is the history of American culture.

Somewhere around or about the year of 1810, John Lewis Krimmel of Philadelphia pulled out his pencil to illustrate with line and wash a noisy family gathered around their table-top Christmas tree. Fashion has changed since then, but the sentiments remain much the same.

THANKS FOR THE MEMORY

It was in 1941 that Bob Hope started taking a Christmas show on the road to entertain American troops at home and overseas. His basic formula: a big band, some busty starlets, and his own acerbic wit. In Korea and Vietnam, Hope's troupe tried to bring a balm of light relief to the stark realities of war. "The sight packed enough emotion into this unsentimental frame to last a lifetime," Hope said of Christmas Day 1957, when 7,000 GIs filled Korea's Bayonet Bowl. Generations of American fighting men far from home will thank him to the end of their days for those memories.

Home for Christmas

This is meeting time again. Home is the magnet. The winter land roars and hums with the eager speed of return journeys. The dark is noisy and bright with late-night arrivals—doors thrown open, running shadows on snow, open arms, kisses, voices and laughter, laughter at everything and nothing. Inarticulate, giddying and confused are those original minutes of being back again. The very familiarity of everything acts like shock. Contentment has to be drawn in slowly, steadyingly, in deep breaths— there is so much of it. We rely on home not to change, and it does not, wherefore we give thanks. Again Christmas: abiding point of return. Set apart by its mystery, mood and magic, the season seems in a way to stand outside time. All that is dear, that is lasting, renews its hold on us: we are home again. . . .

This glow of Christmas, has it not in it also the gold of a harvest? "They shall return with joy, bringing their sheaves with them." To the festival, to each other, we bring in wealth. More to tell, more to understand, more to share. Each we have garnered in yet another year; to be glad, to celebrate to the full, we are come together. How akin we are to each other, how speechlessly dear and one in the fundamentals of being, Christmas shows us. No other time grants us, quite, this vision—round the tree or gathered before the fire we perceive anew, with joy, one another's faces. And each time faces come to mean more.

Is it not one of the mysteries of life that life should, after all, be so simple? Yes, as simple as Christmas, simple as this. Journeys through the dark to lighted door, arms open. Laughter-smothered kisses, kiss-smothered laughter. And blessedness in the heart of it all. Here are the verities, all made gay with tinsel! Dear, silly Christmas-card saying and cracker mottoes— let them speak! Or, since still we cannot speak, let us sing! Dearer than memory, brighter than expectation is the ever returning *now* of Christmas. Why else, each time we greet its return, should happiness ring out in us like a peal of bells?

Elizabeth Bowen
Home for Christmas, 1955

The only real blind person at Christmastime is he who has not Christmas in his heart.

Helen Keller
Ladies' Home Journal
December, 1906

CHRISTMAS TONIGHT

Everywhere, everywhere,
Christmas tonight!
Christmas in lands of the palm
tree and vine;

Christmas where snow-peaks stand
solemn and white,
Christmas where cornfields lie
sunny and bright.

—*PHILLIPS BROOKS*

It is Christmas Eve at Waikiki, and Mary Margaret and Bill Aiton, now in their 80s, are at St. Clement's for the midnight Eucharist. In the crowded church, which is lavishly decorated with orchids and poinsettias, many congregants of every racial origin are wearing the season's traditional bright red muumuu. As the organ peals, Mary Margaret and Bill rise with the congregation to sing the Doxology—in Hawaiian.

On Christmas Day, the couple will entertain their family with a traditional mainland Christmas dinner at their house, poised on the slope of an extinct volcano. Before dinner, they will all have a nice swim in the solar-heated pool. "Sometimes," says Mary Margaret, "I think it would be nice to see some snow. But we feel fortunate living here."

On Christmas Eve in Santa Fe, the town is ablaze with light from thousands of bags filled with sand and lighted candles and hundreds of brilliant bonfires from wood piled three feet high.

Theo and Peter Raven can see the broad spectacle from their house on a plateau overlooking the town, and they always drive down to take a closer look and some deep breaths. "The smell of the piñon saturates the air," says Theo, "and it's as if you'd died and gone to heaven."

In the Aleut village of Old Harbor, Alaska, the Russian Orthodox Church of the Three Saints begins its Christmas Eve service in the afternoon, with (as customary) the men's pews on one side and the women's on the other: Among the men is Mike Rostad, who has just flown 50 miles from Kodiak (there is no road to Old Harbor) to celebrate Christmas with friends in this isolated place.

As the congregation sings hymns in Russian and Aleut, altar boys twirl six-pointed tinsel stars, three to five feet in diameter, on wide-looping chains. "The Orthodox church relives the birth of Christ as if it were happening today," Mike says. "It's very jubilant."

By 7:00 P.M. on Christmas Eve, the Grimsbo family of Grand Rapids, Minnesota, is just about to sit down to their premier Christmas celebration of the season. Outside, a heavy snow covers the potato fields that have been worked by generations of Grimsbo men.

On the table are *julbockar* (Swedish straw reindeer), and high above the heads of the seated celebrants, angels spin in the heat waves that rise from triple-decker brass candlesticks. *Lutfisk*—dried cod with drawn butter or cream sauce—is the main dish, and with it comes venison sausage, potato sausage, roasted beef spareribs, potate *lefse* (flat bread spread with butter), green beans, and beets. For dessert: cardamom-flavored tea cakes, sugar-dusted *fattigmanns*, rosettes, *sandkakers*, rum balls, and fruit soup, made with dried fruits and pearl tapioca.

On Christmas Eve at the Mission in Nashville, a group of men and women are dishing up a holiday dinner to the poor and handing out presents to people who would otherwise have no Christmas. Later in the evening, they will stop off at their favorite pub before celebrating Christmas Eve together at someone's home.

"We call ourselves Christmas waifs." says organizer Robert Wynne, a writer for the TV show "Nashville Now." "Most of my friends are in TV and music," he says, "and most are divorced. Nobody spends the holidays with family anymore, so we do something different every year, together. We've all gone from tremendous bomb-outs in our lives to significant victories. We're all between 30 and 40 and we're settling down now, being less self-indulgent and more benevolent."

Christmas Eve service for the Lewis family of Wayland, Massachusetts, is at the Unitarian Church, an early 19th-century frame "Christmas card" church, on this occasion bright with lighted candles and festooned with aromatic pine boughs. The choir sings selections from the *Messiah* and carols are sung by all.

On Christmas morning, stockings are the first order of business. "Everyone gets a stocking," says Martha Lewis. "A big felt stocking appliquéd with a snowman or a sleigh or an angel. Every one is different." And every one has a fat tangerine in the toe.

Three generations of Lewises take a long walk through open fields and woods before Christmas dinner which, for them, is always a hearty joint of meat. And afterward they play board games and card games and listen to recordings of baroque music—and always go to bed without picking up the crumpled Christmas wrappings. That is traditional, too. "My mother is a meticulous housekeeper," says Martha, "but never on Christmas Day."

BE IT EVER SO HUMBLE

Historians tell us that George and Martha Washington always had a good time on Christmas Day, filling their Mount Vernon home with guests and considerable merrymaking. Thomas Jefferson liked to play the fiddle for his family and friends, while Franklin D. Roosevelt entertained his children by reading aloud from Dickens's *A Christmas Carol*. The Kennedys and the Carters and the Reagans scattered from Cape Cod to Plains to California for the holidays, but some part of a presidential Christmas is always celebrated in our nation's capital. Many people will be surprised to learn that the holiday food preferred by the first families does not consist of caviar and truffles and, in fact, is remarkably like the meals all families share together.

At the first real White House party in 1811 Dolly Madison introduced her famous cinnamon-laced eggnog. FDR enjoyed a glass of bubbly with his chicken sandwiches and Jimmy Carter looked forward to a Southern Christmas breakfast that included country ham, eggs, and grits with cheese. And at a December 25th dinner dance Eleanor Roosevelt served eggs, sausages, and raw onions—obviously unconcerned with any face-to-face effects on those under the mistletoe.

The Great Seal of the United States

For most of us, the idea of being invited for Christmas dinner with the President is as remote as having igloo pie at the North Pole. Yet we are endlessly fascinated to know what foods the first families serve and always delighted to discover that they eat in very much the same way as the rest of us. Indeed, glancing over some of these recipes, it seems we may even be eating better than some of the folks who hobnob with kings and presidents, prime ministers and pop stars. Did Harry and Bess Truman *really* include toasted Triscuits on their menu? Be that as it may, sharing these recipes is one way we can vicariously invite ourselves to the President's table.

At Hyde Park: FDR joins daughter Anna and a fair slew of grandchildren.

Franklin Delano Roosevelt's Roast Duck with Potato Dressing

1 onion, coarsely chopped
4 tablespoons butter
¾ cup dry bread crumbs
1 cup mashed potatoes
1 egg
1½ teaspoons salt
½ teaspoon pepper
1 4- to 5-pound duckling

Sauté the onion in the butter until it starts to brown. Add bread crumbs, and sauté another minute. Then add potatoes, egg, and seasonings. Stir together until well blended; then stuff the duckling. Roast in 350-degree oven approximately 2 hours. Serve with a side dish of applesauce. Serves 4.

A Treasury of White House Cooking

Bess and Harry S. Truman's Christmas Dinner

THURSDAY, DECEMBER 25, 1952

Oysters on Shells

Clear Soup with Egg Balls
Celery Hearts • Assorted Olives
Melba Toast

Roast Stuffed Turkey
Sage Dressing • Giblet Dressing
Small Link Sausage Garnishing
Cranberry Sauce
Candied Sweet Potatoes • Spinach Goldenrod
Artichoke Hearts In Lemon Drawn Butter
Rolls

Stuffed Endive & Cress Salad • French Dressing
Toasted Triscuits

Plum Pudding • Hard Sauce

Nuts • Candies • Demi-Tasse

"Give-'em-hell" Harry, Bess, and Margaret Truman pose on the north portico of the White House.

Ike and Mamie spend a golfing Christmas.

Dwight and Mamie Eisenhower's Stone Crab Bisque

(For 8 people)

If you cannot find stone crabs on the market, use regular crab meat.

Using fresh stone crab I [the White House chef] cook enough to make 1½ cups crab meat. If you use canned crab meat you will substitute chicken consommé for the fish stock which I make by cooking my stone crabs in salt water to which I have added carrots, celery, onion, thyme, bay leaf, and fish seasoning which you can buy at the store. Cook 25 minutes for fresh crabs, 10 minutes for canned. Now I make a *roux* of 3 tablespoons butter and 3 tablespoons flour, adding 4½ cups chicken consommé or stone crab stock. Next, I add 2½ cups cream just before taking off. Then I pass the bisque through the blender, adding half of the crab meat only. I strain to make sure that there are no little bits of shell, of course, before I put the liquid in the blender. When the bisque is nice and creamy, I take it off the blender, add ⅓ cup dry bread crumbs, the remaining ¾ cup of crab meat, and serve with a sprinkling of chopped parsley and little croutons which I have fried in butter to golden brown.

White House Chef

MARTHA WASHINGTON'S GREAT CAKE

Take 40 eggs and divide the whites from the yolks, then beat them to a froth. Then work 4 pounds butter to a creamy state, and put the egg whites into it, a tablespoon at a time, until it is well worked. Then add 4 pounds (8 cups) sugar, finely powdered, to the butter mixture. Then add the egg yolks, 5 pounds flour, and 5 pounds fruit. Add ½ ounce (1 tablespoon) mace, one nutmeg, ½ pint of wine, and some French brandy. Two hours will bake it.

The Presidents' Cookbook

Jacqueline and John F. Kennedy's Christmas Eve Dinner

Drinks

Hot Chocolate and Christmas Cookies

Billibi (Cream of Mussel Soup)
Turkey with Chestnut Stuffing and Gravy
Creamed Celery • String Beans
Endive and Bibb Lettuce Salad
Pepperidge Farm Rolls

Champagne

Praline Ice Cream on Holly Leaves
Rum Chocolate Cake

Café Filtre or Medaglia d'Oro Espresso

Lyndon and Lady Bird Johnson's Deer Meat Sausage

One-half deer
One-half hog
25 ounces of salt
20 ounces of black pepper
8 ounces of red pepper
2 ounces of sage

Mix together for 200 pounds of sausage. Now, for how to prepare this delicacy:

BAKED DEER MEAT SAUSAGE

Place uncut sausages in a 400-degree oven, in an open pan with a small amount of water. Cook 10 minutes on one side; then turn and repeat on the other side. Slice in inch-long pieces and serve.

A Treasury of White House Cooking

Jack and Jackie give a pre-Christmas staff party.

Pat Nixon's Christmas Tree Cookies

4 cups sifted flour
⅔ teaspoon baking soda
¼ teaspoon each cinnamon, allspice, ginger, and mace
8 ounces honey
2 tablespoons dark corn syrup
½ cup sugar
1 egg
Colored sugar or melted chocolate to decorate

Preheat oven to 350 degrees. Combine flour, baking soda, and spices. Blend honey, syrup, sugar, and egg. Combine the dry ingredients with the honey mixture, and roll dough to ¼-inch thickness. Cut into desired shapes with cookie cutters. Brush with water, and sprinkle with colored sugar; or after baking, dip in melted chocolate. Bake 10 to 12 minutes, or until firm. Makes 50 to 60.

A Treasury of White House Cooking

GEORGE WASHINGTON'S EGGNOG

1 quart milk, 1 quart cream, 1 dozen eggs, 1 dozen tablespoons sugar, 1 pint brandy, ½ pint rye whiskey, ¼ pint Jamaica or New England rum, ¼ pint sherry.

Mix liquor first. Separate yolks and whites of eggs. Add sugar to beaten yolks. Mix well. Add liquor mixture, drop by drop at first, slowly beating. Beat whites of eggs until stiff and fold slowly into mixture. Let set in cool place several days.

Christmas in the White House

Rosalynn Carter's Cranberry Ring Mold

2 envelopes unflavored gelatin
½ cup cold water
¾ cup boiling water
¼ cup fresh lemon juice
2 cans (1 pound each) jellied cranberry
  sauce
½ cup cold water
½ teaspoon bottled horseradish
2 to 3 dashes liquid red pepper seasoning
¼ teaspoon salt

In a large mixing bowl, sprinkle gelatin over ½ cup cold water to soften. Add boiling water and stir until the gelatin is dissolved. Stir in lemon juice.

Combine cranberry sauce and ½ cup cold water in a saucepan. Stir, then beat with whisk until it is smooth; do not allow to boil. Add horseradish, hot pepper seasoning, and salt. Stir in gelatin mixture. Pour into a 6-cup ring mold that has been rinsed with cold water. Chill about 4 hours, or until firm. Unmold onto round serving plate.

Serves 6 to 8.

Christmas in the White House

Ron and Nancy celebrate Christmas Eve in the family quarters at the White House.

Nancy Reagan's Monkey Bread

¾ ounce yeast or 1 package dry yeast
1 to 1¼ cups milk
3 eggs
3 tablespoons sugar
1 teaspoon salt
3½ cups flour
6 ounces butter, room temperature
½ pound melted butter
two 9-inch ring molds

In bowl, mix yeast with part of milk until dissolved. Add 2 eggs, beat. Mix in dry ingredients. Add remaining milk a little at a time, mixing thoroughly. Cut in butter until blended. Knead dough, let rise 1 to 1½ hours until double in size. Knead again, let rise 40 minutes.

Roll dough onto floured board, shape into a log. Cut log into 28 pieces of equal size. Shape each piece of dough into ball, roll in melted butter. Use half of the pieces in each of the buttered, floured molds. Place 7 balls in each mold, leaving space between. Place remaining balls on top, spacing evenly. Let dough rise in mold. Brush tops with remaining egg. Bake in preheated oven at 375 degrees until golden brown. Approximately 15 minutes.

The White House

BENJAMIN HARRISON'S CHRISTMAS TURKEY

Turkey **Sherry**
English walnuts

The turkey should be cooped up and fed well some time before Christmas. Three days before it is slaughtered it should have an English walnut forced down its throat three times a day, a glass of sherry once a day. The meat will be deliciously tender, and have a fine nutty flavor.

The Presidents' Cookbook

A
KALEIDOSCOPE
OF CHRISTMAS

JINGLE-BELL ROCK!

From the Mountains, to the Prairies, to the Oceans White with Foam

BY ANDREA ISRAEL

From coast to coast we celebrate this beloved holiday with events designed to bring the spirit of Christmas past, present, and future into the season. An American Christmas, as captured in the picture portfolio that follows, is at once a 50-state send-up of a favorite holiday and a smorgasbord of individual celebrations that belong to a land that pulsates with diversity.

Tradition reigns supreme, but with a novel twist: In every state one can find Nativity pageants—Lilliputian ones under a tree on the common or bigger-than-life spectacles launched in drive-ins. Parades on water as well as on land abound and festivals of lights lure airline pilots away from their flight paths to observe cities glittering in the night like multicolored stars. Trees are decorated by celebrities and local merchants alike—and even turned into singing human pyramids. Early settlers' log cabins, resplendent antebellum mansions, and simple adobe huts are adorned with garlands and wreaths.

There are madrigal feasts, crafts shows, productions of *A Christmas Carol* and choruses singing the *Messiah*—from the local Baptist church to professional choirs of over 200 voices. On Fifth Avenue in New York, men and women wear furs and camel's hair overcoats to sit on hard wooden pews for Midnight Mass in St. Patrick's Cathedral, while in New Mexico's Mexican-Indian churches, worshipers spread Navajo blankets on earthen floors.

Like other Americans, the North Pole's man of the hour knows that anything goes. In Texas, where he is Pancho Claus, he dons a ten-gallon Stetson. In Louisiana, he answers to Papa Noel. In California, his sunglasses match the black belt of his familiar red outfit.

It is the contrasts, the combinations of events both outlandish and serenely spiritual which comprise an American Christmas. One can plant one's feet firmly on Alaskan tundra and stare at the natural Yuletide blessing of the aurora borealis or stand on a New York City street corner and see the Empire State Building twinkle with red and green lights.

When all is said and done, just about everyone can find some special way of summoning up a Merry Christmas. For where else but in America could you celebrate a Norwegian Christmas in Milan and still be in Minnesota?

Kansas City's Country Club Plaza is outlined with tiny lights: enchanting.

A nation's hopes light up on the National Tree as the President throws the switch.

For 32 years, Tiffany's Christmas windows have created jeweled dreams in miniature.

Bethlehem, Pennsylvania-style, goes modern.

The Bracebridge Dinner caps the celebration at Yosemite's Ahwahnee Hotel.

Brave soldiers lend dash to Disneyland's Christmas splash.

In Boston, the stockings are hung on a clothesline with care, in hopes that some customers soon will be there.

On Maui, Santa comes from the sea.

Macy's in New York: From a retail view, this is where it all started.

At Longwood Gardens in Pennsylvania, a world of bright dreams emerges from the winter landscape, a world of giant sugar plums dipped in light.

Every December, triumph of the tutus: *The Nutcracker* is danced by the New York City Ballet and some 200 other companies nationwide.

Santa does a Jingle Bell schuss!

As always, Salvationists burnish brass.

From tree to tip, 30 Rock is unequaled
in urban splendor.

Silver out of the dark: A yacht joins Fort Lauderdale's Holiday Boat Parade as half a million spectators watch.

Four glittering elkhorn arches punctuate Christmas displays at Jackson Hole, Wyoming.

At The Metropolitan Museum in New York, seraphim soar.

The village of Leavenworth, Washington, twinkles in the Cascades' Icicle Valley, a bit of Bavaria on the Pacific rim.

Brilliance on the banks of the Cane River at Natchitoches, Louisiana.

A Christmas on Temple Square in Salt Lake City resounds with the music of the Mormon Tabernacle Choir.

At New York's South Street Seaport, a living Christmas tree bursts into song.

Santa's carriage clops across the cobbles on Nantucket Island.

Still, snowy, and decked with wreaths: Weston, Vermont, says "Home for Christmas."

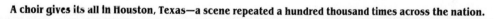

A choir gives its all in Houston, Texas—a scene repeated a hundred thousand times across the nation.

Oh, to be in Chicago, Chicago . . .

Season's Celebrations

ALABAMA

Christmas at DeSoto Caverns

What's larger than a football field, higher than a 12-story building, and able to conjure up Christmas spirit in a single sound? The Great Onyx Cathedral, which reverberates with seasonal music and a light show. Contact: DeSoto Caverns Park, Childersburg AL (205) 378-7252

Bellingrath Gardens

Ten thousand red and white poinsettias, some up to six feet tall, bloom in the Bellingrath Gardens at Christmastime. The highlight is a 12-foot Christmas tree fashioned from the plants. Contact: Bellingrath Gardens, Theodore AL (205) 973-2217

Annual Glenn Miller Christmas Concert

"Joy to the World" and other favorites swing with be-bop and big band sound. Contact: Montgomery's Civic Center, Montgomery AL (205) 861-6992

ALASKA

Christmas in Sitka

Imagine yourself by the Volga River as six-pointed wooden stars

Carolers sing on cue and occasionally on key.

adorned with colored paper and bells are twirled during the Russian Orthodox Christmas Eve church choir procession. Also: Lighted boat parade in the harbor. Contact: Sitka Convention & Visitors Bureau, Sitka AK (907) 747-5940

Governor's Open House

Even politics becomes personalized at this once-a-year opportunity to greet the governor with a Merry Christmas handshake. A house tour is included. Contact: Alaska State Chamber of Commerce, Juneau AK (907) 586-2323

ARIZONA

Phoenix Christmas

What do you do with a ton of sand, 700 candles, and paper bags? Make *luminarias*! Join the spectacular hike, *luminaria* lighting, and carol sing, 1¼ miles up Squaw Peak. Six thousand similar candles also glow at the Desert Botanical Garden on Arizona *Luminaria* Night.

On a cooler note, a six-foot ice angel adorns Civic Plaza as a 52-foot human Christmas tree sings. Contact: Phoenix & Valley of the Sun Convention & Visitors Bureau, Phoenix AZ (602) 254-6500

It takes 5,700 feet of evergreens to dress the Georgetown Mall for Christmas in Washington, DC.

ARKANSAS

Ozark Christmas
Toe-tapping mountain music sets the tone for a regional country Christmas. Contact: Ozark Folk Center, Mountain View AR (501) 372-4000

Toys Designed by Artists Exhibition
American artists compete in creating under-the-tree fantasies for this show, touted to be the only one of its kind. Contact: Arkansas Art Center, Little Rock AR (501) 372-4000

CALIFORNIA

World's Tallest Living Christmas Tree
The hook-and-ladders aren't putting out a fire, they're putting up 900 bulbs on a 150-foot Sitka spruce in California's giant redwood country. What size are the presents underneath? Contact: Ferndale Chamber of Commerce, Ferndale CA (707) 786-4000

Christmas in the Adobes
Vibrant Mexican decorations— huge radishes carved into people and animal shapes, piñatas, candelabras, and Nativity scenes— abound in Monterey, where 12 sand-colored adobe homes are opened to the public. But the American Victorian Christmas is recaptured also, as are Scottish traditions re-created in the adobe house once occupied by Robert

Louis Stevenson. Contact: Christmas in the Adobes, Monterey CA (408) 649-7118

Hollywood Christmas Parade
Santa "takes a screen test" and parades with some 100 movie and television stars that have ranged from Gene Autry to Angie Dickinson and Stevie Wonder. Over 20 floats glide along Hollywood and Sunset Boulevards as a million viewers cheer. Contact: Hollywood Christmas Parade, Hollywood CA (213) 469-2337

The Bracebridge Dinner
Washington Irving's *Sketch Book* serves as the inspiration for a four-hour dinner and pageant at the Ahwahnee Hotel in Yosemite National Park. Festivities include trumpeters, singers, and a Lord of Misrule with a pet bear. Reservations are requested a year in advance by some 10,000 people, and guests are selected by lot every January. Contact: Yosemite National Park, CA (209) 252-4848

COLORADO

Rocky Mountain Christmas
Every Christmas is different at Denver's opulent Brown Palace Hotel, but each year the lobby and atrium balconies become a gossamer Christmas fantasy of greenery and lights. A host of holiday happenings is launched when the year's debutantes sweep down the curved staircase to their

Yuletide ball. Contact: Christmas in the City, Denver CO (303) 534-6161

CONNECTICUT

Mystic Seaport Christmas
Hear tall ships rock and creak, and climb aboard a lantern-lit whaler. Walk along village pathways guided by *luminarias* on your way to old captains' homes decked out for Christmas. Contact: Mystic Seaport Museum, Mystic CT (203) 572-0711

Huck Finn's & Uncle Tom's Christmas
Walk through Mark Twain's and Harriet Beecher Stowe's homes decorated with Victorian trimmings. Contact: Nook Farm, Hartford CT (203) 525-9317

The Second Continental Light Dragoons Christmas
With the firing of muskets and the Yuletide hail of Revolutionary soldiers returning home, Christmas as it was 200 years ago is re-enacted. Contact: Putnam Memorial State Park, Redding CT (203) 938-2285

Santa's Trolley Ride
Bells clang, whistles blow, and pistons rise up and down while jolly "ho-ho-ho's" signal the giving of presents to visiting children. Contact: Shoreline Trolley Museum, East Haven CT (203) 467-6927

Christmas Village
The North Pole re-created:
Santa's parlor is complete with
giant record books of good and
bad children and elves hammer-
ing away in a toy shop. Contact:
Parks & Recreation Department,
Torrington CT   (203) 489-2274

DELAWARE

Farmer's Christmas
How're you gonna keep 'em down
on the farm? It's easy in this reconstructed, self-sufficient farm
where Christmas is celebrated
with decorations made of natural
materials, craft demonstrations
true to the 1800s, music, and
warm cider. Also: Lantern-lit
tours of the old farmhouse, blacksmith shop, schoolhouse, gran-
ary, and other historic buildings.
Contact: Delaware Agricultural
Museum, Dover DE
(302) 734-1618

DISTRICT OF COLUMBIA

Pageant of Peace
It's "Capitol!" Musical programs
on the Mall include caroling
around a huge Yule log. The festivities are opened when our Commander-in-Chief—the President—
hits the button . . . to light the
National Tree. Contact: The
Ellipse, Washington DC
(202) 462-6700

A Season of Song
The nation's largest outdoor caroling songfest harmonizes to kick
off the holiday season. Contact:
Western Plaza, Washington DC
(202) 639-4011

Christmas in the White House
If Santa had grown up to be President this might have been his
home, and he could have led the
candlelight tours himself. A highlight is the 18th-century Neapolitan wood and terra-cotta crèche
flanked by twin blue spruces.
Contact: White House, Washington DC   (202) 456-7041

FLORIDA

Fort Lauderdale Winterfest
Truckloads of snow are imported
to bring "a Christmas look" to
this palm-fringed beach resort,
but the real razzle-dazzle comes
from the parade of over 100 luxury yachts and motorboats, whose
Christmas decorations light up
the Intracoastal Waterway. Contact: Fort Lauderdale/Broward
County Chamber of Commerce,
Fort Lauderdale FL
(305) 462-6000

Santa Fly-In
A reindeer might be quieter, and
you can't put a red nose on a helicopter blade, but the chopper is
a spectacular way for Santa to
transport presents. Contact:
Santa Fly-In, Miramar FL
(305) 989-6205

Walt Disney World Christmas
Goofy, Donald, and Mickey deck
the halls of the Magic Kingdom

with boughs of holly and build the
world's largest gingerbread village. Also: Candlelight Processional and the Very Merry
Christmas Parade. Contact: Walt
Disney World Information, Lake
Buena Vista FL   (305) 824-4500

GEORGIA

Christmas in Savannah
Since the city itself was once a
Christmas present, from General
Sherman to President Lincoln,
there is an annual Civil War re-
enactment of this gift—a *tour de
force* that even Santa can't top.
Also: River Street Lighting and
Parade. Contact: Savannah Area
Convention & Visitors Bureau,
Savannah GA   (912) 233-6651

A Country Christmas at Callaway Gardens
Flowers galore—with poinsettias
as the guests of honor—form the
setting for traditional celebrations
throughout December, day and
night. Madrigal dinner concerts
cap the festivities. Contact: Calla-
way Gardens, Pine Mountain GA
(404) 663-2281

Macy's Egleston Christmas Parade & Festival of Trees
Celebrities march down Peach-
tree beside floats and street per-
formers as giant helium balloons
hover over all. Trees decked out
in every conceivable fashion
adorn the Atlanta Apparel Mart.
Contact: Parade or Festival of
Trees, Atlanta GA
(404) 222-2123 (parade),
(404) 634-6099 (festival of trees)

Christmas 1900

A tram ride takes you through a time capsule to a turn-of-the-century Christmas party in Rockefeller Cottage, featuring readings, music, and games. Contact: Jekyll Island Information Center, Jekyll Island GA (800) 841-6586 (outside Georgia), (800) 342-1042 (in Georgia)

HAWAII

Christmas in Volcanoes National Park

The lava isn't flowing but hot apple cider is; and music helps create a festive atmosphere for craft displays and gift booths. Santa himself appears on opening day. Contact: Volcano Art Center, Volcanoes National Park HI (808) 967-7179

A Christmas Tradition

Missionaries shunned pineapple in favor of plum pudding. Now Hilo commemorates its New England-style Christmas with music and arts and crafts demonstrations. Contact: Lyman House Memorial Museum, Hilo HI (808) 935-5021

Santa Comes to Wailea

Reindeers can't swim, so St. Nick opts for a dugout canoe and arrives in a red and white lava-lava.

Contact: Maui Inter Continental, Wailea, Maui HI (808) 879-1922

IDAHO

Torchlight Parade

We're not talking small potatoes here. Dollar Mountain becomes a zigzag of light on Christmas Eve as the Sun Valley ski instructors wind down the trails with hand-held torches. Then fireworks explode above the snowy slope. Contact: Sun Valley-Ketchum Chamber of Commerce, Sun Valley ID (208) 726-4471

LEGAL RECOGNITION OF CHRISTMAS DAY*

1836 Alabama	**1858** Maine	**1873** Nebraska
1838 Arkansas	**1861** Colorado	**1875** Indiana
Louisiana	Illinois	South Carolina
1845 Connecticut	Nevada	**1876** New Mexico
1848 Pennsylvania	New Hampshire	**1877** Missouri
1849 New York	Wisconsin	South Dakota
Virginia	**1862** Iowa	**1879** Texas
1850 Georgia	Maryland	**1880** Mississippi
Vermont	Oregon	**1881** Arizona
1851 California	**1863** Idaho	Florida
1852 Rhode Island	North Dakota	North Carolina
1854 New Jersey	**1864** Kentucky	**1882** Utah
1855 Delaware	**1865** Michigan	**1886** Wyoming
Massachusetts	Montana	**1888** Washington
1856 Minnesota	**1868** Kansas	**1890** Oklahoma
1857 Ohio	**1870** District of Columbia	
Tennessee	West Virginia	

*It was not until 1836 that the first state, Alabama, established Christmas as a legal holiday, but by the end of the century all the then states and territories had followed suit.

ILLINOIS

Christmas Around the World
Chicago's many ethnic groups are honored at a month-long festival offering music, dance, crafts, pageantry, and Christmas foods. Also: Lunch with Santa. Contact: Museum of Science and Industry, Chicago IL   (312) 684-1414

The Frank Lloyd Wright Home & Studio Victorian Christmas
For those who have designs on the perfect Christmas, this architect's house is a festive place to celebrate, as well as a national landmark. Contact: Frank Lloyd Wright Home & Studio, Oak Park IL   (312) 848-1978

Caroling to the Animals
Come, all ye faithful and sing to the sea lions with children's choirs. Contact: Lincoln Park Zoo, Chicago IL   (312) 294-4660

Annual Teddy Bear Walk
It's an invasion of cuddly creatures: more than 800 teddy bears take to the street for Christmas frolicking. B.Y.O.B. (Bring Your Own Bear). Contact: Annual Teddy Bear Walk, Mount Prospect IL   (312) 398-6616

The Star of Bethlehem
Simulate a walk through the desert with the Wise Men and view the heavens from their perspective. Contact: John Deere Planetarium, Rock Island IL (309) 794-7327

INDIANA

Conner Prairie Christmas
Wander from house to house in this 1836 village to meet historical characters who tell tales of Christmas long ago. Start at the Eagle Taproom with a sooty-faced Belznichol (an early Santa Claus) and follow the candlelit paths, ending at the Campbell House for caroling around the piano and drinks from the wassail bowl. Contact: Conner Prairie Settlement, Noblesville IN (317) 776-6000

Ho-Ho-Ho Hometown
Yes, Santa, there is a town nestled in the hills of southern Indiana named in your honor. Here, Christmas, Noel, and Holly Lakes are surrounded by roads with names such as Three Kings and Blitzen and all are lit up in competitive displays ranging from Nativity scenes to golfing Santas. Contact: Festival of Lights, Santa Claus IN   (812) 544-2345

IOWA

Santa's Village
More than 150 animated characters, some dating back to the early 1900s, are moved realistically by hidden electric motors, levers, clockworks, gears, and switches. Many are old electromechanical department-store window displays. Contact: Santa's Village, Storm Lake Chamber of Commerce, Storm Lake IA (712) 732-3780

Frontier Christmas Windows
Storefronts of 30 historic shops frame 19th-century Christmas scenes re-created by costumed participants. Also: Festival of Decorated Trees. Contact: Christmas in the Village, Davenport IA   (319) 322-3426

KANSAS

Christmas Through the Windows
The blacksmith works at the forge as the locals gather at Fritz Snitzler's bar; the one-room schoolhouse and Wichita's first city jail are decorated to greet Father Christmas, who mingles with strolling carolers. Also: a rousing performance by the Dixie Lee Saloon Girls and "A Visit from St. Nicholas" for the children. Contact: Old Cowtown Museum, Wichita KS   (316) 264-0671

St. Lucia Festival
Candles flicker on shimmering trees, folk dancers twirl, and St. Lucia is crowned. Contact: St. Lucia Festival, Kindsborg KS (913) 227-3706

Ye Olde Englishe Feaste
This version of the groaning board practically sinks beneath the medieval plenty, which includes boar's head, wassail bowl, and a Christmas pudding served flaming hot. Contact: Ottawa University, Mobray Union, Ottawa KS (913) 242-5200

KENTUCKY

"Silent Night" in the Caves

Subterranean Christmas echoes warble through the depths of the longest known cave system in the world at the Candlelit Carol Sing on the Friday before Christmas. Contact: Mammoth Cave National Park, Mammoth Cave KY (502) 758-2251

Frontier Christmas

Tomahawks land with a swift thud; they're thrown in one of the many contests and Christmas events held in this 1786 log cabin village, which boasts a log church and museum and the last existing cabin built of flatboat planks. Contact: Frontier Christmas, Maysville KY (606) 564-3555

LOUISIANA

Christmas in Roseland

A rose by any other name . . . would smell sweeter surrounded by 300,000 lights, a carillon tower ringing seasonal music, fiddlers, bell choirs, and Japanese folk dancers. Make a Yuletide wish at an elf-guarded well or watch the Louisiana Christmas gator pull a gift-laden pirogue. Also: Wire sculptures of the Nativity, the Statue of Liberty, and the Eiffel Tower. Contact: Shreveport–Bossier Convention & Tourist Bureau, Shreveport LA (800) 551-8582 (outside Louisiana), (318) 222-9391 (in Louisiana)

City of Lights

Dusk looms. Thousands gather on the banks of the Cane River to watch fireworks explode overhead. A moment of silence. Darkness. Suddenly, a flip of the switch and the oldest permanent settlement in the entire Louisiana Purchase territory lights up. Contact: Natchitoches Parish Chamber of Commerce, Natchitoches LA (318) 352-4411

Bonfires on the Levee

Cajun bonfires glow along the bayous and foggy Mississippi River, lining the way to plantations for Papa Noel in his pirogue. Contact: Tezcuco Plantation, Darrow LA (504) 562-3929

MAINE

Scottish Christmas Walk

The bonnie banks of Loch Lomond could be underfoot for this Christmas stroll of plaid-clad pipers and dancers. Santa in a tam-o-shanter? Why not! Contact: Scottish Christmas Walk, Boothbay Harbor ME (207) 633-2353

Kennebunkport Christmas Prelude

A long early-December weekend of Maine activities launches the season with verve in this picturesque harbor: tree lighting in Dock Square, hayrides and trolley rides, pancake breakfasts and a lobster dinner at the firehouse, carol sings, and a bonfire party. Contact: Christmas Prelude, Kennebunkport ME (207) 967-2751

MARYLAND

Christmas in Annapolis

Spirits are literally raised high during the Candlelight Pub Crawl, in which guides in colonial garb lead tours of historic taverns for a progressive dinner. Also: An 18th-century Christmas reenacted at historic William Paca House. Contact: Christmas in Annapolis, Annapolis MD (301) 263-5401

MASSACHUSETTS

Storrowton

The quintessential New England Christmas. A steepled meeting house, blacksmith shop, village gazebo, general store, taverns, one-room schoolhouse, and private residences swathed in wreaths and garlands. Contact: Storrowton's Winter Holiday Festival, West Springfield MA (413) 787-0137

Nantucket Christmas

Captain Ahab's spirit rides again when a town crier announces the annual Christmas Shoppers Stroll in this 19th-century whaling village. Amble along cobbled streets where historic homes, carolers, and Christmas trees are dressed up for the holiday. Contact: Nantucket Tourist Information Bureau, Nantucket MA (617) 228-0925

Edaville Railroad Christmas

An 1,800-acre cranberry bog is the setting for a five-and-a-half-mile train ride through a carnival of 200,000 lights, past animated Christmas tableaux for children. Contact: Edaville Railroad Christmas, South Carver MA (617) 866-4526

Bells of Boston

Handbells ring carols and chime seasonal songs in steepled Faneuil Hall, while the hustle-bustle of Quincy Market gives everyone "that Christmas feeling." Contact: Bells of Boston, Faneuil Hall, Boston MA   (617) 523-1300

A Shaker Christmas

The Brick Dwelling House offers a behind-the-scenes look at how Shakers observed Christmas in Massachusetts more than 100 years ago. Contact: Hancock Shaker Village, Hancock MA (413) 443-0188

MICHIGAN

Holly Christmas

Tiny Tim and Scrooge walk the streets. Vendors sell piping-hot potatoes. This aptly named town becomes a spectacle of Dickens's Christmas characters. Contact: The Holly Board of Commerce, Holly MI   (313) 634-1900

Huckleberry Christmas

Board the Huckleberry Christmas Train, on an authentic narrow-gauge railroad, and watch 40,000 colored lights sparkle in a restored 19th-century village. Contact: Crossroads Village and Huckleberry Railroad, Flint MI (313) 736-7100

Home for the Holidays

Deck the halls of a 100-room Tudor mansion, place Santa in a cottage filled with toys, and the stage is set for two weeks of Christmas celebrating. Contact: Meadow Brook Hall, Oakland University, Rochester MI (313) 370-3140

Annual Gingerbread House Contest

If you have four walls and a roof over your head—one that you can eat—you've succeeded in America. At least that's the case in this competition. Contact: Annual Gingerbread House Contest, St. Paul MN   (612) 646-8629

1900 Logging Camp Christmas

The cookshack is filled with the aroma of Christmas turkey on a wood stove as lumberjacks take a break for blackjack (coffee) and pregnant woman pie (dried apple pie). The bunkhouse swells with sounds of old-time lumberjack music and Christmas song. Also: Storytelling—tall tales of loggers' exploits in the woods. Haywagon rides drawn by Belgian draft horses. Contact: Forest History Center, Grand Rapids MN (218) 327-4482

Christmas City of the North Parade

Can't get a round-trip flight to the North Pole? Compromise. This march launching the Christmas season is sure to be accompanied

by the appropriate cold weather. Santa makes his first appearance amid floats and marching bands. Contact: Christmas City of the North Parade, Duluth MN (612) 339-3433

MISSISSIPPI

Christmas in Natchez

Clip-clop, clip-clop . . . carriage tours wind through this twinkling Southern city and pillared antebellum mansions open their doors to the public. Also: *Cochon de Lait*, a Christmas pig roast. Contact: Natchez Adams Chamber of Commerce, Natchez MS (601) 445-4611

"Apples and Cinnamon" Christmas

Hoop skirts skim the floor and Confederate soldiers lead a waltz, when suddenly the violins stop. There are Union gunboats coming up the river! It's a reenactment of the 1862 Christmas Ball at Balfour House. Also: Antebellum house tours, including Cedar Grove, where a Federal cannonball is still lodged in the parlor wall. Contact: Vicksburg-Warren County Tourist Promotion Commission, Vicksburg MS (800) 221-3536

MISSOURI

Country Club Plaza
Can you believe it?—a multi-colored light show 47 miles long and 156,000 bulbs strong. Contact: Country Club Plaza Christmas Activities, Kansas City MO (800) 523-5953 (outside Missouri), (816) 221-5242 Ext. 10 (in Missouri)

Send the Very Best
Or go see Hallmark Cards' Crown Center Complex for yourself. Seventeen decorated trees each represent a Christmas gift created by Hallmark artists each year for the company's founder, the late Joyce Hall. Contact: Hallmark Cards, Kansas City MO   (816) 274-7251

MONTANA

St. Nick's Nordic Festival
Attention all Santa Claus skeptics: Forty-five miles of groomed cross-country ski trails, skis, lessons, draft-horse-drawn sleighs . . . all free! Who else could give such a Christmas gift? Contact: Lone Mountain Ranch, Big Sky MT   (406) 995-4644

Holiday Torchlight Parade
Blazing torches held by adept skiers seem to float down the mountain, as fireworks light up the sky. Contact: Bridger Bowl, Bozeman MT   (406) 587-2111

NEBRASKA

Light of the World
That glow in the sky isn't a UFO. It's the Christmas lights of this small prairie town of 3,000. Residents gather at the courthouse as bells ring, a pageant is performed, and the entire dome becomes illuminated by webs of hand-painted bulbs. Contact: Minden Chamber of Commerce, Minden NE   (308) 832-1811

Ogallala's Fantasyland
The name itself—pronounced trippingly on the tongue—evokes images of fairy tales, which are indeed acted out on the County Fairgrounds at Christmas. Contact: Ogallala Chamber of Commerce, Ogallala NE (308) 284-4066

Homesteader's Christmas
When the wagons were unloaded and the sod houses evolved into wooden homes, Christmas in Nebraska became a way to celebrate permanence, with tree trimmings and taffy pulls. It still is. Contact: Homestead National Monument, Beatrice NE (402) 223-3514

NEVADA

A Gift to Reno
Dealer doesn't take all when the spirit of giving is exemplified in this gambling town. Two 60-foot Douglas firs are shipped to Reno and Sparks by the citizens of the tiny coastal town of Garibaldi, Oregon, because the Nevada deserts can't grow Christmas trees. Garibaldi's own Santa delivers the trees. Contact: Reno Chamber of Commerce, Reno NV (702) 786-3030

Sierra Nevada's Living Christmas Tree
"This Little Babe" and "Christmas Day" are part of the repertoire of the 125-member Sierra Nevada Chorale, who stand in pyramid form as they serenade the audience. Contact: Reno Chamber of Commerce, Reno NV (702) 786-3030

NEW HAMPSHIRE

Candlelight Stroll at Strawberry Banke
Candles flicker in the chill air. Carolers sing, classical guitarists strum, and bell ringers sound the season's good tidings; New England's past is present here. Contact: Strawberry Banke, Portsmouth NH   (603) 433-1100

Dickens of a Christmas
Like old Ebenezer, folks in Hanover are dancing in the streets. They're also wearing stovepipe hats and riding horse-drawn sleighs to the tune of carols and handbell choruses. Also: Christmas Tree Lighting on the Green with Santa and the Dartmouth Glee Club. Contact: Hanover Chamber of Commerce, Hanover NH   (603) 643-3115

The night sky, ablaze with a thousand stars, is echoed by earth's luminous *luminarias.*

Full Moon Ski Tour

The werewolves are probably too cold to howl, but in Wolfboro, luminescent snow shimmers along the woodland trails. Also: Lighting of the Trail Christmas Tree. Contact: Full Moon Ski Tour, Nordic Skier, Wolfboro NH (603) 569-3151

NEW JERSEY

Cape May Christmas

The ocean laps at a deserted boardwalk, but gas-lit streets, a gazebo, gingerbread architecture, and a trolley car create 19th-century charm in this ultimate Victorian seaside town. Featured is a Dickens Extravaganza, including dramatic readings and lectures. Contact: Greater Cape May Chamber of Commerce, Cape May NJ   (609) 884-5508

Washington's Delaware Christmas

A dramatic reenactment of December 25, 1776, when Washington led 2,400 soldiers across the river for an unexpected Christmas "bash" with British mercenaries. Contact: Washington Crossing State Park, Titusville NJ (609) 737-0623

Holiday Turkey Skeet Shoot

Bag that dinner. Each person can shoot at 50 clay targets for a chance to win a turkey. Contact: Trap & Skeet Range, Lenape Park, Cranford NJ (201) 276-0225

NEW MEXICO

City of Little Lights

Thousands of *luminarias*—bags containing lighted candles—shine along narrow streets, garden walls, and flat rooftops—as if the stars have fallen from the sky to help celebrate Christmas. Suddenly, a crowd gathers at the door of a house and a young man and his wife, veiled in blue, request lodging for the night. In a centuries-old Spanish verse drama, *Las Posadas*, Joseph and Mary seek shelter. Contact: Albuquerque Visitors & Convention Bureau, Albuquerque NM   (800) 321-6979 (outside New Mexico), (505) 243-3696 (in New Mexico)

Sante Fe Christmas

New Mexico's capital is outlined with millions of shimmering *luminarias*, also called *farolitas* here. A candlelit *Las Posadas* is played out for nine days in San Miguel Mission, the oldest church still in use in the United States. And during Christmas at the Palace, the courtyard of the Governors' Palace glows with bonfires, carolers sing, and San Juan Indians perform ceremonial Christmas Eve and Christmas Day dances called Bow and Arrow, Black-Cloaked Turtle, and Buffalo. Contact: Santa Fe County Tourist Information, Santa Fe NM   (800) 221-7051 (outside New Mexico), (505) 988-8871 (in New Mexico)

NEW YORK

Angel Tree Unveiled

A hush fills the Medieval Court of The Metropolitan Museum. One by one, the branches of a giant blue spruce are lit as if by evening stars that cast a glow over hosts of 18th-century Neapolitan cherubs and angels. Underneath the tree: a baroque crèche. Contact: Metropolitan Museum of Art, New York NY   (212) 535-7710

Rockefeller Center

Golden Prometheus presides over the lighting of a 70-foot tree, adorned with 18,000 multicolored lights strung on more than five miles of wire. Five hundred tuba players provide brassy music as skaters twirl and carolers sing. Contact: Rockefeller Center, New York NY   (212) 698-8676

Eleanor Roosevelt's Christmas

The famous toothy smile no longer brightens her Hudson River home, but the former First Lady's fun-spirited Christmas is still carried on. Contact: Val-Kill, Hyde Park NY   (914) 229-9422

Ships and a Chorus Tree

At a restored 19th-century waterfront—once one of the world's great sailing ports—65 carolers form a human Christmas tree to welcome the public to another era. Contact: South Street Seaport, New York NY (212) 669-9424

Christmas at the Falls

Water thunders a triumphant fanfare as holiday lights are reflected in thousands of tiny drops and splashes. Contact: Convention Center & Wintergarden, Niagara Falls NY   (716) 695-8530

NORTH CAROLINA

Coastal Christmas Celebration

Santa arrives aboard a yacht and climbs into a horse-drawn carriage for a ride to the center of town and the lighting of the tree. Contact: Swiss Bear Inc., New Bern NC   (919) 638-5781

Old Salem Christmas

Visitors to this restored village watch as the resident Moravians celebrate with traditional tree-shaped pyramids, hung with greenery and lit candles, and Czechoslovakian music. Also: Wagon rides and nighttime bon-

fires. Contact: Old Salem, Inc., Winston-Salem NC (919) 723-3688

Biltmore House

An 1895 Christmas fête opened this magnificent Vanderbilt mansion in the Blue Ridge Mountains. Today, 30 of 250 rooms are decorated with miles of garlands and bushels of holly, paper bells, feather wreaths, poinsettias, azaleas, and ferns. Cinnamon-stick trees and hot cider scent the air, and there are candlelit tours of the baronial rooms. Contact: Christmas at Biltmore Estate, Asheville NC   (704) 274-1776

NORTH DAKOTA

Little Christmas on the Prairie

Bonanzaville! The name conjures up a gold strike, and at Christmastime it is. The whole community turns out to celebrate grass roots, literally, in this reconstructed prairie village. Contact: Fargo-Moorhead Convention & Visitors Bureau, Fargo ND (701) 237-6134

Merriment in Minot

Elizabethan characters in North Dakota? Yes—a bevy of royal singers, dancers, and jesters herald the season with madrigals, mead, and mutton. Contact: Minot Chamber of Commerce, Minot ND   (701) 852-1923

OHIO

Light Up at the Zoo

Santa makes his appearance, but where is Dr. Dolittle? Visit the live Nativity scene en route to greet the elephants and apes, or take a camel ride amid 300,000 sparkling white lights. Contact: Cincinnati Zoo, Cincinnati OH (513) 281-4701

Zoar Christmas

One of the first communal living villages in the United States comes alive when the Christkind (Christ Child) passes out treats to children (as was the custom in the early 19th century), and German carols are sung by candlelight. Contact: Zoar Village, Zoar OH (216) 874-3211

OKLAHOMA

Territorial Christmas

Guthrie regains its former status as capital of Oklahoma Territory when it puts on its Christmas show. Some 245,000 feet of tiny lights outline the Victorian architecture, and residents dress up in period finery. Newsboys hawk the evening paper, carolers sing, and U.S. marshals preserve law and order. Also: Christmas parade with horse-drawn vehicles, handbell concert, and Christmas steer roping. Contact: Guthrie Chamber of Commerce, Guthrie OK (405) 282-1947

OREGON

Living Trees

When the wind ruffles the pine needles of these decorated trees, you don't have to worry about picking them out of the carpet. These are rooted, growing evergreens that are decked with an international array of ornaments from Europe and the Orient. Contact: The World Forestry Center, Portland OR   (503) 228-1367

Christmas Flotilla

Tiny sailboats and grand yachts dot the Columbia and Willamette Rivers in Portland, displaying a myriad brilliantly colored lights against a starry sky. Contact: Oregon Economic Development Department, Salem OR (503) 581-5115

Gingerbread House Contest

This is a real estate development that will leave you hungry for more. Contact: Bush Barn Art Center, Salem OR (503) 581-2228

Christmas Wildlife Safari

Does Santa need a pith helmet? Take a Christmas drive through this 600-acre reserve and see elephants, rhinos, hippos, lions, tigers, and . . . reindeer? Also: A Christmas Party for the Animals to which children are encouraged to bring food for the wildlife. Contact: Wildlife Safari, Winston OR (503) 679-6761

PENNSYLVANIA

Brandywine Christmas

At Longwood, a former Du Pont estate, four acres of indoor gardens come alive with Christmas music in a colorful setting of greenery and flowers banked around gushing fountains. And in Chadds Ford, the Brandywine River Museum delights children with Christmas treasures, including O-gauge trains and antique dolls. Contact: Chester County Tourist Bureau, West Chester PA (215) 431-6365

With the Troops at Valley Forge

On the 2,800-acre site of General George Washington's winter encampment (1777–78), the pre-Christmas arrival of the Continental Army takes place once again. Contact: Valley Forge Country Convention & Visitors Bureau, Valley Forge PA (215) 278-3558

America's Bethlehem

"And in the dark night shineth the everlasting light. . . ." A giant eight-pointed star glimmers over America's not-so-little town of Bethlehem, ablaze with thousands of illuminated parchment stars and candles. Also: The Central Moravian Church's Christmas Putz, a small-scale sound and light presentation of carved figures representing scenes from the Christmas story. Contact: Bethlehem Area Chamber of Commerce, Bethlehem PA (215) 868-1513

RHODE ISLAND

Newport Christmas
Opulent 19th-century million-aires' mansions, decorated in Victorian style, and historic colonial homes open their doors for daytime and candlelight tours. Everyone puts on winter finery for the lavish parties, dinners, balls, pageants, Christmas readings, and musicales that comprise Newport's most sumptuous season. Contact: Christmas in Newport, Newport RI   (401) 847-0563

SOUTH CAROLINA

Drive-In Christmas Pageant
Some 20,000 visitors line up bumper-to-bumper to watch actors perform two Biblical scenes. Eight live angels on the roof beckon worshipers. Contact: North Trenholm Baptist Church, North Trenholm SC (803) 787-2133

Charleston Christmas
Church bells ring. Carriages bump over cobblestones for views of 18th-century homes wreathed in popcorn berries, magnolia, and South Carolina holly. Civil War plantations and gardens are festooned with garlands, and walking tours often end with Southern teas. Also: Christmas at Boone Hall, an 18th-century cotton plantation. Contact: Charleston Trident Convention & Visitors Bureau, Charleston SC (800) 723-7641

SOUTH DAKOTA

Capitol Rotunda Christmas
Pierre's Capitol Building becomes an indoor forest of Black Hills spruce, ponderosa pine, and cedar trees. Decorations include the blue and gold state flag. Contact: Capitol Building, Pierre SD (605) 773-3011

TENNESSEE

Christmas in Olde Jonesborough
In the heart of the Appalachians, storytelling, recipe swaps, and wreath-making parties figure in a real hill-country Christmas. Contact: Christmas in Olde Jonesborough, Jonesborough TN (615) 753-5961

Christmas at Twitty City
If there's a twang in the name it's because Conway Twitty, country music superstar, has brought the magic of Christmas to this nine-acre fantasyland with 250,000 lights. Also: Santa's Candy Castle. Contact: Twitty City, Hendersonville TN   (615) 822-6650

Nashville Christmas
Dolly Parton standards are replaced by odes to St. Nick, and nearly everyone in the country music capital, led by Minnie Pearl, gets into the swing of Christmas. Highlights include: The Nashville Gas Christmas Parade for over 100,000 spectators; a tree ornament display by 100 music stars; Rudolph's Red Nose

Run for athletes; and Opryland's "A Down-Home Country Christmas Musical Celebration," which promises intimacy but is enjoyed by 3,000 people in the Presidential Ballroom. Contact: Nashville Area Chamber of Commerce, Nashville TN (615) 259-3900

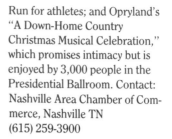

TEXAS

Christmas Fiesta
Spanish dancers' skirts flare, mariachi bands play along River Walk, lined with brilliant *luminarias*, and carolers serenade from floating barges. The highlight is the *Las Posadas* procession. Also: Pancho Claus visits the Mexican market, where children burst piñatas and bring their animals for a Christmas blessing. Contact: San Antonio Convention & Visitors Bureau, San Antonio TX (800) 531-5700 (outside Texas), (800) 292-1010 (in Texas)

Dickens on the Strand
Along a shore road named for London's Strand, parades of Dickensian characters read from *A Christmas Carol* and make music on scores of handbells. Contact: Galveston Historical Foundation, Galveston TX (409) 765-7834

Cowboys Christmas Ball
They've been "Yee-hawing" since the 1880s at this traditional Yuletide stomp. Contact: Cowboys Christmas Ball, Anson TX (915) 823-2390

Fairy-Tale Christmas
Mother Goose, Snow White, Rudolph, and many other childhood favorites appear, along with Santa, in three-dimensional settings covering several acres. Best seen when lit up at night. Contact: Richmond State School, Richmond TX   (713) 342-4681

UTAH

Santa Claus Express
Santa jumps aboard and the little old steam train chugs its way from the Heber Creeper Railroad depot through the scenic "Alps" of Utah. Contact: Heber Creeper, Heber City UT   (801) 654-2900

Temple Square Christmas
The Mormon Tabernacle Choir belts out Christmas cheer and 210,000 lights glisten in downtown Salt Lake City. Contact: Salt Lake Area Chamber of Commerce, Salt Lake City UT (801) 364-3631

Let the tubas sound and the Christmas bells ring their merry music.

VERMONT

Early Vermont Christmas
Old New England is recalled with a rural Christmas that includes horse-drawn wagon or sleigh rides, wandering carolers, and meeting-house hymns. Contact: Shelburne Museum, Shelburne VT   (802) 985-3346

Woodstock Wassail
In the snow-blanketed Green Mountains, jugglers, court jesters, and wenches cavort and the entire town gathers on the village green to light the Yule log and toast the season around the wassail bowl. Contact: Woodstock Chamber of Commerce, Woodstock VT (802) 457-3555

VIRGINIA

Scottish Christmas Walk
Bagpipers in full tartan regalia play as Highland dancers fling their way into the Christmas season. Contact: Alexandria Chamber of Commerce, Alexandria VA (703) 549-SCOT

Williamsburg Christmas

No Christmas tree? No Santa Claus? What kind of Christmas is this? It's a true colonial Christmas, complete with a cannon blast to signal the season's start, fife and drum corps drills, and dancers whirling in a Virginia reel. At night, candles light up every window and carolers stroll from house to house. Contact: Colonial Williamsburg, Williamsburg VA (804) 253-0192

Carols at Wolf Trap

It's cold outside, but when the U.S. Marine Corps Band exchanges "Yes, Sir!" for "Merry Christmas!", everyone warms up. Contact: Wolf Trap Music Festival, Vienna VA (703) 255-1900

Familiar Face Christmas Pageant

Everyone knows someone in this perennial favorite put on by a cast of more than 300 local residents. The hometown spirit is contagious. Contact: The Nativity, Richmond VA (804) 780-8136

WASHINGTON

Bavarian Christmas

With oompah music, twinkling lights, and handbells, carolers surround Alpine-style "gingerbread" houses. Food booths serve German specialties and snow is practically guaranteed in the Icicle Valley of the Cascades. Contact: Leavenworth Chamber of Commerce, Leavenworth WA (509) 548-7914

Seattle Boat Parades

Catamarans, power yachts, sailboats, speedboats . . . all the decks decked out for the season cruise Puget Sound, Lake Union, and Lake Washington. Contact: Seattle-King County Convention & Visitors Bureau, Seattle WA (206) 447-4240

WEST VIRGINIA

Old Tyme Christmas

No time like the right time for an old-time 1900s gathering at the scenic junction of the Shenandoah and Potomac Rivers. Contact: Old Tyme Christmas Celebration, Harpers Ferry WV (304) 535-2514

Wine-Tasting Christmas

Are those "ho-ho-ho's" the result of one sip too many at this caroling and wine-tasting given by the Purgitsville Winery? No matter. The Christmas spirit comes from the heart, rather than from the bottle, and could even be enhanced by a tipple or two. Contact: The Winery at Purgitsville, Purgitsville WV (304) 289-3493

WISCONSIN

Lunch with Santa at the Zoo

Two hundred children join 5,000 exotic animals and Santa and his elves for lunch—and get a pre-Christmas present. Also: Evening carols and brass ensemble performances in this festively decorated zoo. Contact: Milwaukee County Zoo, Milwaukee WI (414) 771-3040

WYOMING

Torchlight Parade

No, it's not a bolt of lightning skimming down the side of Après-Vous Mountain, but 45 skiers waving blazing lights above their heads to welcome Christmas Day. Contact: Jackson Hole Area Chamber of Commerce, Jackson WY (307) 733-3316

Yuletide Yee-haw

"Oh, give me a home where the buffalo roam. . . ." Christmastime, cowboy style: Two thousand people turn out for a gala get-together, with a Stetson replacing the traditional angel or star atop the tree. Contact: Buffalo Bill Historical Center, Cody WY (307) 587-4771

Andrea Israel writes for television and travel publications.

A TIME
FOR GIVING

THE GIFT
BEHIND THE GIFT

The most splendid Christmas gift, the most marveled and magic, is the gift that has not yet been opened. Opaque behind wrapping or winking foil, it is a box full of possibilities. An unopened present might be anything—gems, crystal, oranges, a promise of devotion. While the present is unopen, it can rest under the tree to be regarded and speculated upon at length, becoming whatever the recipient wishes.

Opening the present, by comparison, is often anticlimactic—no matter what the contents. For once opened, the gift passes from the enchanted realm of promise into the constrained reality of material possessions. Then it begins to impose terms on its owner—terms like sizes, warranties, colors, maintenance, accessories, storage space, assembly, extremely thick books with instructions. (Anyone receiving a personal computer this year should not expect to speak to loved ones again until next year.) Open a gift and, like the vacuum in a coffee can, the possibilities whoosh away, never to be recovered.

So it is that Christmas Eve is the best part of Christmas. Compared with the clamor and urgency of the day itself—the schedules to satisfy, the near-strangers to pretend to be close to, the post-gift frenzy to compare windfalls—Christmas Eve is serene. It is the moment, still and expectant, when the warmth of the season may be felt for its own sake—the moment to light candles and listen for a sound in the distance. It is the moment when the meaning of the day, for those who wonder at it, may be contemplated without distraction from timetables or remote-controlled robots.

If anticipation is the essence of Christmas, Christmas Eve is the essence of anticipation. All the holiday's elves and henchmen revel in it. Snow is most beautiful while it falls, noiseless and free: Once on the ground, it succumbs to soot and stumbling tracks. The solitary country house is most beautiful observed from the cold hill above, as it shines out yellow squares of light and firesparks, promising friendship. The smell of Christmas cookies baking can be as satisfying as eating them, the first cup of Christmas cheer as gratifying as the next five combined. Lighting the tree is the finest part by far.

Often what precedes is better than what follows, even when, like Christmas Day, what follows is good. The first kiss, clumsy as it always is—first kisses generally have all the grace of two freight trains colliding on a dark siding—can be the most moving. However physically inadequate, it conveys the promise of further kisses, more esthetic or athletic, and the promise of proximity before and after, the companionship that a kiss seals. By that way of thinking, the most excitement available under the mistletoe is not the touch itself, but the instant just before, when she (or he, depending) steps forward to join you there. This is the moment when you know someone else wants to be near you, a moment blushing with what might be.

The original point of Christmas, now better reflected on tranquil Christmas Eve than on the madcap day itself, was to proclaim what might be. Wise men and shabby shepherds alike went to Bethlehem that first Christmas Eve because they hoped what was happening there would begin to elevate humankind—to make us more truly humane and deserving of each other.

So far, it has not worked out that way. But that does not mean the ideal was wrong or the goal unattainable. What might be is only elusive, not impossible. Peace on earth and mercy mild are still possible. On Christmas Eve all things are possible.

Gregg Easterbrook
The New York Times
December 24, 1983

"Mark my words, Balthazar, we're starting something with these gifts that's going to get way out of hand!"

THE BUSINESS BEHIND THE GIFT

Backstage at Marshall Field's

BY ROBERT OSTERMANN

Most gifts given at Christmas come from a department store, and in a world-class department store, performance comes first. The aim of the store is to attract you to its cornucopia of treasures, so artfully that you pay no attention to the creative planning, supervision, and discipline of legions of people that ensure the merchandise you want will be where you expect it to be, when you want it.

For a department store, this is, during the Christmas season, a steadily escalating challenge.

Few retail merchants can match the Christmas record of Marshall Field's, with 25 stores in Wisconsin, Illinois, and Texas. And fewer still can bear comparison to Field's flagship store in Chicago.

Illusion, Enchantment, and Memories

Every year, the 27-member staff of Visual Merchandising (the store's design group) transform Marshall Field's State Street store into one huge Christmas ornament.

Says Homer Sharp, Vice President, Display, and a 40-year Field's veteran, "We're starting a new Christmas when our customers are still trying to recover from the previous one."

Christmas throughout Field's is built around a different theme each year. The most memorable in a sequence of national themes was "The Eagle and the Crown," which memorialized a

British Christmas and emphasized the Victorian era.

The following year Field's featured an American Christmas based on the classic Christmas movies of the '30s and '40s. One in particular, *It's a Wonderful Life* starring James Stewart, was the inspiration for Field's overall design.

Annually, the decorations start with animated window displays, move to the main aisle, then overflow onto the selling floors. A team of 125 workers scrambles through the store for two weeks before the season opens, putting in 12-hour days and six-day weeks, to deck Field's halls top to bottom.

But the centerpiece of Field's Christmas is the giant tree raised every year for almost a century in the Walnut Room restaurant, known to

Glittering lights shower happiness on all.

It takes 35 people—scaffolding experts, electricians, carpenters, and artists—to assemble The Great Tree and ready it for its full-dress appearance.

Then, switch on.

Ooooh! Aaaah!

Couples who became engaged while dining under the tree return annually to celebrate their anniversaries. Parents bring their children to share their own childhood experience of eating under The Great Tree.

Helen Ewert, associated for many years with the Walnut Room and now in charge of catering at the State Street store, told me about the couple who in 1985 celebrated their 50th annual Christmas visit to the Walnut Room and are still counting. They share the anniversary now with children, grandchildren, and great-grandchildren.

The pair, both in their 80s, wear the same costumes each year. His is a black velvet Tyrolean jacket and a hat adorned with pearls and sequins. His wife regularly tops her outfit with a sequined hat shaped like a tree. "Everyone calls her 'the Christmas-tree lady,'" Mrs. Ewert says, "and everyone looks forward to the day the family comes to visit us."

all as "The Great Tree." Visitors stream into Field's from surrounding states and even from overseas, and wait uncomplainingly for an hour or more to sit under its spreading branches.

The Great Tree is an awesome spectacle. Cascading down from its 45-foot crown are streams of tiny white bulbs, 12,000 in all, that lace the tree with light. The branches drip with 5,000 ornaments that replicate the season's theme, every one of them designed and crafted in Field's own shop.

BOXING DAYS

Field's gift boxes come already set up, not folded flat. During the Christmas shopping season it takes at least one trailer every night to bring a daily supply to the store.

A special staff distributes them to the selling floors, and early every morning an obstacle course of boxes fills the aisles, waiting to be stowed out of sight before the store opens. No one really knows what the store total might be, but 20 cartons of gift boxes for men's shirts, for example, are delivered every night.

And the Trailers
Keep Rolling Along

The storm is about to break below the land-mark clock that hangs like a beacon from Marshall Field's at the corner of State and Randolph Streets. You can feel it inside the building, as if thunder were already starting to rumble down through the store's 2 million square feet.

Most of the year, except during one of Field's spectacular sales, some 20,000 to 25,000 shoppers daily make the store their own. But on the Friday after Thanksgiving—Black Friday in the vernacular of the trade, because that is the day when department stores cross over from the red side of the ledger into the black—Field's

must handle 75,000 shoppers with their sights trained on Christmas, still more than a month away.

Field's began gearing up for the challenge many months ago, and the Operations people are on the front line. It is their job to make sure that the merchandise gets in and out of the store without a hitch. And the logistics of stocking ten sales floors with the right items, in the right quantities, and in the right locations are as complex as keeping an army on the move.

"It really starts in September," explains Rick Johnson, who directs Operations at State Street. "That's when Christmas merchandise begins to arrive in bulk. From that point on we race to keep up with the numbers."

During July, the slowest month in the year for the delivery of new merchandise, some 80 trailers arrive at the store to unload. In September the number soars to 210, in October to 218, in November to 283, then, in December, it climaxes at 291 trailers.

These trailers bring merchandise from Field's warehouses. A huge variety of outside suppliers are also pouring their trailers into the system—upward of six times the number of Field's own. This means that from 3:30 A.M. till 11:00 P.M., each truck discharges 400 to 500 cartons on the loading dock, more than 28,000 cartons a day at the season's peak.

Imagine State Street—"that great street"— and Chicago's Loop as one gigantic parking lot. That is what downtown Chicago would be if the scores of trailers arriving daily were not scheduled with split-second timing to be unloaded quickly and moved on.

Logistics, phase two. Arriving in successive waves, hundreds of tons of merchandise end up on Field's back porch; now it all has to be moved to destinations inside the store, with the absolute assurance that Linens will not be selling perfume nor Women's Accessories hawking men's sweaters the following morning.

Again, timing and speed are all. The Operations team, expanded by 25 percent for the Christmas rush, transfers all the arriving merchandise to a second basement. There it is

---

FEEDING THE CHRISTMAS SPIRIT

The store begins planning its Christmas food activities in February, says Susan Hanson, manager of Food Work Groups. The candy kitchens on the 13th floor start turning out their first Christmas candy around April. All in all, the kitchens produce a million pounds of candy a year, with Field's best-selling original Frango Mints selling about 400,000 pounds during the Christmas season alone.

The bakeshops also work overtime, preparing 10,000 fruitcakes, 21,000 Yule logs, and 8,000 plum puddings, the three most popular bakery items. Decorated cookies in the shapes of dolls, Santa Claus, and The Great Tree —also prepared in Field's kitchens especially for Christmas—sell in the countless thousands. The menu of items offered in the bakery is two pages long.

Children squeal with joy to see animated fairy tales and nursery rhymes in the sparkling store windows along State Street; at left Cinderella arrives triumphant at the ball. On the right, a re-creation of a lavish Victorian boudoir offers temptations for giving and receiving, or just viewing.

sorted, then relocated to two remote stock floors during the day. After hours, when the store is empty of shoppers but swarming with workers, the merchandise—already ticketed with price and inventory data at the warehouse—is delivered to the appropriate selling floors. Mountains are moved every night for weeks.

Every day during the Christmas season, about 3,000 of the items trailered in are turned around and shipped out as purchases—almost four times the daily volume for the rest of the year and requiring three times the usual number of people needed to facilitate the flow.

Getting the Story Out

Creating an effective print ad—typically, more than 700 in November alone—is a ferocious challenge in itself for Russ Hardin's shop. The next stage, getting an ad released, is an even greater challenge.

Seven people in Mr. Hardin's department check that an ad is letter perfect. Another five to seven people representing the account review the copy, art, and layout. A dozen or more specialists—writers, proofreaders, designers, art directors, production people, color separa-

tors—screen the entire work for the slightest imperfection.

Each day, the same army of perfectionists repeats this exhaustive examination for 50 to 60 print ads. Says their general ruefully: "Sometimes I wonder why we don't just set up cots and live here until Christmas is history."

THAT EXTRA MILE

- *Field's Christmas Directory.* **A special road map of the store is created for holiday shoppers.**

- *White Carnation Program.* **Executives and managers, wearing white carnations, spend certain hours at highly visible posts, to direct Christmas shoppers to their destinations and to deal on the spot with any problems.**

- *Gifts-for-Her-Shop.* **For ten months of the year this shop bears the name Field's Fashion Service, where skilled sales associates help women upgrade their wardrobes. During Christmas, and by appointment only, men are offered one-on-one assistance in choosing gifts for their ladies.**

SAFETY FIRST

Loss Prevention is what Field's calls the unit of professionals, 150 strong, that is charged with assuring the security of everyone and everything in its stores.

Lewis Shealy, Loss Prevention executive, quickly corrects the common misperception of his unit as primarily a private police force. "There's a lot more, and a lot less, to the job," he told me, "than most people think. More duties and much less drama."

Among Loss Prevention's less dramatic duties are making sure that fire doors, aisles, and stairways are always clear, in compliance with safety codes, and that empty cartons are removed from work areas so that employees won't take a tumble into a glass showcase. During stormy weather, Loss Prevention people lay safety mats at every entrance so that water and snow are not tracked inside to create slippery floors.

Undramatic, to be sure. But the Loss Prevention group also has many ways to keep theft, by employees and visitors, at a tolerable level.

Not all of them are for public discussion. One that Mr. Shealy will talk about is Field's awards program. This offers $500 to a staff member whose report of an employee theft results in arrest or termination, and $100 for reporting a shoplifter. It works. In 1986, in all Field's stores, 800 employees participated and were awarded a total of $114,000.

Mr. Shealy's people go about their business inconspicuously. "A store is no place to play cops and robbers," Mr. Shealy says. "Our job is to keep Field's safe. Safety first—that's where it begins and that's where it ends."

The Customer Is Always Served

Quality customer service commands unremitting effort from Field's Personnel management and staff in hiring and training the massive influx of part-time help (5,000 throughout the Field's network, 500 at the State Street store), most of whom have limited experience in the art of retail selling—and sometimes none at all.

Quality staff are pivotal at any time of the year, but their importance ratchets up during the Christmas season. Phil Johnson, head of Personnel for all of Marshall Field's, explains why:

"More people come through the store in the five Christmas shopping weeks than we'll see probably in three normal business months. We're under a giant magnifying glass. You let your service standards slip at Christmas and the store has a black eye that will last the whole year through."

Temporary "sales associates" are needed in almost every area. Some departments, such as Women's and Men's Apparel, Cosmetics, Jewelry, and Gift Wrap, are simply extra busy at Christmas; others are Christmas exclusives, like Greeting Cards, Christmas Wrap, "Trim-a-Home" shops, and counters offering seasonal gifts.

Field's relies on three sources for additional personnel: people who have worked there before, hundreds of them repeaters; college students on Christmas break; and those who respond to ads for extra help.

Training of newcomers is brief and intensive. They are taught how to operate the register system, and in the computer age, that means they have to do a lot more than ring up a sale. They learn the codes for the department, the section, the item (for inventory control), cash or credit-card sales, and how to run a check on a card's validity.

More important is to school the temps in Field's "culture," the attitudes and behavior

As you enter Field's the main aisle enfolds you like the atrium of a grand hotel. In the space soaring up to the distant ceiling, arabesques of light perform their festive dance.

that are expected of them in dealing with customers—Field's way of doing business. A lot of candidates flunk one or the other of these vital programs.

Critical though it may be, hiring is the easiest part. Where to assign permanent and seasonal people, and at which hours, in order to match shopper needs with the right number of staff is the million-dollar question.

It is "million-dollar" quite literally. Sales could sag if there were too many sales people in the shoe department and too few in Men's Accessories. Multiply that through ten floors of merchandise and you have some sense of the potential crunch on Christmas revenues, which represent some 35 percent of Field's annual total.

Lodged in the canny brain of the store's computer are the historic traffic patterns for every department at every hour of every business day. In September it receives the sales plan and weekly amount of business expected for each department through to the end of the year. Data whip around the electronic circuits, and the computer arrays this blizzard of numbers into an assignment pattern. It then schedules all of the permanent staff plus the additional temporary people needed, including in its calculations such factors as lunch breaks and the timing of shifts.

The system is not foolproof, of course. The computer cannot predict the weather, always a big influence on buying decisions. Several years ago, during a particularly frigid winter, gloves, scarves, hats, and coats were hot—information duly entered in the memory banks. The following year, unfortunately, Chicago enjoyed a balmy winter. Gloves *et al.* turned cold.

MUSEUM CATALOG SOURCES

The Brooklyn Museum Gallery Shop
200 Eastern Parkway, Brooklyn
NY 11238

Colonial Williamsburg
P.O. Box CH, Williamsburg VA 23187

Cincinnati Art Museum
Publications Department
Eden Park, Cincinnati OH 45202-1596

The Freer Gallery of Art
Smithsonian Institution
Washington DC 20560

The Metropolitan Museum of Art
255 Gracie Station, New York NY 10028

Museum of Fine Arts, Boston
Catalog Sales Department
P.O. Box 1044, Boston MA 02120

National Gallery of Art
Publications Service
Washington DC 20565

The Pierpont Morgan Library
Mail Order Department
29 East 36th Street, New York
NY 10016

San Francisco Museum of Modern Art
P.O. Box 306
125 Main Street, Half Moon Bay
CA 94019

The Mails Have It

Let's pretend that last year a family called Wilson joined the mounting millions who decided not to fight the crowds in the malls. Instead, they did all their Christmas shopping "in the comfort of their very own home." Their very own mailbox, the Wilsons realized, was a portable store stuffed with catalogs offering an almost bewildering variety of choices. All they needed were a credit card, a telephone, and the patience to sift through the myriad temptations.

Their confidence in prompt and reliable service was not misplaced, and from early December onward, dozens of packages began to flood across the country, destined for the friends and family who would not be joining them for the holidays. The week before Christmas, UPS trucks began lining up behind the mail vans in the Wilsons' own driveway.

On Christmas Day, the Wilsons displayed a magnificent North Carolina balsam fir tree ordered from American Express, fully decorated with ornaments from The Metropolitan Museum. Beneath it were exquisitely wrapped presents (in designer paper from Boston's Museum of Fine Arts): a pair of lined mooseskin slippers for Dad from L.L. Bean, a memory typewriter for Mom from 47th Street Photo, a rocking horse for the kids from F.A.O. Schwarz, and an electronic flea collar for their dog from The Sharper Image. The table was laden with Laura Chenel's chèvre, D'Artagnan Inc.'s foie gras, Neiman-Marcus's quail, Zabar's smoked salmon, and DiCamillo Bakery's foccacia. For dessert they chose Mother Sperry's plum pudding. . . .

There are estimated to be at least 6,500 gift catalogs, making mail order a $40 billion-a-year industry. The prime shopping season begins in late August and ends the week before Christmas—but for buyers who *really* like to procrastinate, some companies will take orders two days before Christmas and send them out by express mail.

The gamut runs from retail stores in major cities to burgeoning cottage industries in small towns. Traditional companies offering clothes and household items, such as Sears, Spiegel, and L.L. Bean, compete with upscale "yuppie toy" marketers that include The Sharper Image, which has offered a $5,000 tanning bed, or small independent merchants such as Patterns of History, which supplies 19th-century women's dress patterns. Lillian Vernon mails out 82 million catalogs every year, and it is almost impossible to browse through one without finding dozens of gift ideas: musical Christmas cards, for instance (210,000 sold), or His & Her matching eye masks. Or how about Hammacher Schlemmer's two-way indoor putting green, or a solar-powered, ventilated pith helmet?

Department stores are increasingly relying on their mail-order catalogs to boost sales. Marshall Field's 84-page Christmas catalog, for example, now goes to 1.6 million people. Cultural institutions of all kinds send out beguiling shopping magazines (see box for a listing of museum gift shops with catalogs that accept mail-order sales). *The Directory of Mail Order Catalogs* (available in good libraries or from Grey House, Bank of Boston Building, Sharon, CT 06069) lists an amazing variety of special interest businesses from which one can also order by mail.

There are catalogs designed for new fathers, and catalogs devoted to cookbooks (Jessica's Biscuit, Box 301, Newtonville, MA 02160, is the most comprehensive). Catalog browsers can also find oak casks for the home winemaker, vintage guitars, seashells, sun-dried tomatoes, nautical prints, a clambake for two, video memberships, fur coats, fir wreaths, jet-propelled surfboards, sexy underwear, computerized chess sets, robots that pour and serve champagne, physicians' scales, snorkel masks, electronic cat doors, iceless skating rinks, and cast-iron sake warmers.

Prices? From affordable to outrageous—but if you phone in your order, it's toll-free.

Another call, another gift . . .

Commercials, Now and Forever

No more zapping of the sound to avoid the commercial message on TV. Instead, millions of Americans can now be found sitting transfixed before the tube, often for hours at a stretch, willingly watching *only* commercials.

This is television shopping, chiefly available on cable but increasingly found on UHF channels, too. Big players are Home Shopping Network (HNS), Cable Value Network, and QVC Network, which scored when it signed with Sears to offer the giant retailer's products to its cable subscribers. Your very own shopping mall.

As it is for all retailers, Christmas is boom time for TV selling. Home Shopping Network, for example, recently sold more than $3 million worth of merchandise a day.

The format of this nonstop retailing varies with the sponsor, but the basic components remain the same.

The camera focuses on a product and a voice-over praises it with an intensity that would make a used-car dealer blush. All you need is a telephone to make your purchase.

Except for an occasional camera pan to the announcer, that's it. The appeal is strictly "Buy cheap. Buy now. Buy lots."

Next Year from Neiman's: Half of Lake Havasu? All of Algiers?

1960: HIS AND HER AIRPLANES

His: A 7-seat Beechcraft Super G18. Hers: the 4-seat Beechcraft Bonanza; both 3 miles a minute, choice of color, style, cabin arrangement, and any number of combinations of individual navigational equipment. His: $149,000. Hers: $27.000.

In days of yore it was quite enough for Mary to have a little lamb—but not for Mary Lou or Sue Ellen from Dallas, not by a long shot. Every year since 1960 they and a wondering nation want to find out what will be the Gift of the Year from Neiman-Marcus. Is it only in Texas that the folks home on the range dream on a starry Christmas Eve of owning his and her ostriches, his and her jaguars (full-grown) or their very own pair of camels? Conspicuous consumption is the order of the day—the bigger, the better, and the more outrageous, the more fun.

1963: HIS AND HER SUBMARINE

The MiniSub Mark VII, a freely flooded underwater craft, is designed to carry two people and cruise at a speed of 3 to 7.3 mph. A hull of plastic-impregnated laminated glasscloth, the sub is 14 feet long, 46 inches high, and 90 inches wide. $18,700.

1967: HIS AND HER CAMELS

For people who have been promising themselves to slow down: a matched pair of the slowest, surest beasts on land will be flown from California to your private oasis (anywhere in the Continental United States). $4,125.

1968: HIS AND HER JAGUARS

A pair of Neiman-Marcus pussycats: for him, Britain's magnificent Jaguar XKE Grand Touring Coupe; for her, a natural Brazilian jaguar coat trimmed in natural ranch mink. His: $5,559. Hers: $5,975.

1971: HIS AND HER MUMMY CASES

A gift of gifts from the ancient land of Mother Nile: richly adorned, but gratefully vacant, authenticated mummy cases, both approximately 2,000 years old. $16,000.

1979: HIS AND HER DIRIGIBLES

These hot-air dirigibles have a compartment that will comfortably accommodate two passengers and a well-stocked picnic basket. A 72-hp engine enables each dirigible to cruise at 25 mph, and all 120 feet of each craft are collapsible and portable. Full flight instructions included, and the dirigibles may be had in any color and design. $50,000.

1978: HIS AND HER NATURAL SAFETY DEPOSIT BOXES

Deep within a 9,000-foot mountain of granite in Utah's Wasatch Range is a cavern, over 150 feet long, for those seeking maximum security and preservation for their really valuable possessions. Temperature and humidity never vary. Security is assured by an elaborate system of surveillance, closed circuitry, and hair-triggered alarms—all powered by waterfall-generated electricity. Available for a 50-year lease. $90,000.

1981: HIS AND HER ROBOT

ComRo I, the domestic robot system, designed for Neiman-Marcus by Ultimation, Inc. The 4½-foot-high, acrylic-encased robot operates either by remote control from a hand-held transmitter, or with a preprogrammable microcomputer "brain." $15,000.

THE FINE ART OF GIFT-GIVING

Once, at a Christmas Eve party, I was presented with the most gorgeous box, which, by its sateen flourishes and embossed logos, I instantly knew contained a bottle of Chivas Regal. Thrilled, and beaming at the giver as he stood beaming beside me, I tore through the sealed sides of the box and drew forth a bottle completely enveloped in a sack of royal purple velvet. At once I saw that a legend was sewn into the velvet in gold thread: HAPPIEST CHRISTMAS TO WATSON B. TAIT.

Now, this was somewhat puzzling, as my name is not, nor was it then, Watson B. Tait. I looked questioningly at the giver, who was no longer beaming, but rather was standing stock-still as if turned to stone. It turned out to be, of course, the old story. Long ago and far away, someone had ordered a personalized sack of Chivas Regal for Watson B. Tait, whomever that might have been. On receipt, Mr. Tait had presented same, unopened, to some associate who, in like fashion, had moved the benefice on until, at last, it came into the hands of my friend, who gave it to me as if it were fresh-plucked from the Chivas factory by his own hands.

But the truth would out.

Fortunately, I did not have the least reluctance about drinking from Mr. Tait's sack, and I hastened to assure my embarrassed friend of that. I also pointed out that, had he not been present at the gift-giving, I might well have stashed the box myself and given it later to someone else on some subsequent occasion—Valentine's Day, for example. Imagine the confusion.

(On the other hand, the box might not have been opened even then, and, like some ghost ship, it might still be circling through the considerable population of people who give liquor to each other but don't necessarily drink it.)

I suspect that the box with the Chivas in it started out as a business gift—that some hapless salesman had been hoping to impress Watson B. Tait. Poor soul! Business gifts can be so difficult. There is always a whiff of sulfurous self-interest about them.

Consider the time I gave a beautifully framed mirror to a big buyer of my products who had recently had a face-lift. In lipstick I wrote on the mirror, "Here's looking at you, Babe." My hope was that every time she looked in the mirror, she would see me as well as her ravishing new face and that, putting the two together, she would reach for the telephone and place a big order. She didn't, though. Did she see

"Gift wrap it, please."

the mirror as the tacky device it really was? If so, I don't feel a bit guilty. All gift-giving, and particularly gift-giving at Christmas, is laced with guile.

The fact is that there is a purpose behind every gift we give. We start with a lie—that Santa Claus brought all this stuff—and move right along: with the watch so glittering and thin and expensive that our spouse is reassured of our undying love; with the Italian epergne so tall and flamboyant that Aunt Gladys will remember us in her will; with a lifetime supply of Grateful Dead T-shirts to assure our son that, though we are mystified by his addiction to that group, we love him anyway.

I don't think we ought to blame ourselves for having these kinds of hidden agendas when we go out shopping and buy and give. These behavior patterns have been with us since people started to be wary of Greeks bearing gifts. Most of what we inherit from the Attic mind is frozen in books and statuary, but the giving of gifts is as lively today as it was in the fifth century before Christ.

Speaking of whom, the Magi set the tone by bearing gifts to the Christ Child with the purpose of honoring him, using the common practices of that time, and thus it is that gift-giving has always been a featured part of Christmas behavior. Although it has occasionally been condemned as a pagan practice, the model of the Magi has been kept custom-safe.

In that context, and later reinforced by the Dickensian sentimental mood, Christmas gift-giving takes on a purity of purpose which probably underlies most agendas. There is no getting away from the fact that while my gift to you at Christmas says "I love you," it also says, silently but eloquently, "Please love me."

And there is nothing in the world wrong with that.

Selecting the "Right" Gift

The Christmas gifts we buy—and hope others will buy for us—are remarkably accurate mirrors of the times in which we live. Today, our choices reflect an America fascinated with luxury, opulence, and tradition. We are looking for our pasts while we forge our futures.

Television has an enormous influence on the gift-giving season, gift consultants unanimously report. Taking our cue from shows that subliminally suggest the good life is hidden in the gleam of a diamond ring, the sheen of a satin sheet, or a designer perfume's haunting scent, we create an instant demand for a designer label (or an item of status): Ralph Lauren sheets, a Chanel crystal necklace, Fabergé eggs, an an-

tique pine wardrobe, cashmere sweaters, and a trip on the Orient Express.

These are the Christmas gifts, it seems, that all kinds of people long for and a surprisingly large number—from young college graduates to the middle-aged and on up into the ranks of what used to be called the elderly—actually receive. And it isn't only the upscale crowd, wooed by the adman's love song, who are conditioned to want not just a food processor or a VCR but a particular brand with a particularly formidable price tag.

This fascination with the "right" commodity filters down to less upwardly mobile markets as well. The result: Americans can choose from K mart's more accessible line of clothes designed by Jaclyn Smith or the lacy lingerie being promoted by Joan Collins, or find the perfume counters of department stores selling such scents as Passion, created by Elizabeth

"A microwave oven? That's your idea of a gift fit for a king?"

Taylor. Even street hawkers can find gift-seekers galore to haggle over their "Pierre Cardin" T-shirts or imitation Cartier watches.

The most-wanted gift today is indulgent and lavish, not necessarily sensible, though sometimes functional—and almost always creative. Lord & Taylor, for example, offers "theme" gifts such as a baby's wicker carrying crib filled with bibs, toys, and feeding spoons, or a winter hunt hamper overflowing with wild rice, cornbread, and quail. To give the "right" gift is to know that a napkin-lined reed basket stuffed with black squid-ink pasta and New York State chèvre is preferable to a traditional fruitcake in a tin with an "Old Master" painting on it. Raw silk kimonos are more popular than your basic terry robe—unless, of course, it has a Christian Dior tag at the neck.

Specifically, who would like what?

The single corporate woman needs clothes, clothes, clothes—for her work image, her weekend playtime, and her evenings out.

The "DINK" crowd (Dual-Income-No-Kids, so pegged by *Time*) are intrigued by items such as a pants-pressing machine that enables the couple to ogle a silent gadget rather than a possibly squalling baby.

The Filofax is the perfect gift for a friend who has everything except enough time; it provides organization that will enable the recipient to find "that extra 20 minutes," and in a handsome crocodile cover ($600) it both looks and costs a whole lot more than a datebook.

Department-store food halls always provide gourmet inspiration, ranging from an advent calendar whose doors open upon exquisite morsels of chocolate to gorgeous jars through whose clear glass sides whole fruits can be glimpsed, deliciously drowned in liqueurs.

And at some stores—New York's B. Altman's, for one—entire rooms of designer furniture and fabrics can be transplanted in your loved one's home.

On a less extravagant scale, men's fragrances

A ROAD MAP FOR YOUR CHRISTMAS SHOPPING

• If you give a tested and approved carpet sweeper to a newly married daughter, you'll give plenty of joy and satisfaction to last for many years.

• Here are useful gifts for business or college girls. The fluted vacuum washer will take care of lingerie and sweaters; the iron is light, speedy—and how she'll need the stocking frames for knee-high socks!

• A chummy family will simply love an electric corn popper for evening get-togethers. It is an ideal gift, too, for children in their teens, who are past the toy age. Then they can give their own popcorn parties.

• Any woman would like an extension dryer for lingerie, towels, hosiery. Add gay dishcloths or dish towels to make it complete.

• Haven't you a neighbor who would welcome a rubber-coated dish drainer on Christmas morning? Give it with mat for drainboard.

• Just the gift for Aunt Jane, who's so short she can never reach the china on the top shelf—a gay red step-stool, sturdy and safe.

• A collection of pie-making tools is an ideal gift. The plates are paper; the knitted cover for rolling pin keeps piecrust from sticking.

• For an inexpensive holiday gift, why not choose a set of refrigerator-bowl covers? Easy to pack, they make a good send-away gift.

Good Housekeeping
December, 1940

THE GOLDEN AGE OF LITTLE BLACK BOOKS

Ladies' sets of books, three in number, for recording visits made and received, for accounts, and for journals are twice as large this season. As one's circle increases and distances in the city become greater, the visiting-list is a matter requiring constant care, hence the visiting book is enlarged, and is arranged in columns for names, addresses, receptions, dates, and finally remarks. This is done on parchment paper, very elegantly bound in lizard-skin and lined with cream-colored moiré silk. The three books are mounted in a frame which can be locked, and it is therefore safe anywhere.

Harper's Bazaar
December 14, 1895

are a growing industry, and unisex products are in great demand as gifts, thanks in part to the health and fitness craze which has heightened body awareness. The next time you wonder who is wearing that interesting perfume, it might not be the Roberta at your table but the Robert.

For a new friend, there are "fluff" gifts, such as a giant bucket of popcorn. Functional yet innovative items, such as an electric mixer in cobalt blue, will please the cook in your life.

But while Americans today are looking for what's new and fun in colors and sizes, they also want security. Heirloom gifts such as Waterford crystal are more appreciated than ever, and for those who can—and wish to—afford it, such a present can be part of a Christmas Club arranged by Saks Fifth Avenue. Starting with a price of $1,000 and escalating up to $100,000, one can arrange for a limousine to deliver a gift on each of the 12 days of Christmas, ranging from a pedicure to a sable coat—by Revillon, of course.

"Fire is a wonderful gift, Oog—it's just that I was hoping for a fur coat."

When Nothing Comes to Mind, Think of a Book

H. Berinsky

I have a friend who owns a department store. What do you give to a friend who not only has everything, but could buy anything else she wants—wholesale?

My solution was: A BOOK.

I don't mean a book from a bookstore, I mean a book about her, a book about her professional life. I made it with my own hands.

This is the way it was for her. She inherited some land. It was a useless piece of land, outside a very small town. She built a building, intending to open a specialty food store. Days after the building was completed, the only road leading to it was diverted, isolating the building. Thus she now had a useless building on a useless piece of land.

However, with incredible determination, she built a business that now grosses many millions of dollars every year. People come from all over the country, embarked on the great adventure of finding the store; when they see it, they are so excited that they stumble in with their wallets open, eager to spend heaps of money on all the good things my friend has waiting for them.

Even in the first year the word spread and the cash registers jingled and jangled at such a rate that one day hardly anyone noticed that there was an armed robber in the store. He had to fire his gun into the air to rivet everyone's absolute attention. He got away with hard-earned dollars and cents and generated the kind of free publicity that stores can't buy.

The next year, just before the big selling season started, there was a flood, and all the merchandise was ruined. But my friend overcame that, and many other troubles, and carried on.

Admiring her grit, I made her a book.

I got a huge pile of magazines, cut out apt pictures, and pasted them on blank pages.

The first page showed a picture of a bar-

ren piece of land with the caption "In the beginning . . ."

Page 2 featured a golden palace of a hotel, pasted down with a caption along the lines of "She dreamed of building a great building . . ."

Page 3 was a photograph of the actual store, and so on.

You will have got the idea by now. It was then easy enough to find a photo of three little kids playing cops and robbers to depict the robbery. For pictures of floods and pestilence, I looked every week in *Time* magazine.

The gift was a great success.

You could do this for anyone whom you admire, who has ever had a life.

NOTORIOUS NOVELTY

A novelty of the season is the Cleopatra pen-rest, in the shape of a silver snake. This costs $2.

Harper's Bazaar
December 7, 1895

Suiting a Man

I know that Robert Burns once said something about seeing ourselves as others see us, but he said it with a Highland accent, which somehow turned the obvious into finer stuff. About the time of last Christmas, one of my young relatives brought the point home to me that I was a problem—something, I admit, I have become used to hearing.

"I don't know what to get you," she said. "You're a man who has everything."

Me? A man with everything? Could she be serious? Later that day, on a long drive, I pondered the extraordinary idea. The fact of the matter is that during the last decade or two, I've accumulated a certain amount of impedimenta. It does not mean, however, that I am difficult to get things for. Quite opposite. My tastes are an open book. I like classical records, biographies and 19th-century novels, preppy sweaters and socks that come over the calf. I also like cufflinks, most kinds of food, odd gadgets, pajamas in extra-large sizes, anything representing Jack Russell terriers, and ties for summer in a single loud color such as turquoise or lemon yellow. All I want is more of the same. Lots and lots.

What I do not want, not at all, are Madras trousers or pants with hibiscus, ponies, or anything else printed on them. I also do not want open-net shirts or fancy sandals. Not being a dashing Italian, I have never learned how to wear an ascot. Few American men have. I do not want any garment conventionally made of cloth that is now cleverly turned out in suede or leather. I want no costumes. I am not a frontiersman or a rock singer, nor do I wish to disguise myself as one.

I hope I have made myself as plain as possible. I have left one thing out. My birthday is July 24. Should you miss me for Christmas, there is plenty of time to shop.

Frederick Eberstadt
Vogue
December, 1986

Gifts Which Embarrass: A Protest from Men

Christmas I love, but not Santa Claus! He brings me, usually, but chains and fetters. For who knows my tastes and needs so well as I? Who can tell how the handle of a knife will fit into *my* hollowed palm? The size of my collars one may discover; but it needs a detective to sleuth out the secrets of my private liking, my subtle fancies and my secret abominations. How dares another select a tool for *my* particular use? How much less should he hazard outraging the idiosyncrasies of my aesthetic sense? I desire nothing merely ornamented; but if I did, I am the one to select it, not he. Can a friend pick out a fountain pen that fits my mood? How can a sweetheart choose a necktie without flinching at the risk of disapproval? Let others lend me their books—there's a rare charity!—but not load them on my shelves to gather dust!

No, Christmas is become a formula, and I, for one, would become emancipate from its

dogmas, its pocketknives for the boy, its collar boxes for the adolescent, its "military" hair brushes for the youth and its boxes of handkerchiefs for the stripling.

When I want a camera I'll buy one and get the proper size and quality. If presents must be given, let them be money—or kisses! When you wish me a Merry Christmas, do not let the embossed paper label seal a potion that will poison my freedom! Use gold cord about your package if you will, so you do not tie me into a mood of impossible gratitude for an unwished gift. I hate silver, for one thing, this I now inform my friends; but how can I catalog my abhorrences. They are infinite. From silk-knit ties to little boxes devised to hold six matches. I loathe everything that money can buy—unless I have bought it myself!

Gelett Burgess
Good Housekeeping
December, 1910

"Are you interested in a gift with or without an emotional attachment?"

DAD COULD BE SURE OF THREE THINGS: DEATH, TAXES, AND SLIPPERS

Mother's gift to father was yearly the same but always received by him with surprise and gratitude. She made him slippers of cross-stitched wool which, when completed, she took to our good old cobbler who attached leather soles and heels to the embroidered wool uppers. Mother had obtained the design of crimson roses and green leaves on a black wool background many years before from *Godey's Lady's Book* and felt it could not be improved upon. Father often remarked that they gave him perfect comfort and proved it by wearing them in the evening and all relaxed hours.

Diary of Polly McKean Bell
Portland, Oregon, 1880s

T'was the night before
Christmas
and deep was the need
To find something besides
Clement Moore's poem to read.
The children were pacing the hallways
in fear
That nothing much new would be
offered this year.
But back on the bookshelf were classics
galore,
Teeming with faith, hope, and humor
and more—
All the right thoughts for a holiday
season
But much less familiar, and thereby
more pleasin'.
So herewith a list, filled with promising
choices—
Stories to read them, in fatherly voices.

Timeless Stories with Timely Morals

The Animal Family
By Randall Jarrell. Illustrations by Maurice Sendak. The little-known and very powerful story by the late poet about the importance of family and the need to see.

The Little Prince
Text and illustrations by Antoine de Saint-Exupéry. Consider this: "You become responsible, forever, for what you have tamed." And imagine this: that a child can grow up knowing the importance of the snake, the rose, and the well.

King Midas and the Golden Touch
By Nathaniel Hawthorne. Retold and illustrated by Kathryn Hewitt. Wall Street take note.

The Phantom Tollbooth
By Norton Juster. Illustrations by Jules Feiffer. This is a book about a fantastic land where numbers war with letters, and sunrises are conducted like symphonies, and the deadliest monsters are those of the spirit. It is funny, wise, and ageless, and, most important, it is a celebration of the search for meaning.

The Giving Tree
Text and illustrations by Shel Silverstein. Tree meets boy; tree loses boy; tree gets boy.

Where the Wild Things Are
Text and illustrations by Maurice Sendak. The classic story of home: what it means to wander away from it and what it means to come back. Most beautiful drawing: the wild things in the land where the wild things are.

Winnie-the-Pooh
by A.A. Milne. Illustrations by Ernest H. Shepard. Try rereading "Eeyore Has a Birthday and Gets Two Presents." See, Eeyore figures he can fit the pieces of his broken balloon into the useful pot—and proceeds joyfully to put them in and take them out again and again. Not a bad message come Christmas Eve.

The Marzipan Pig
By Russell Hoban. Illustrations by Quentin Blake. An owl falls in love with a taxicab meter, a mouse dresses in hibiscus petals, and a marzipan pig sets the whole thing in motion. Really it's a book about the adventure that is love.

The Selfish Giant
By Oscar Wilde. Illustrations by Dom Mansell. A hundred years later, the struggle is still between the selfish and the brave.

How the Grinch Stole Christmas!
By Dr. Seuss. You know exactly how. But what the heck. It's Christmas.

Esquire
December, 1987

Christmas Books

The holidays are just around the corner, bringing with them the good cheer and onerous duties of the season. Since most people can read, books make the ideal present. We at the Culture Press are happy to announce our "Christmas lineup" of books for every age group and level of intelligence.

Toeing the Line: Feet in History by B. F. W. Cafritz. We walk around on our feet every day, but how many of us are aware that feet have a history going back thousands of years? In this lively chronicle B. F. W. Cafritz takes a not-so-solemn look at feet through the ages: from Alexander the Great (who had no toenails) to Neil Armstrong, "the most famous footprint since Man Friday." Illustrated; parental guidance suggested. 331 pp. $29.95.

Blank and Pitiless: W. B. Yeats's Letters to Zenia Gonne, edited and with an introduction by Fr. James O'Shaughnessey, S.J. Only recently discovered, these letters tell the intriguing story of Zenia Gonne's unrequited love for the great Irish poet. Zenia, the younger sister of the better-known Maud, fell passionately in love with "Willie" Yeats and wrote to him daily for seventeen years. Her letters have not survived (all were burned upon receipt), but Yeats's replies to her are now available for the first time. 6 pp. $5.95.

The Films of Evita Peron by Justin Sperling, B.S. Justin Sperling analyzes all facets of Evita Peron's brief film career, from *¡Segundos Afuera!* to *La Prodiga*. Contains stills from her movies, plus pronunciation guide. Soon to be a major motion picture. 19 pp. $9.95.

Sub-Zero: Toward a New Theory of "Literature" by Samuel F. B. Hofstock, Ph.D. In this thought-provoking study Samuel Hofstock, dean of the Meta-Meta Critics, performs what he calls "a literary autopsy" on two paragraphs written by Roland Barthes. In the process he evolves a new theory of "literature" and gains tenure at a prestigious East Coast university. Comes complete with glossary, blueprints, and decoding ring. 438 pp. $25.00.

PLUS: *The Chronologion* by Robert T. Weidaw. This book represents a "first" for the Culture Press: for the first time in our publishing history we are offering a work of fiction. *The Chronologion* is called by author Weidaw a cross between "H. G. Wells, Giorgio Vasari, and A. Conan Doyle." A winning combination! In this intriguing novel Leonardo da Vinci invents a time machine that carries him into the future, where he collaborates with Sherlock Holmes in solving a mystery that has baffled Scotland Yard and the Sûreté. You won't want to miss this exciting story, told by one of America's best-known copy-editors. "It's a book, all right," raves Umberto Eco. "The words run right across the page." 362 pp. $19.95 or best offer.

John Harris
The Atlantic
December, 1985

Sending Your Gift Through the Mail

Some guidelines from the U.S. Postal Service:

Selecting the Proper Container

Fiberboard containers are generally strong enough to ship material of average weight and size; these are the common brown boxes that are readily available in supermarkets or hardware stores. An "average" parcel is defined as one which is no more than 34 by 17 by 17 inches and weighs 25 pounds or less. These are the dimensions which can be handled by automated parcel processing.

Other acceptable containers include reinforced (padded) bags, cardboard boxes, metal cans and tubes, wooden boxes, and fiber mailing tubes with metal ends. The container should be large enough to allow adequate cushioning to prevent damage to the contents, but not so large as to permit the contents to shift or joggle about. Liquids should be sent in leakproof interior and exterior containers. Package powders in siftproof containers, and place items that have an odor in a container that is completely airtight.

Cushioning the Contents

Cushioning distributes and absorbs shocks and vibrations while preventing the contents from shifting. When several items are packaged in a container, they should be separated from each other and protected from outside forces. Even items packed alone should be cushioned for safety. Heavy items should be securely braced. Suitable cushioning materials include poly-

styrene, shredded or rolled newspaper, "bubble" plastic wrap, and fiberboard inserts.

Wrapping the Package

It is *preferred* that you not wrap the outside of the container in brown (kraft) paper if the box itself is adequate for shipping. However, wrapping paper equivalent in strength to the average large grocery bag may be used if required. Pressure-sensitive, filament-reinforced strapping tape should be used for closing and reinforcing parcels whenever possible. Although twine and cord are permitted, it is *preferred* that they not be used as they may catch and bind in mail-processing equipment.

Mailing the Package

PARCEL POST

Parcel post is one of the most economical means of mailing a package that weighs be-

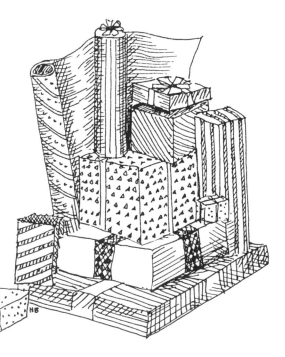

tween 16 ounces and 40 pounds and is smaller than 84 inches in combined length and girth. (Mail smaller items via third-class mail, first-class mail, or priority mail; larger packages are accepted at some post offices, but check with your postmaster first.)

Rates are determined by the weight of the parcel and the distance it is being sent. Mail three to four weeks before Christmas, earlier if you are sending gifts overseas.

Protection against loss, rifling, or damage to domestic mail can be obtained for parcel post items in any amount up to $400.

For an additional handling fee, Special Delivery provides delivery outside normal delivery hours, and on Sundays and holidays, at all destination post offices served by city carriers or within a one-mile radius of any other post office.

THIRD-CLASS MAIL

Third-class mail is an especially economical way to ship small packages that are not heavy enough to qualify for parcel post. While there is no maximum limit on size, packages must be *at least* 3½ inches wide (high) by 5 inches long. Any piece ¼ inch or more in thickness must also be rectangular in shape.

PRIORITY MAIL

Priority mail gets your package almost anywhere in the country in two to three days.

Any acceptable package weighing 70 pounds or less can be sent by priority mail. Size can go up to 100 inches in combined length and girth. Packages weighing up to four pounds can be mailed to almost any country in the world.

EXPRESS MAIL NEXT-DAY SERVICE

Express mail next-day service offers dependable overnight delivery to major cities throughout the country. A directory of over-

SENDING YOUR GIFT VIA UNITED PARCEL SERVICE

UPS offers door-to-door service for parcels weighing up to 70 pounds and measuring no more than 108 inches in length and width combined.

To send a package, phone the UPS office nearest to you and your package will be picked up the next day. The delivery charge is determined by the weight of the package, the zone to which it is being sent, and the service requested, either ground service, next-day air, or second-day air service. You need to establish all these details prior to making the call and UPS will quote you the cost, including a pick-up fee, so that you can prepay all the charges.

UPS will not accept packages in damaged cartons or cartons without intact flaps. Packages may not be tied with string but should be fastened only with pressure-sensitive plastic tape, 2 inches or more in width; water-activated paper tape, water-activated reinforced tape, cellophane tape, and masking tape may not be used.

night destinations can be obtained from your local post office.

Express mail packages mailed by 5:00 P.M. at any express mail post office enter a streamlined system that expedites handling to make sure your package is delivered the next day by 3:00 P.M. at latest. Or it can be picked up by your addressee at the destination post office as early as 10:00 A.M. on the next business day.

You can send anything mailable weighing up to 70 pounds by express mail.

EXPRESS MAIL SAME-DAY AIRPORT SERVICE

This provides service between 56 major airports in 54 of the largest U.S. cities at a cost comparable to that of post-office to post-office express mail.

You bring your shipment to the mail facility at the airport (usually located in the cargo area) and it will receive expedited preferential treatment to the destination airport. You will be told the scheduled arrival time, so that you can arrange for it to be picked up at the corresponding airport mail facility the same day.

Goods and merchandise shipped via express mail next-day service or same-day airport service are insured against loss or damage for their actual cash value up to $500—at no extra charge.

Mom is getting a head start on the day; don't get in her way!

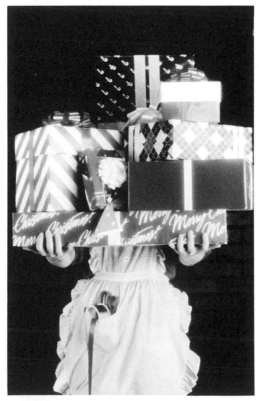

Making Sure Your Gift Gets There Safely

CERTIFIED MAIL

For less than a dollar, you can certify any piece of first-class mail, but this simply provides proof that you mailed it. You cannot insure certified mail.

RETURN RECEIPT

For proof that any letter or package arrived at its destination, you can pay a further small fee and fill out a form at the post office, which will be returned to you when signed by the recipient.

REGISTERED MAIL

This is the most secure method of mailing that the Postal Service offers, to be used for really valuable and irreplaceable items, such as jewels or the special sweater you spent months knitting. For an additional fee, it incorporates a system of receipts for an article that has been prepaid at first-class mail rates, enabling its progress to be monitored from the point of acceptance to the point of delivery. Additional insurance can be purchased to cover articles valued up to $25,000.

INSURANCE

You can buy up to $500 worth of insurance for items sent by third- and fourth-class mail, and in higher amounts for materials sent by priority mail or first-class mail. Insuring an item at minimum valuation ($25 and under) does not provide proof of delivery; for packages insured for more than $25, the recipient signs a receipt that is filed at the delivery post office.

It is a fallacy that the Postal Service pays more attention to a package that has been insured. All packages receive the same treatment—except registered materials, which travel under lock and key.

THE TIP OF ALL TIME

The largest Christmas tip on record was given by James Gordon Bennett, Jr., the *bon vivant* millionaire publisher of his father's *New York Herald*. He had frequently breakfasted amidst the silver and crystal of the old Delmonico's. After his Christmas morning breakfast in 1876, he gave the waiter who always served him a small roll of bills. As soon as the man had the opportunity, he looked at the roll, and when he recovered his equilibrium he took it to Mr. Delmonico. There were six $1,000 bills. The proprietor, sensing that a mistake had been made, put them in the safe. When the publisher next visited the café, Delmonico told him the waiter had turned the money in. He added that he would return it as Bennett departed.

"Why return it?" said the millionaire publisher. "Didn't I give it to him?"

"Yes, but of course it was a mistake. You gave him $6,000."

"Mr. Delmonico," replied Bennett, rising to his full considerable height. "you should know that James Gordon Bennett never makes a mistake."

December 25th:
The Joys of Christmas Past
Phillip Snyder

To Tip, Or Not to Tip

That is the question. Whether 'tis nobler to grease the super's palm or simply to wish him a Merry Christmas and not partake in a sea of *quid pro quo* donations. It is a pleasant thought, but in the real world the biggest dilemma is simply "to whom and how much?"

The ultimate tipping tip: It *is* up to you. A Christmas tip should be an expression of gratitude for year-round service and be in proportion to the quality of same. Whether this expression takes the form of a present or cash is also a personal decision. Though most hairdressers, for example, receive a gift, often in the form of food or liquor, a building staff member (including the night doorman who does not know you because he is always asleep) expects to see Jackson's face. The boy who delivers the soggy paper on rainy mornings and the trashmen who grind the garbage at 5:00 A.M. are also contenders for recognition. And don't forget the house cleaner, babysitter, and garage attendant.

As for the one who delivers *all* in inclement weather, braving yapping dogs and unpredictable sprinkler systems to do so, the mail carrier is not legally allowed to accept tips, but many people slip appreciative envelopes into the outgoing mail.

Below is a useful guide from *Money*.

City	Doorman	Maintenance Worker	Newspaper Deliverer	Babysitter	Housekeeper/ Cleaner	Gardener/ Lawnman	Hair Stylist
Atlanta	$20 to $100	$50 to $75	$5	$15 to $25	$30 to $65	$35 to $40	$10 to $25
Boston	$50 to $150	$5 to $100	$5 to $20	$5 to $10	$20 to $50	$25 to $50	$10 to $100
Chicago	$15 to $20	$25 to $40	$5	$5 to $15	$20 to $25	$10 to $20	$5 to $10
Dallas	$10 to $50	$10 to $20	$10	$5 to $15	$35 to $45	$30 to $55	$10 to $15
Miami	$25 to $50	$25 to $50	$5 to $25	$5 to $10	$35 to $40	$25 to $100	$10 to $50
New York City	$10 to $100	$10 to $100	$5	$20 to $30	$50 to $200	$5 to $25	$5 to $100
Washington, DC	$10 to $25	$10 to $25	$10 to $25	$10 to $25	$35 to $50	$20 to $30	$20 to $100

THE CHRISTMAS STOCKING

BY MERYLE EVANS

Is there any more enduring, cherished reminder of the halcyon days of our childhood than the Christmas stocking? For one night each year that otherwise ordinary article of clothing is miraculously transformed into a captivating catchall—hung, empty, by the fireplace before bedtime, and retrieved gleefully at the crack of dawn, bulging with Santa's bounty.

For almost two centuries the joys—and sometimes the sorrows—of this beloved annual ritual have been recorded by American writers and illustrators looking back at their own early years.

The novelist Lillian Smith, in "Memory of a Large Christmas," wrote about her family celebration in the South:

Mother accelerated the stocking hanging. Twelve were hung. The foresighted had reserved Big Granny's weeks ahead, the laggards settled for the cook's (first choice) or Mother's (second choice). Each long black stocking hung with a name on it in Mother's bedroom. Five o'clock next morning everybody was scrambling round the fireplace, feeling in the dark for his. So you took down your knobby stocking and in the light of the fire you dug in. There on the floor and in the chairs were The Things you had written Santa about.

Washington Irving, writing in 1809 in *Knickerbocker History of New York* (by the pseudonymous "Dietrich Knickerbocker"), is the first to refer in print to "hanging up a stocking on the chimney on St. Nicholas eve; which stocking is always found in the morning miraculously filled—for the good St. Nicholas has ever been a great giver of gifts. . . ."

The very next year, an engraving of St. Nicholas by the prominent New York artist Alexander Anderson included a vignette of a fireplace flanked by two oversized stockings, one replete with toys, oranges and sugarplums, the other stuffed with sticks. Over the mantel are pictures of a happy little girl holding a lap full of toys and a tearful lad with a stick in his buttonhole.

Before long the Christmas stocking made its debut in verse. In 1821, a small illustrated book, *A New Year's Present*, described Santa's nocturnal journey in these stanzas:

> Through many houses he has been,
> And various beds and stockings seen,
> Some white as snow and neatly mended,
> Others that seem'd for pigs intended.
>
> Where e'er I found good girls or boys
> That hated quarrels, strife and noise,
> I left an apple or a tart
> Or wooden gun or painted cart . . .
>
> But where I found the children naughty,
> In manners rude, in temper haughty,
> Thankless to parents, liars, swearers,
> Boxers or cheats or base tale bearers,
>
> I left a long black birchen rod,
> Such as the dread command of God
> Directs a Parent's hand to use
> When virtue's path his sons refuse.

Despite the dire threat of birch rods, stockings were soon "hung by the chimney with care" all across the country. In *The Southern Christmas Book*, Harnett T. Kane writes of the festivities at the White House in 1835, when President Andrew Jackson's niece Mary Donelson and several other youngsters came for Christmas:

If we don't get all we ask for, we can always hope to get more than we deserve.

That night the President invited the children to his room to hang their stockings. (They) were hung from hooks on the mantel, from curtain rings at the foot of Jackson's bed, one from a "boot jack carelessly left on Uncle's green leather armchair." One of the children had an idea: why not hang a stocking for Uncle himself? . . . Jackson agreed, commenting that he had waited nearly 70 years to put up a stocking.

In the morning each child found a silver quarter, cakes, nuts, candy, fruit, and toys, while the President's stocking contained a pair of slippers, a cob pipe, and a tobacco bag.

Although fireplaces were few and far between in the Deep South, Susan Dabney Smedes, the daughter of a Mississippi planter, wrote that everyone in her house hung a sock on a line strung along the hall staircase—23 in all, including the new baby's pink bootie. And out in the Oregon wilderness where presents of any kind were few and far between, pioneer Charles Stevens found a piece of an old pipe, some tobacco, and a penknife in his stocking on Christmas Day.

However, by mid-century, the stocking had a rival as a repository for presents. The anonymous author of *Kriss Kringle's Christmas Tree*, a book published in Philadelphia in 1847, commented:

> The practice of hanging up stockings in the chimney corner . . . is being superseded by that of placing a Christmas Tree on the table to await the annual visit of the worthy Santa Klaus. He has, with his usual humor, accommodated himself to this change in popular taste.

By the 1880s Santa was asked to accommodate another switch—back to the stocking. An editorial in *The New York Times* in December of 1883 noted a definite decrease in the demand for "The German Christmas Tree—a rootless and lifeless corpse." The writer, tongue-in-cheek, speculated that stockings had fallen into disfavor because:

> The New England stocking, though admirably suited for holding presents like paper cutters or knitting needles, did not have sufficient room for the ordinary Christmas presents for even an economical home.
>
> On the other hand the tonnage of the Western stocking—especially that of the Chicago type—was so great that it could not be filled except at a cost which few fathers of families could afford.

What was needed, the *Times* continued, was the newly invented Smith Christmas Stocking, which looked like ordinary hose, but was made of *elastic* and thus "suited to the circumstances of every family. . . . The inventor has also provided it with a watertight metallic compartment in the region of the toes for the reception of molasses candy," the soft, sticky substance responsible for ruining many perishable gifts.

Bigger and better stockings have been a favorite theme of Christmas chroniclers. Frank J. Bonnelle's poem "Greedy Jim" tells the story of a boy who planned to increase his share of toys by hanging a long rubber stocking "That would reach from his head to the floor / And contain quite as much as a tub / Or, if stretched enough, possibly more." Santa, surprised at the size of the stocking, "laughed till giant tears

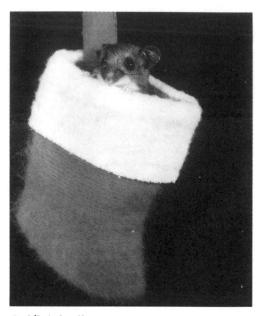

Gerbils to boot!

wet his eyes." In the morning the stocking was so full that to reach it Jim had to climb on a chair, but alas! he "was punished for being so greedy / For the stocking held nothing but air."

Toward the end of the 19th century, bright red, gaily decorated, specially designed Christmas stockings came on the market, along with the first prefilled stockings, ranging in size from 8 inches (10 cents) to 30 inches ($3.00). B. Shackman & Co. advertised that:

> These surprises, so appreciated by the little ones, are made in transparent nets of various colors, through which the contents can be easily seen. They contain Jewels, Curios, Picture Books, Fans, Umbrellas, Dolls, Humming Tops, Cornets, Prizes, Toys, Christmas crackers, etc. These are made separately for boys and girls.

But, of course, it is neither the size nor the quality of the stocking that counts. Jan Struther, in her story of *Mrs. Miniver*, written in 1939, captures the timeless and universal appeal of the tradition. The scene is set at 6:00 A.M. on December 25th. The three Miniver children have claimed their stockings and straggled into their mother's room to empty the contents on her bed:

> To the banquet of real presents which was waiting downstairs, covered with a red and white dust sheet, the stocking toys, of course, were only an *aperitif*; but they had a special and exciting quality of their own. Perhaps it was the atmosphere in which they were opened—the chill, the black window panes, the unfamiliar hour; perhaps it was the powerful charm of the miniature, of toy toys, of smallness squared; perhaps it was the sense of limitation within a strict form, which gives to both the filler and the emptier of a Christmas stocking something of the same enjoyment which is experienced by the writer and the reader of a sonnet; or perhaps it was merely that the spell of the old legend still persisted.

> Meryle Evans is a social historian with a particular interest in holiday customs.

To Stuff a Stocking

You can fill a stocking with delightfully dopey, funny stuff *or* you can make a tiny treasure trove of goodies with a theme. One nice theme is the recipient's known or secret hobbies, as you please; be sure to provide plenty of variety.

For the food lover, consider the following:

Many food companies make miniatures—bottles of herbs and spices, jams, honey, rounds or wedges of cheese, packets of crackers, candies, jelly beans, chocolates, cookies, teas (with a tea ball for infusing loose tea), minibags of different kinds of coffee, and splits (the smallest-size bottles) of champagne. Accompany these with assorted gadgets, such as bottle openers, egg cups, a mother-of-pearl spoon, or a pepper mill.

Include some exotica, too: one or more kinds of caviar, a jar of quail eggs, and some other fancy foods that have special significance—a fresh white truffle, say, for someone who loves them, a box of shortbread for a Brit, some chilies or cellophane noodles or even (if you are really skilled) home-baked fortune cookies with a personal message in each one.

For a photographer, get some rolls of exactly the right kind of film, with some lenses and small accessories that would make the receiver happy. Slip in a copy of a photography magazine, too.

Blank cassettes are always welcomed by all, and there are literally hundreds of small objects in the hi-tech area, such as a personal telephone directory that is the size of a credit card, or a favorite old movie on video that can form the nucleus of a collection.

For a luxurious gift, how about a variety of makeup or soaps and lotions, along with a gift certificate for a makeup session?

Tickets are great to put into stockings. You can tailor them to your budget. Put in a "ticket" good for six hamburgers, or season tickets for a favorite sports team or a tennis tournament. Think in terms of tickets to rock or chamber music concerts, the theater, ballet, or opera; or admission to a series of lectures or cooking classes. Your tickets can cover visits to museums, zoos, gardens, or the next horse show; a journey to a sunny beach or to see a dear friend; a day's rental of a bicycle, a canoe, a Mercedes—or a hot-air balloon.

Now you're soaring!

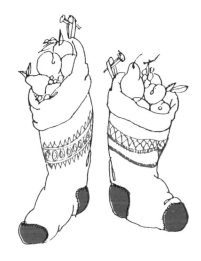

Gift Time in the Corporate World

Recently, Santa received a Christmas letter requesting 300 wineglasses, 200 address books, and 50 boxes of stationery. Normally, the jolly fellow would not be fazed—but this request came from one individual. So Santa politely referred the inquirer to a professional gift consultant.

In the business world, the act of Christmas giving is a business in itself. According to *The New York Times* and Bruce Bolger of *Incentive Marketing* magazine, businesses pay $1.4 billion annually for gifts, and two-thirds of that is spent in the middle of December. That is why most major department stores and exclusive shops such as Tiffany's and Godiva provide gift consultants. These invaluable people specialize in the finances, aesthetics, and psychology of giving, whether en masse or to that one person on whom an individual's future career may depend.

We spoke to the gift consultants at Lord & Taylor, Saks Fifth Avenue, and Bloomingdale's, and they all concurred in the importance of analyzing just what it is that makes a present *presentable* in a given set of circumstances. Noting that it is sometimes important for a gift to be extravagant—or to seem as if it is—they pointed out that the selection is often a subtle way of acknowledging a good year's work, expressing confidence in an employee, reinforcing appreciation for a business transaction, or signaling how well the company is doing.

Although it may not be talked about, many a crystal vase is sized up according to its surmised cost and understood to equal the recipient's status in the boss's good graces. If a gift is too expensive, on the other hand, it can be looked upon as a bribe. In addition, the selection can set a precedent for the years to come. It is not hard to see why many firms have established standard gifts in certain categories for employees, clients, and others who offer services, such as the elevator operators and doormen.

It is considered more appropriate for those who have climbed the corporate ladder to give to those on lower rungs than vice versa. The higher up one is, of course, the more one is expected to spend. Often the price range is considered before the actual present is selected.

Gift consultants can and do handle most corporate giving dilemmas for brokerage firms, banks, Fortune 500 companies, and even mom-and-pop stores that need to show seasonal appreciation. They know just when to recommend the simple route of a gift certificate, propose the solution of offering electronic battery-operated staplers to all middle management, or specifically put two and two together with the inspired suggestion that a $3,600 pair of diamond earrings might be just the thing for a female CEO. As always, it will depend on the size of the company, who the givers and receivers are, motivation, and—perhaps most important of all—budget.

What does one professional give to another?

Something he *really* needs: a miniature train set, with remote control, contained in an attaché case. And only $1,000. Ideal on the Paoli local.

CHRISTMAS COURAGE FOR THE GIRL
WHO EARNS HER OWN LIVING

The Christmas season is the true test of a business girl's courage. This is not because most of us must work harder than ever just before Christmas, but because we must solve holiday problems which our stay-at-home sisters are spared. . . .

The self-supporting girl must decide —and stick to that decision—that she should, first of all, do the square thing by herself and the man she works for. And the square thing does not consist of getting into debt or sacrificing the strength which belongs to her employer, in order to make presents to her family and friends. . . .

Which brings us to the question of Christmas presents in business! This is especially puzzling to the inexperienced girl. She begins to feel vaguely anxious when the elevator-man hangs up his holly-decked box, when the office-boy becomes Christmasly solicitous, when she hears rumors of a subscription paper. . . .

Do not in a moment of enthusiasm start a subscription paper to give your chief a pair of gold cuff-links or a brass desk-set. You may feel particularly friendly toward him for promotion, but the girl at the next desk who was not promoted may entertain entirely different feelings for him. . . . If your employer is a well-bred man—and you want to keep your distance from any employer who is not—he will be annoyed if you send him an expensive Christmas present which represents nothing but your fear of him or your desire to secure advancement or a "raise."

If, however, your relations with your chief employer have been more than ordinarily friendly, if, as it often happens, you have been invited to his home to meet his family, then you can send a picture, a book, an artistic card or a few flowers to the husband and wife who have shown that you are more to them than a stenographer or clerk.

Perhaps you ask, "Well, to whom (else) do I give?" To those you love—precisely as your stay-at-home sister does. You have a certain contempt for her if she tries to pay social debts with Christmas gifts beyond her purse or if she uses a Christmas present as a social wedge. Well, look at yourself and your giving from precisely the same standpoint. If the girl on your left has been a good office friend and the girl on your right has been unfriendly, give the girl you like a present—simply because she's a friend, not a desk-mate. If the office-boy has been courteous to you or you know he has a hard time in life and you want to scatter Christmas cheer his way, remember him as you would someone in your own home, but don't toss him a quarter as if it were a Christmas tax.

Woman's Home Companion
December, 1910

One New York company regularly orders $10–$15,000 worth of chocolates to give away. Tiffany's silver screwball key rings are popular, and so are their small crystal bowls and perpetual calendars. At the department stores, clocks do well for those watching the company time, and stemware will suit anyone who likes to take the edge off a hard day's work. Desk-top items such as picture frames, stationery, and expensive pens are always excellent choices because they do not outride the office boundaries, yet they invite personalization with photos and monograms. Organizational devices such as desk calendars or portfolios in faux alligator have the look of quality without the major expense.

In the under-$50 category: For those in New York, Los Angeles, Boston, and Washington, D.C., the "Foodfile" provides an index-card guide to food sources, including restaurants, catering outfits, and publications, while the "Cityfile" offers an equivalent directory of shopping, theaters, transportation, and other vital features. The "Calling Card," a compact computerized address book which can hold up to 150 names and is not much bigger than a credit card, has been a best seller all over the country. "The Message Mike"—a tape recorder in the shape of a 1940s microphone—allows word to be left by anyone entering an office and finding its occupant out.

If you are baffled about what to give that hard-to-please associate, consider this request received not so long ago by Bloomingdale's.

A head of state wanted something for a man who has everything, who is accustomed both to black-tie dinners and to riding Western-style on a ranch, someone of great importance with a sense of humor.

The gift consultant put together a food basket that included Petrossian caviar and jelly beans. The recipient? Ronald Reagan, of course.

"This year, Ms. Wilson, instead of giving you a regular Christmas bonus, the law firm will sue for you anyone of your choice at a 20 percent discount."

BUY·A·PAL

WANTED: Perfect companion for over-worked, lonely, sometimes anxious executive. Someone huggable who will be there when the going gets rough. Looking to share a life of unconditional love and agreement with someone who speaks up and has unusual looks.

Know the feeling? According to *USA Today*, you are not alone, and to fill your need, Santa has put several versions of a new hi-tech toy in his sack. Pete, Repeat, and Friends are two stuffed bears, a hippo, and a rabbit with a multi-microchip device tucked in their tummies which automatically records your voice for four seconds, then plays it back. These new friends will always answer back—but only to say what you want to hear.

You cannot get that through the personals.

Corporate Carrots at Christmastime

When Ebenezer Scrooge gave Bob Cratchit a Christmas turkey he started a trend. And in today's workaday world, which often demands impersonal behavior, employer and employee have come to expect—at the very least—a holiday token of personal good cheer.

In fact, Yuletide business protocol has now become predictable enough to be statistical. When the Bureau of National Affairs recently surveyed 408 businesses ranging from manufacturing firms to hospitals, the following gift-giving patterns emerged:

- Holiday gifts and bonuses are given by over 42 percent of those who responded. Employees at all levels are included, and most gifts bestowed on non-management employees consist of food (60 percent) or merchandise rather than cash or a bonus.

  If food is given, turkeys are more popular than hams.

  If a gift certificate is given, the average is $100 for management and $87.50 for non-management.

- When it comes to receiving, many employers insist that a gift may be accepted only if it is of "normal" value (depending on the company, the price of normalcy can vary from $10 to $250). Non-business employers such as the government or a school are more likely to put a curb on the acceptance of gifts.

- Almost half of those surveyed sponsor Christmas parties. A company-wide party to which spouses and/or other guests are invited is the most common format, but very few include children. More than half of those polled hold parties away from the work environment and after hours.

- Christmas "cheer"—be it hard liquor, champagne, wine, or beer—is served at some 64 percent of the parties.

A bible for the briefcase brigade from Franklin Watts, Inc.

In December, 1903, New York's ladies bountiful set out some spectacular largesse for the poor: a bird in every basket and dinner to feed five. Some recipients eked it out for days.

Ring Them Bells!

The wealth of holiday charity fund-raisers has been an American phenomenon since the turn of the century. Today there are more than 785,000 public charities and countless private ones. The spirit of giving seems to increase proportionally during the busiest shopping season, as the Salvation Army kettles, filled by more than $50 million, bear witness.

The giving takes many forms. For example, donations to the Alternative Christmas Markets of Pasadena, California, provide 23 heifers, 48,484 tree seedlings, and 49 village water pumps for some impoverished villagers in third-world countries, thus insuring them an income and drinkable water.

Holiday causes range from funds to combat AIDS to benefits for the local ballet. One man hands out 200 pairs of gloves to homeless people; a black-tie dinner-dance with a three-digit admission charge provides money for medical research; Citymeals-on-Wheels delivers 22,000 holiday dinners to senior citizens and shut-ins; Love for Kids in Dallas, Texas, offers gifts of food to local refugees from Southeast Asia.

A Christmas gift could be a donation in a friend's name to a charity of your choice. The National Charities Information Bureau, Inc., at 19 Union Square West, New York, NY 10003, has a listing of philanthropic organizations.

POOR RICHARD'S ALMANACK

**When other Sin's grow old by Time,
Then Avarice is in its prime,
Yet feed the Poor at Christmas time.**

December, 1757

THE GIFT OF FOOD

Giving a gift of food that you have made yourself is a loving thing to do. Everyone must eat, so you know your present will be welcome, whether it is as simple as a loaf of homemade bread or as luxurious as a picnic hamper crammed with good things to eat.

Some foods can, indeed must, be prepared months in advance. Mincemeat, plum pudding, fruit cake, and summer preserves need only to be wrapped at the last moment. Cookies, cakes, breads, and many other foods can be prepared weeks ahead and frozen, but even if you have not done any advance planning there are many marvelous things that can be made in just a few minutes.

Sending food to faraway places by mail or UPS is a distinct challenge, and great care must be taken to ensure that fragile foods arrive in good condition. Cakes are best sent in the pans in which they were baked; and, to prevent jostling, pack cookies in an airtight container cushioned with miniature marshmallows. Send jars of preserves and pickles separately in case somebody along the way does not take the "Fragile" label seriously. Or you can minimize the risk of disaster by transferring such foods to plastic containers; even though they will not look as sensational as when they are packed in glass, their safe arrival may justify the aesthetic compromise. Pack the gift food in a carton with rigid sides and use popcorn, whole peanuts in their shells, or styrofoam pellets as packaging material. Enclose a card with storage or reheating directions, or slip in a cassette with taped messages from family or friends.

On the whole, it is considerably easier and certainly preferable to deliver homemade foods by hand, so that both the food and its wrappings are fresh. It is also interesting to match a food gift with another gift. For example, if you are giving a gift of homemade granola, enclose the recipe and measured amounts of all ingredients so that the recipient can make another batch.

Give a gift of homemade cookies with a cookie jar, a set of colorful or antique cookie cutters, or an ice cream maker, filled, of course, with some just-made ice cream.

Give a jug of mulled cider with a set of mugs or a box of highly polished red and green apples.

Give homemade bread with a bread knife or an assortment of unusual and rare honeys from other countries, including the ancestral homes of yourself and the recipient.

Give homemade coffee cake with a coffee pot, a pound of coffee beans, and an electric or hand-turned grinder.

For an artichoke lover, give a freshly cooked but cold artichoke tied onto an artichoke plate and wrapped in green cellophane. The same thing can be done with asparagus on an asparagus plate.

For friends with a fireplace, give some chestnuts with a chestnut roasting pan and include some chestnut stuffing (it can be frozen for later use), *marrons glacés*, and chestnuts in syrup.

Knives are the most essential of all kitchen utensils. Give one or more with a sharpening utensil, a butcher block, a book on carving, and the promise of a roast to be delivered by arrangement with the local butcher.

For a garden lover, give a crock of herbs and spices, put some allspice in a Russian lacquer box, or send a pot of rosemary that you have bought or grown yourself. Enclose some seed catalogs and a book on cooking with herbs.

If you have food-loving friends who have a particular interest in one country, choose a gift that will give them special pleasure. For example, for devotees of all things Italian, give a jar of homemade pasta sauce with a pasta machine, an Italian cookbook, some Italian cheeses, sausages, cookies, chocolates, or wine. For a Chinese cooking enthusiast, give a group of hard-to-find ingredients from a local Chinese gourmet shop or mail-order firm. And make some fortune cookies yourself and include your own "sayings."

For camping, hiking, and boating friends, visit or write to an outdoors supply company and put together a group of freeze-dried foods with a set of nested utensils (for the limited space of a galley) or buy them some outdoor cooking equipment.

And if you cannot, or choose not to, think any further, give beautiful food from a mail-order supplier—country ham; prime steak; frozen quail; smoked goose; smoked salmon from Scotland, Ireland, Nova Scotia, or the Pacific Northwest; lobsters and clams from Maine; crayfish from California; Russian caviar; fresh foie gras; fresh fruits; dried, tropical, glacéed, and crystallized fruits; nuts (whole, in the shell, salted, roasted, dry roasted, candied, and chocolate-covered); sauces; spreads; pickles; mustards; vinegars; chocolates; cookies; candies; gingerbread houses, or a take-home pizza.

Pâté Maison

It would be very kind to give an attractively wrapped homemade pâté, but even kinder to give it in the pâté mold or terrine, casserole, or earthenware pot in which it was cooked. To estimate the quantity of ingredients you will need, fill the pot you have selected with water, and then measure it. One cup of water will occupy the same space as half a pound of ground meat.

Allow 2½ pounds of ground meat to fill a 2-quart pâté mold to the brim. (Mound it slightly in the center to allow for shrinkage.) A 2-quart pâté should be cooked for approximately 1½ hours. However, the deeper the container the longer the mixture will take to cook. (The reverse is also true; cooking time for a 1-quart container should be reduced to 1 hour.)

Makes a 2-quart-sized pâté

½ pound thinly sliced bacon
1 pound raw ground veal
1 pound raw ground pork
½ pound raw ground beef
½ pound raw ground calves' liver
1 teaspoon dried thyme
1 teaspoon dried sage
¼ teaspoon nutmeg
1½ teaspoons salt
Freshly ground black pepper
¼ cup Madeira
¼ cup brandy
¼ cup heavy cream
2 eggs, lightly beaten

Preheat the oven to 350 degrees.
Line the bottom and sides of a 2-quart terrine or casserole with three-quarters of the bacon slices.
Put the ground meats into a large bowl and fold in all the remaining ingredients. Fill the terrine with the mixture, mounding it slightly in the center. Cover with the remaining bacon slices and put on the casserole lid, or cover with aluminum foil.

Put the terrine into a larger container and add sufficient hot water to come three-quarters of the way up the sides of the terrine. Bake in the preheated oven for 1½ hours, or until the internal temperature reaches 150 degrees on a meat thermometer.

Remove the casserole lid and cover the terrine with aluminum foil. Allow the pâté to cool completely, then weight it with a bottle of wine or cans of food to make it more compact and easier to cut. Chill the pâté for at least 48 hours before serving.

Pecan Ball

This is a small gift of food that could be given with an assortment of other cheeses, a wooden cheese board, a jar of imported pickles or mustard, or a bag of Georgia or Texas pecans. You can form the cheese into one large ball or make many bite-sized morsels with a toothpick inserted into each.

Makes 1 large ball

8-ounce package cream cheese
¼ cup finely chopped parsley
2 tablespoons finely chopped chives
½ teaspoon Worcestershire sauce
Dash Tabasco sauce
¾ cup finely chopped pecans

Combine the cheese, parsley, and chives with the Worcestershire and Tabasco sauces. Chill until the cheese is firm. Form into one large or several small balls and roll in the pecans.

Gingerbread

Gingerbread is for delivering by hand, fresh from the oven, and is meant to be eaten with a spoonful of whipped cream. However, if you are giving it to all the neighbors, the mailman, the hairdresser, and dozens of other people who have been kind throughout the year, it can be frozen very successfully until the time comes for distributing gifts.

Cut the gingerbread into squares and present it in a box lined with a paper doily or in a basket lined with a gingham napkin. Don't forget to enclose the recipe!

Makes 6 large squares

½ pound butter
1 cup boiling water
2 eggs
¾ cup dark brown sugar, packed
¾ cup molasses
2½ cups all-purpose flour, sifted
½ teaspoon baking powder
2 teaspoons baking soda
2 teaspoons powdered ginger
1 teaspoon cinnamon
½ teaspoon allspice
½ teaspoon ground cloves

Preheat the oven to 375 degrees.

Butter and flour an 8-inch-square baking pan.

Cut the butter into small pieces and dissolve it in the boiling water. Cool to room temperature.

Beat the eggs and brown sugar together in a mixing bowl until they are very thick. Stir in the molasses.

Sift together all the dry ingredients in a separate bowl. Add them to the egg mixture, alternately with the butter and water, beating well after each addition.

Pour the batter into the prepared pan and bake in the preheated oven for 40 minutes, or until a cake tester inserted into the center comes out clean.

Remove the gingerbread from the oven and allow it to cool in the pan for 15 minutes before cutting into squares.

Lemon Curd

This is a delicious, easy-to-make sweet lemon butter that is very popular in England. It is used as a spread on crumpets, muffins, and toast. Put it in a glass or china pot for gift-giving and tie it with a yellow ribbon. Store it in the refrigerator if you are making it a few days ahead of time.

Makes 1⅓ cups

3 large lemons
5 eggs
1 cup granulated sugar
8 tablespoons unsalted butter

Grate the lemon rinds and set aside. Squeeze the juice and put into a blender or food processor. Add the remaining ingredients and process until smooth.

Pour the mixture into a very heavy saucepan or the top half of a double boiler. Stir in the lemon rind and cook over low heat or over simmering water for about 10 minutes, until thickened. Stir the mixture with a wire whisk if it appears lumpy.

Chill the lemon curd before serving. It becomes thicker as it cools.

Marinated Mushrooms

First, find an attractive glass jar with a lid. It could be an apothecary jar, a large English candy jar, even an empty mayonnaise jar. I once gave a gift of a jar of marinated mushrooms accompanied by a small basket lined with green leaves and filled with meringue mushrooms dusted with cocoa powder. . . .

Makes about 1 quart

½ pound button mushrooms, washed

VINAIGRETTE:

1 clove garlic, finely chopped
6 tablespoons salad oil
2 tablespoons tarragon vinegar
1 tablespoon finely chopped parsley
1 teaspoon Dijon mustard
½ teaspoon sugar
½ teaspoon salt
¼ teaspoon dried or 1 teaspoon chopped
    fresh tarragon
Freshly ground black pepper

Fill the jar with uniformly sized button mushroom caps.

Combine all the dressing ingredients in a food processor, or in a bowl, using a wire whisk. Pour enough dressing into the jar to cover the mushrooms completely. Raw sliced scallions and a sprig or two of fresh tarragon or thyme can be added to the jar if you wish. Store in the refrigerator.

Almond Cookies

These bites of almond-buttery goodness literally melt away as you press your tongue against the roof of your mouth—and you *have* to have another one to be sure they were really as divine as you thought they were.

Makes about 60

½ pound unsalted butter, softened
¾ cup granulated sugar
½ teaspoon almond extract
1 teaspoon vanilla extract
2 cups sifted flour
1 cup ground almonds or filberts
1½ cups confectioners' sugar

Preheat the oven to 350 degrees.

Beat the butter and sugar together until they are light and creamy, using an electric mixer or a food processor. Beat in the almond extract, vanilla, flour, and ground nuts. (The nuts must be very finely ground or the cookies will fall apart.) Chill the mixture for 2 hours until very cold.

Butter and flour 2 baking sheets. Form the dough into bite-sized balls and put them on the sheets. Bake in the preheated oven for 10 minutes. The bottoms should be barely browned.

Remove the cookies from the oven immediately and transfer to wire racks to cool. Roll them in confectioners' sugar while they are still warm. Allow them to cool and roll them again. Store in an airtight container.

Mincemeat

This recipe will produce enough filling for two 9-inch pies. Mincemeat can also be used as an accompaniment for roast pork, roast game, or as a filling for dessert omelettes or crêpes.

If you are making a homemade mincemeat pie as a present, it should be delivered on the day it is baked, or frozen until you are ready to part with it. Give a gift of year-old mincemeat in a canning jar or a beautiful pot.

Makes 2 quarts

¼ pound beef suet, ground
½ cup light brown sugar
2 cups raisins
2 cups currants
1 cup chopped glacéed fruits
½ cup chopped almonds
1 tart apple, peeled, cored, and grated
1 cup fine freshly made bread crumbs
Grated rind and juice of 1 lemon
1 teaspoon cinnamon
1 teaspoon allspice
1 teaspoon almond extract
½ teaspoon mace or nutmeg
½ teaspoon ground cloves
½ cup apricot preserves
1 cup brandy or applejack
Port wine (optional)

Combine all the ingredients except the port wine in a bowl or crock with a lid. Cover, and leave in a cool place for 1 month. Stir the mixture once a week. Add a little port wine if the mixture seems too dry, though there should be sufficient brandy to keep it moist for a year.

Banana Bread

This is an easy bread to bake even if you have never made bread before. It is at its best still warm from the oven, but it can also be prepared in advance and frozen.

Makes 1 8-inch loaf

2 cups flour
½ teaspoon salt
½ teaspoon baking soda
8 tablespoons butter
½ cup brown sugar
2 tablespoons honey
2 eggs
2 fully ripened bananas, mashed
½ cup chopped citron
½ cup chopped walnuts

Preheat the oven to 350 degrees.
Butter and flour an 8-by-4-inch loaf pan.
Sift together the flour, salt, and baking soda. Beat the butter and brown sugar in an electric mixer until thick and creamy. Stir in the honey. Fold in the eggs alternately with the flour mixture. Fold in the bananas, citron, and walnuts.

Turn the dough into the prepared pan and bake in the preheated oven for 1¼ hours, or until a cake tester inserted into the center comes out clean. Remove the bread from the loaf pan and leave to cool on a wire rack.

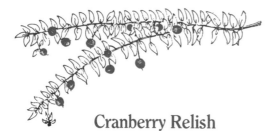

Cranberry Relish

This little gift can be presented on its own in a pretty jar—or, to be especially festive, with a country ham.

Makes 2 8-ounce jars

2 cups fresh cranberries
Grated rind and juice from 1 large
  thick-skinned orange
1 cup granulated sugar
1 teaspoon dry English mustard powder
  dissolved in 1 teaspoon cold water
1 tablespoon vinegar

Wash the cranberries and put them in a heavy saucepan. Add the orange rind and juice and the sugar. Bring to the boil and simmer for 5 minutes. Remove from the heat and stir in the mustard and vinegar.

Chill for 24 hours, then pack into jars. Store in the refrigerator if you are not presenting them as gifts immediately.

Homemade Mixed Fruit Marmalade

You will be amazed how much beautiful, clear, fresh-tasting marmalade can be made from just one orange, one lemon, and one grapefruit. It has an excellent spreading consistency, neither too firm nor too runny, and can be given in a brandy snifter, a handmade pot, or any other attractive container you can find. If this lacks a lid, tie transparent wrap over the top with rib-bon—marmalade sets firmly and, being acid, keeps well even without a paraffin wax seal.

If you have a food processor, you can make a supply of marmalade for hostess gifts—to be given with a loaf of homemade bread.

Makes 8 half-pint jars

1 thick-skinned orange
1 large lemon
1 large grapefruit
Water
Sugar

Cut each fruit in half. Remove the seeds and tie them into a bag made from cheesecloth. (The seeds contain pectin, which helps the marmalade to set.) Set the bag aside.

Slice the citrus rinds and pulp thinly, using a sharp knife or the slicing disk in the food processor. Save any juice that results from the slicing in a bowl. Measure the combined fruit and juice into a large bowl and add 3 times that quantity of cold water. Submerge the cheesecloth bag of seeds in the liquid, cover the bowl, and leave at room temperature for 24 hours.

Transfer the contents of the bowl to a large heavy saucepan or casserole and simmer gently for about 1 hour, until reduced by half.

Measure again and add an equal quantity of sugar. Return the mixture to the pan and bring slowly to the boil, stirring from time to time until the sugar has dissolved. Stop stirring and bring to a full rolling boil. Boil steadily for about 40 minutes, or until the temperature reaches 222 degrees on a candy thermometer. Stir the marmalade occasionally to make sure it is not scorching on the bottom of the pan.

Discard the cheesecloth bag and skim off the surface foam. Let the marmalade stand for 30 minutes, stirring occasionally to distribute the fruit evenly in the jelly.

Have ready at least 8 sterilized half-pint jars. Fill them with marmalade and cover with transparent wrap. Store the jars in a cool, dark place. Just before parting with them, tie the jars with a ribbon.

White Bread

This recipe makes an excellent loaf of white bread with a good, golden crust. You can make a single loaf in a food processor or, if you are kneading it by hand, you can double the recipe. Give the bread on its own or with a gift of homemade pâté, a group of cheeses and cocktail sausages, or a jar of your own preserves. The bread can be frozen until gift-giving time.

Makes 1 8-inch loaf

1 package dry yeast
½ cup lukewarm water (110 degrees)
½ cup milk
2 tablespoons butter
1 teaspoon sugar
1 teaspoon salt
3 cups all-purpose flour

GLAZE:
1 egg yolk stirred with 1 tablespoon milk

Sprinkle the yeast over the surface of the lukewarm water and let stand for 5 minutes.

Meanwhile, heat the milk to a simmer and stir in the butter, sugar, and salt. Let the mixture cool to room temperature.

Put all these ingredients in a food processor, add the flour, and process just until combined. Do not continue to mix the dough or the food processor will overheat and turn itself off. Alternatively, combine the dough ingredients in a bowl, using a wooden spatula.

Knead the dough until it becomes smooth and elastic and put it into a lightly oiled bowl. Cover the bowl and let the dough rise in a warm place for 1½ hours, until doubled in bulk.

Butter and flour an 8-by-4-inch loaf pan.

Knead the dough again for 5 minutes and shape it into a loaf. Put the shaped dough into the pan, cover, and let rise for another hour, until again doubled in bulk.

Preheat the oven to 350 degrees.

Brush the dough with the egg yolk and milk glaze. Bake the loaf in the preheated oven for 1 hour, until golden. Remove, turn the loaf out on a wire rack, and let it cool.

A Crock of Spices to Give with a Jug of Country Apple Cider

Put these spices in a crock or an attractive container and keep them handy for making mulled cider to greet yourself or your family and friends on cold wintry days. The proportions are not that important—the cider will just end up tasting slightly more of one thing than another—but here is my favorite combination.

12 cinnamon sticks, broken in half
¼ cup whole cloves
¼ cup allspice berries
¼ cup juniper berries
1 teaspoon nutmeg
Grated rinds of 2 oranges, 2 lemons, and 2 tangerines

Combine all the ingredients and store in an airtight container.

To make spiced cider, measure a heaping teaspoon of the mixture for each mug of cider. Simmer the cider with the spices in a large saucepan for 10 minutes. Strain before serving.

Lemon Butter Cookies

You can double this recipe and keep the dough in the refrigerator until you feel the urge to eat or give a gift of homemade cookies.

Makes 60

8 tablespoons unsalted butter, softened
½ cup granulated sugar
1 egg yolk
¼ teaspoon salt
1 tablespoon water
2 teaspoons fresh lemon juice
Grated rind of 1 lemon
1 teaspoon vanilla extract
1 cup all-purpose flour
½ cup superfine sugar

Preheat the oven to 350 degrees.

Beat the butter and sugar together, until light and creamy, using an electric mixer. Beat in the egg yolk, salt, water, lemon juice and rind, and the vanilla. Beat in the flour. (Or you can put all the ingredients into a food processor and combine them, using the steel blade.) Form the dough into a ball, wrap it in wax paper, and chill for at least 2 hours.

Roll the dough out thinly on a well-floured surface. (There is a high proportion of butter to flour, so if you have any difficulty rolling the dough, knead it between your hands for a minute to soften and warm it a little.)

Cut the dough into 1¼-inch circles, using a cookie cutter. Put the circles on unbuttered baking sheets and bake in the preheated oven for 8 to 10 minutes, until the edges are lightly browned. Remove the cookies from the baking sheets immediately and cool on wire racks. They will become crisp as they cool. Sprinkle with superfine sugar just before serving.

Chocolate Truffles

These are enough trouble to make that I share them only with my dearest friends. Roll the truffles again in cocoa before finally parting with them. Nest them in paper truffle cups, in a small covered container—a glass bowl, a china dish, or a lacquer box.

Makes 4 dozen

PRALINE:

1 tablespoon oil
½ cup sugar
½ cup whole almonds

FILLING:

6 ounces semisweet or bittersweet chocolate
8 tablespoons unsalted butter
2 tablespoons Grand Marnier or rum
Grated rind of 1 orange
2 tablespoons heavy cream

COATING:

4 ounces semisweet chocolate
½ cup unsweetened good-quality cocoa
    powder

Oil a baking sheet for the praline.

Put the sugar in a small heavy saucepan and heat over a low flame until it has melted into caramel. Add the almonds and continue cooking until it becomes a rich dark brown color. Be careful not to let the caramel burn. Pour the hot mixture onto the oiled baking sheet and, using a metal spatula, spread it to form a thin layer. Let cool.

When the praline is cold, grind it to a fine powder in a blender or food processor.

Now you can make the filling. Melt the 6 ounces of chocolate in the top of a double boiler over simmering water. Stir in the butter, Grand Marnier or rum, grated orange rind, cream, and praline powder. Chill for 1 hour, then shape into balls about ½ inch in diameter. Freeze until firm.

To make the coating, melt the remaining 4 ounces of semisweet chocolate, then allow it to cool to lukewarm. Roll each truffle in the melted chocolate. (The best—and most deliciously messy—way of doing this is to put a little melted chocolate in the palm of your hand and roll the truffle in the chocolate until it is very thinly coated.)

Spread the cocoa powder on a piece of wax paper and roll the chocolate-coated truffles in the cocoa. Store in an airtight container. The truffles can be frozen and eaten directly from the freezer. They will melt slowly in your mouth if you allow them to.

A Crock of Herbs and a Pot of Glorious Beef Broth

Look for a handmade clay pot or a similar container that has a lid. Fill it with equal quantities of oregano, thyme, dried parsley, crumbled bay leaves, and black peppercorns. With the crock at hand, the recipient can reach into it at will for a pinch of the herb mixture to flavor soups, stews, and sauces. You can give the herb mixture on its own, or with a casserole filled with homemade beef broth, below.

Leave on the fat that will rise to the surface of the chilled broth—it will act as a lid and prevent the broth from spilling as you carry it to a friend in need of nourishment.

Makes 1 quart

4 pounds veal bones
2 onions, peeled and sliced
2 carrots, sliced
2 stalks celery, sliced
Generous pinch of Herb Mixture (above)
2 pounds stewing beef, cubed

Preheat the oven to 400 degrees.

Put the veal bones in a large heavy casserole and cook, uncovered, in the preheated oven for about 30 minutes until well browned. Remove from the oven and add the onions, carrots, celery, and herb mixture. Add the beef and pour in enough cold water to cover.

Partially cover the casserole and bring just to a simmer over low heat. Continue to simmer for 8 hours, checking from time to time. The surface of the liquid should barely simmer.

Strain the broth into a bowl or an elegant casserole; chill.

Apricot Vodka

Here is an unusual gift to put into an antique or modern decanter.

1 pound dried apricots
1 cup granulated sugar
1 fifth (or 750 ml) vodka
3 tablespoons apricot brandy

Cut the apricots into small pieces and put them in a saucepan with the sugar and 1 cup of the vodka. Bring slowly just to boiling point, then remove from the heat and let cool. Add the remaining vodka and the apricot brandy. Pour into a glass jar and cover tightly.

Leave in a cool place for 2 months, then strain into a decanter.

Fruitcake Is Forever

Thirty-four years ago, I inherited the family fruitcake. Fruitcake is the only food durable enough to become a family heirloom. It had been in my grandmother's possession since 1880, and she passed it to a niece in 1933.

Surprisingly, the niece, who had always seemed to detest me, left it to me in her will. There was the usual family backbiting when the will was read. Relatives grumbled that I had no right to the family fruitcake. Some whispered that I had "got to" the dying woman when she was *in extremis* and guided her hand while she altered her will.

Nothing could be more absurd, since my dislike of fruitcake is notorious throughout the family. This distaste dates from a Christmas dinner when, at the age of 15, I dropped a small piece of fruitcake and shattered every bone in my right foot.

I would have renounced my inheritance except for the sentiment of the thing, for the family fruitcake was the symbol of our family's

roots. When my grandmother inherited it, it was already 86 years old, having been baked by her great-grandfather in 1794 as a Christmas gift for President George Washington.

Washington, with his high-flown view of ethical standards for Government workers, sent it back with thanks, explaining that he thought it unseemly for Presidents to accept gifts weighing more than 80 pounds, even though they were only eight inches in diameter. This, at any rate, is the family story, and you can take it for what it's worth, which probably isn't much.

There is no doubt, though, about the fruitcake's great age. Sawing into it six Christmases ago, I came across a fragment of a 1794 newspaper with an account of the lynching of a real-estate speculator in New York City.

Thinking the thing was a valuable antique, I rented bank storage space and hired Brink's guards every Christmas to bring it out, carry it to the table, and return it to the vault after dinner. The whole family, of course, now felt entitled to come for Christmas dinner.

People who have never eaten fruitcake may think that after 34 years of being gnawed at by assemblages of 25 to 30 diners my inheritance would have vanished. People who have eaten fruitcake will realize that it was still almost as intact as on the day George Washington first saw it. While an eon, as someone has observed, may be two people and a ham, a fruitcake is forever.

It was an antique dealer who revealed this truth to me. The children had reached college age, the age of parental bankruptcy, and I decided to put the family fruitcake on the antique market.

"Over 200 years old?" The dealer sneered. "I've got one at home that's over 300," he said. "If you come across a fruitcake that Julius Caesar brought back from Gaul, look me up; I'll give you $10 for it."

Russell Baker
The New York Times
December 25, 1983

CHRISTMAS GRAPHICS

CHRISTMAS GRAPHICS

Gift-wrap papers, posters, magazine covers, even the once-humble shopping bag have become fresh canvases for the host of graphic artists whose influence touches each aspect of our daily lives. Their designs enhance everyday objects from tea kettles to fine china, but it is their Christmas art on paper that we celebrate here.

Over the past few years the food that is served in the grandest to the simplest restaurants has altered dramatically and the menus themselves have become works of art, heralding tastes to come. The holiday menu opposite exquisitely reflects the caring attention to detail that typifies the best in both food and graphics.

Though it is true that fashion in art changes as constantly as fashion in fashion, some classic symbols endure the test of time; the Campbell Soup Kid, decked out for Christmas, has captured the nation's affection from one generation to the next.

Christmas magazine covers, however, must embody anew both the times and the essence of what lies within. *New Yorker* designs are predictably brilliant, with a soaring imagination that simultaneously delights the eye and makes us smile. Others, too, like our sample from *Town and Country*, share this special quality of surprise and jubilation.

Every year, thousands toil to produce fresh gift-wrap papers for the millions of presents we give each other. How wonderful it is when a brilliant imagination makes those symbols we know so well into designs of infinitely satisfying simplicity. Comparably, countless great artists have deliberately selected the poster as their medium, seducing us with their personal imagery transformed into lasting art on paper.

"Believe!" is the message spread as shoppers hoist colorful bags brimming with treasures aboard buses, trains, and planes. Each, of course, is advertising, with greater or lesser subtlety, a store or a product, or sometimes, just Christmas itself.

"Bah Humbug!" we may reply, as each season brings forth new interpretations of the Three Kings following the Star or toy soldiers on parade, as The Metropolitan Museum's angels chorus from their tree, or the New York City Ballet announces this year's performance of "The Nutcracker" . . . but we are thrilled, no doubt about it, just as we are when Cartier's wraps itself as an outsize Christmas gift. And when Santa has sprung from the rooftop to a new location on the label for a California wine named Château St. Nicholas, we can close appropriately by saying, "Cheers!"

HAPPY NEW YEAR

THE INN
AT LITTLE
WASHINGTON

Menu

Amuse-Gueule

Fresh Pâté de Foie Gras de Canard
with
Sauternes Aspic

Maine Lobster Bundled in Savoy Cabbage
Coral Beurre Blanc

Black Truffle Consommé

Warm Salad of Baby Lamb Tenderloin
with
Black-Eyed Peas Vinaigrette

Cheeses

Bûche de Nöel
and Other Dessert Selections

A Glass of Champagne
to Toast 1985 with Patrick and Reinhardt

Ninety Dollars per person

New Years Eve, 1984

Holiday menu from Patrick O'Connell's Inn at Little Washington, Virginia.

The Campbell Soup Kid.
Campbell Soup Company.

Gift-wrap designs by Lynne Hugill.
Cooper-Hewitt Museum Shop,
New York.

Dec. 16, 1985

THE NEW YORKER

Price $1.50

New Yorker cover by L.S. Johnson.

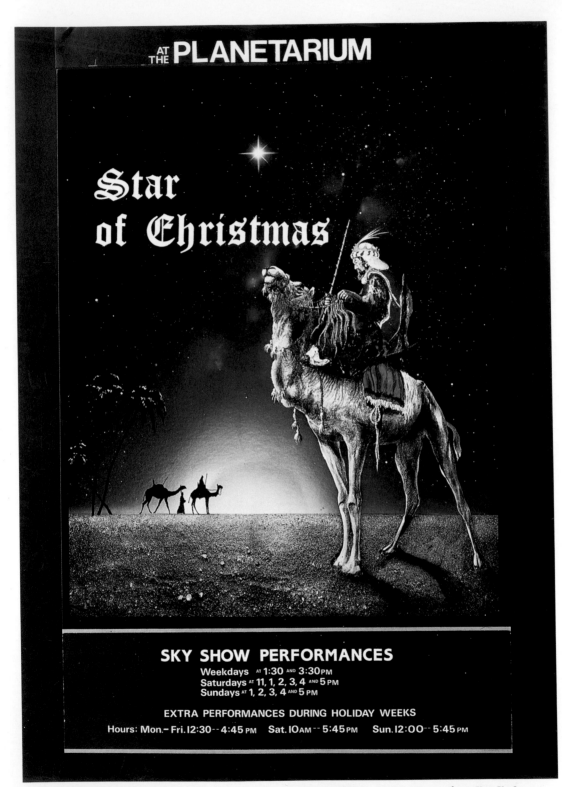

Poster painting by Helmut Wimmer. American Museum of Natural History, Hayden Planetarium, New York.

Angel. Attributed to Salvatore di Franco, Italian (Neapolitan), active 1770–1815. Polychromed terra cotta, wood, and silk.

Angel. Attributed to Giuseppe Sammartino, Italian (Neapolitan), 1720–1793. Polychromed terra cotta, wood, and silk.

Angel. Attributed to Giuseppe Sammartino, Italian (Neapolitan), 1720–1793. Polychromed terra cotta, wood, and silk.

The Metropolitan Museum of Art, New York: Gifts of Loretta Hines Howard, 1964. Bags from The Metropolitan Museum of Art Shop.

Cover painting by Oscar de Mejo.

Gift-wrap illustrations by Gillian Naylor and Mark Faulkner.
Cooper-Hewitt Museum Shop, New York.

Shopping bag illustration by Mary Engelbreit.

Cartier, Inc., Fifth Avenue, New York.

Shopping bag by Gordon Fraser.

GEORGE BALANCHINE'S THE NUTCRACKER / 1000th PERFORMANCE / DECEMBER 6, 1983
NEW YORK CITY BALLET

Sachet from Crabtree & Evelyn,
Madison Avenue, New York.

Poster design by Ira Robbins.
New York City Ballet.

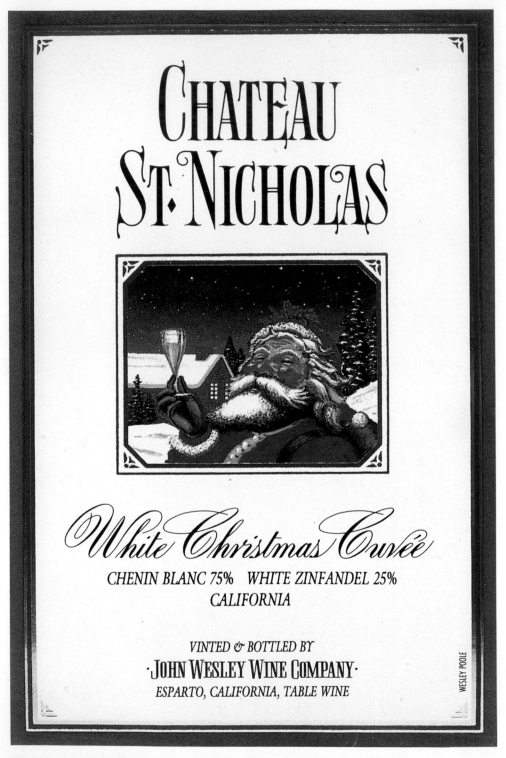

Chateau St·Nicholas

White Christmas Cuvée

CHENIN BLANC 75%   WHITE ZINFANDEL 25%
CALIFORNIA

VINTED & BOTTLED BY
·JOHN WESLEY WINE COMPANY·
ESPARTO, CALIFORNIA, TABLE WINE

WESLEY POOLE

Wine label artwork by Wesley Poole. John Wesley Wine Company, Esparto, California.

SANTA
THE GIVER

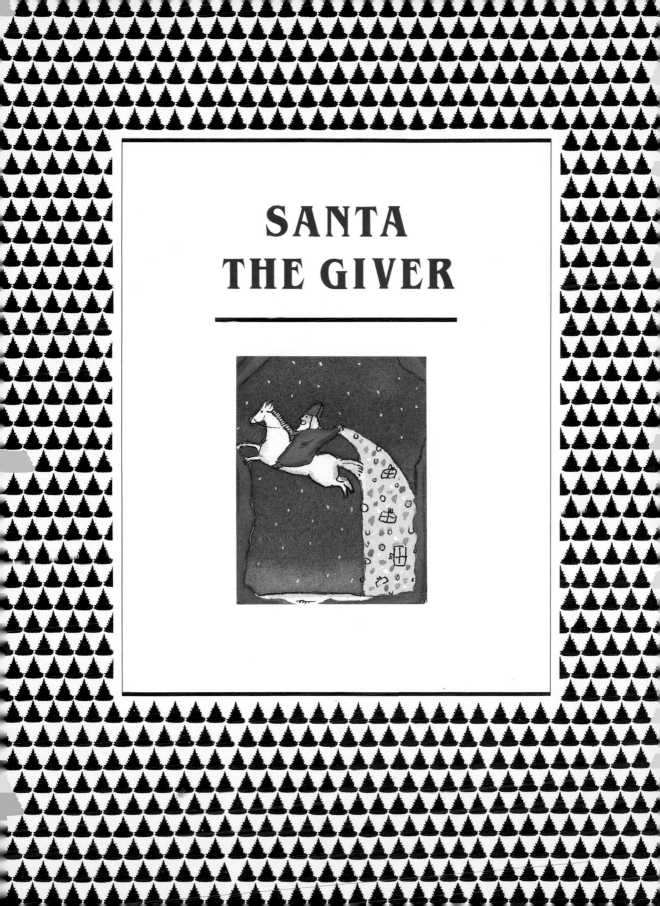

Poseidon Claus

Marc Rosenthal

THE MYTH BEHIND THE MYTH

BY RICHARD ATCHESON

Let's try to get one thing perfectly clear about Santa Claus: He is not a lie. For well over 1,500 years, Santa Claus was an etiological myth and, in many countries in the world, he still is. But when he came to America with the Dutch adventurers he underwent, as all American immigrants do, a kind of metamorphosis. His Dutch name, *Sinterklaas*, was evidently found unpronounceable by immigration officials and they told him that thereafter his name would be Santa Claus. It was soon after that, acculturating himself in the New World, that he converted from religious myth to American legend.

Like everyone else who came here from far parts, his transition into a new life makes an exciting story, full of adventure and reverses and fabulous deeds, some of which must be taken with a grain of salt. But there is no doubt that, whatever may be said of his antecedents, Santa Claus is today a great American hero.

Like comparable figures of American legend—some of the robber barons of the 19th century, for example, or Billy the Kid—Santa Claus's origins are shrouded in mystery. At the same time, it is clear that he is closely linked to a very good family—such a good family as to be Olympian in stature. Of course, he has long since put off all his foreign titles and decorations, his high office in the Church—a bishopric, no less—and all foreign associations generally. He has become a true democrat.

His credentials are such that he would be welcomed to tea by those crowned heads of Europe that are still affixed to their bodies, and the most exclusive clubs in New York City would throw open their doors to him and grant him credit on the strength of his signature alone. But all that is nothing when compared with his secret and *true* identity—an identity of such lofty distinction as to beggar all earthly associations.

Who is Santa *really*? Well, he doesn't like it known, but Santa Claus (*Sinterklaas*, St. Nicholas, Father Christmas, Kris Kringle, etc.) actually started out life as a sort of Christian version of Poseidon, Greek god of the sea and of all waters, also known as Neptune by the Romans. Poseidon was born, of course, into the first family of the world, son of Kronos and Rhea, and he had two brothers, Zeus and Hades. And, as we know, Hades took the underworld, Zeus took the earth, and Poseidon took the kingdom of the sea, establishing himself in grand style in a golden palace under the waters of the Aegean. (Well, he was young.)

Brothers are often contentious and indeed Poseidon and his brother Zeus did not get along; they were always arguing about where the sea stopped and the coastline began. They never solved their disputes. No sooner would Zeus throw a thunderbolt than Poseidon would summon up a tidal wave.

The early Greek sailors were afraid of Poseidon because he could send them terrible storms at sea. But they also noticed that if he were in a good mood, he would grant them calm seas and safe journeys in their little boats. They came to love him not only for his kindness but for the gift of the sea itself, with all its delicious goodies, and for the health-giving properties they found in salt water and air.

Poseidon had charge over fresh water, too, and could strike a rock with his trident and make a spring of sweet water jet forth. He became known as giver of all good things and of life itself. So even back in the third century B.C., when people started erecting temples to him, he was already a kind of Santa Claus and his festival was celebrated by the Greeks and Romans on December 6 (which, after the fourth century A.D., became the feast day of St. Nicholas).

Now, all good things cannot go on forever, even with the gods. The rise of Christianity in Rome destabilized the Olympian family terribly. Poseidon lost himself in the wind and waves and for a time was nameless. Still, even as Christianity gained a firm grip upon the civilized world, sailors called out to him when they saw his white-capped "horses" galloping across the waves and they thanked him when they made a successful crossing, reaching their voyage's end.

All revolutionaries have known the wisdom of incorporating some popular figures of the *ancien régime* while executing the others, and this is what the early Christians did with Poseidon; they rehabilitated him under another name, just as they had converted the beloved god Dionysus into the Good Shepherd.

Tales circulating in Asia Minor, impossible to verify in those days, told of a benevolent bishop of Myra, whose name was Nicholas and whose church stood on a promontory over the sea on the site of a temple of Poseidon. This bishop was said to have all the powers and good disposition associated with Poseidon and then some. He was known, among other things, to go about on a white horse, giving anonymous gifts by night. This attractive new saint was at once taken up by Greek sailors as their patron. Thus it was that, after the initial Terror of the Christian ascendency, Poseidon was rehabilitated with a new name and the tacit protection of the authorities—which proves that Santa Claus, like so many who have undergone persecution for their beliefs and their family connections, is nothing if not a survivor.

His story ever since is one of elusive quick-wittedness, adaptability, undercover work, and the mastery of intelligence and illusion over his enemies and detractors. He has many aliases. His bag is ever packed for a quick getaway. He always knows who's naughty and nice, and, like the Scarlet Pimpernel, he has never been *caught* giving anything away.

Stories of St. Nicholas spread widely in the emerging Christian era and children in most European countries came to know him quite well as a bringer of gifts and rewards—on December 5, the eve of his (formerly Poseidon's) feast day; on Christmas Eve; on New Year's Eve; or even on the feast of Epiphany. For hundreds of years, his traveling clothes were bishop's red and he wore a miter and carried an episcopal staff; his white steed, symbolic of his rule of the waves, could fly him anywhere.

He was a sterner figure in those days. While he might put goodies into the wooden shoes of a little Dutch boy who had been good all year, he might also put a bundle of switches into the shoes of a naughty one.

judgemental Santa

Santa on the run

Though Santa made an early arrival on our shores, he was compelled to keep a very low profile in parts of colonial America, for in those days the idea of a gift-giving saint was near profane in the minds of the Puritans. But finally, in the early part of the 19th century, all Americans embraced him at last as their own.

It was an expansive time and the popular weekly and monthly magazines began to celebrate Old St. Nick in fable and illustration. Santa's sleigh and reindeer would appear to have been an invention of the era. The red suit and the ermine trim belong, of course, to His Excellency Nicholas, Bishop of Myra. And nobody knows where the white horse went.

We *do* know, though, that Santa Claus has been losing an awful lot of weight of late. Formerly so fat that when he laughed he shook like a bowl full of jelly, he has since apparently joined a health club and presumably jogs daily, because in some current representations he is as slim as a rail and ready to model for Calvin Klein.

Santa survives by keeping up with the times. Sailors live a perilous life and admire a figure with a knack for survival; that is why they have stuck with St. Nicholas since long before he answered to that name. He lends his patronage to an extraordinary collection of other groups, too: bankers; all Russians; thieves; scholars; little children; even New York City.

Yet because there is no evidence other than oral tradition that St. Nicholas ever existed, Pope Paul VI as part of his extensive revisions of the Church calendar in 1969 decided to drop December 6 as a compulsory celebration for Roman Catholics, and the old gentleman's day was made an optional memorial only—along with celebrations assigned to other beloved but possibly legendary colleagues such as St. George and St. Christopher.

But, in fact, St. Nick is with us every time any poor soul in reduced circumstances goes to the pawnbroker with his last silver spoon or piece of Meissen, for Nicholas is the patron saint of pawnbrokers, too, and those three golden balls over the pawnbroker's door symbolize a famous kindness that he is alleged to have done in his undocumented tenure as bishop of Myra.

It seems that there were three girls in the town whose father had not enough money to provide them with dowries. In consequence, he could not marry them off and saw no other course but to put them on the streets to earn their livings the old-fashioned way. Getting wind of this, Nicholas dropped by one night under cover of darkness and, astride his faithful white steed, he flung three sacks of gold pieces over the garden wall. Or, as some versions have it, down the chimney where the girls had hung up their stockings to dry.

Wherever the gold landed, a sack of it was a dowry fit for a queen, and the father was spared the shame of having to prostitute his own daughters. Presumably, the girls were delighted, too.

Nick didn't *have* to do it. He just did it. And, like us, he often gives without a thought of getting, in secret. In doing so, he symbolizes the relative abundance of our individual lives and of the love in our hearts. Perhaps, even, he hints to us of some ancient home of ours, and of a wine-dark sea that never ceases to give, and of a certain golden palace fathoms down, and of our own eternal long-lost cradle of the deep.

And that's no lie.

Richard Atcheson is a freelance writer based in New York.

Nast's most popular drawings included:
Santa at the front with Union soldiers in
1853 . . .

Thomas Nast:
Image Maker

Our familiar image of a jolly Santa in a fur-
trimmed red suit began with Dr. Clement C.
Moore. Drawing inspiration from a Dutch
friend, he wrote *A Visit from St. Nicholas* in
1822 to entertain his children. A visitor persuaded Dr. Moore to allow the story to be published and it immediately became a favorite of
children everywhere. Several artists illustrated
the jolly Santa sailing over the rooftops with his
eight reindeer, but it was not until 41 years
later, in 1863, that the words became person-

an urgent call, in nightdress, to the North Pole . . .

ified forever when Thomas Nast drew the beloved Santa for *Harper's Illustrated Weekly*.
Nast, a 23-year-old immigrant from Bavaria, got
part of his inspiration from his own childhood
memories of the German *Pelze Nichol*. Nast became a highly successful political cartoonist,
creating the images for both the Republican
elephant and the Democratic donkey.

and the Old Gent's pleasure as the
call goes through . . .

a portrait that stamped the image for our time . . .

Santa holding the attention of a reverent crowd . . .

and a small person with
giant stocking and high
hopes.

Go, Santa!

The times they are a-changin' and Santa, it seems, moves right along with them. The old gentleman always was a good sport and, as can be seen here, he is as ready to jog with his reindeer as to loll with them in his hot tub, toasting a job well done. He is willing to don accouterments that have nothing in common with his snowy habitat and able to undertake some last-minute delivering at the wheel of a car with a grin as wide as his own.

One thing about Santa never changes, though. Like those movie heroines of the past who survived floods, fires, and fleshly advances without, literally, turning a hair, his glistening mustaches and billowing beard are luxuriantly bouffant, radiantly white, whatever the circumstances. Is Mrs. Claus a beautician? Can it be Santa's hair spray that has made that hole in the Pole's ozone layer?

Like all great institutions, Santa keeps abreast of fashion and we may soon see a slim, trim Claus. He is already wearing sneakers; will his pom-pommed hat shrink into a headband?

Don't be fooled into thinking that Santa will take the risk of driving home after drinking a hot toddy in his hot tub. In his mug is a cheery potion of V8 with all the trimmings.

Santa Seminars

It's "Graduation Day at Santa U.," and *Life* is there. The scene is the ballroom of the Grand Hyatt Hotel in New York City. The event: a Santa seminar sponsored by Western Temporary Services.

"At 9:30 jangling sleigh bells summon [the attendees] to attention, and they take their seats at tables arranged throughout the room. For their first assignment, they must review a video that stars a makeup artist and a thin young man. In a matter of minutes, the model's pip-squeak physique miraculously doubles in bulk, a button nose grows bulbous, eyes begin to twinkle with wisdom. When, at last, he is trussed into the velveteen suit, the metamorphosis is complete—from a 99-pound weakling into a dead ringer for Santa Claus. 'Merry Christmas, boys and girls!' he bellows before

the camera. When the tape is finished, a few of the slighter built Santas in the audience heave a sigh of relief.

"Next, Jenny Zink, the University's fashionable headmistress, instructs the group in basics of North Pole etiquette. 'Many of you know from experience that Santa cuts a frightening image for small children,' she warns them, 'so we've eliminated the traditional "ho, ho, ho" from your repertoire.' Instead, Santas must speak softly and avoid the quick, jerky movements that might cause a youngster to scream. Problem children—those who become easily upset during their visit—may require Santa to deploy one of his tactical defense weapons: the rubber sheet. 'If a child has an accident on your lap, stay in character until you can hand them back to their parents,' Zink says, 'then signal a helper that it's time for Santa to go feed the reindeer.'

"Each prospective Santa is issued a pamph-

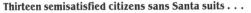

Thirteen semisatisfied citizens sans Santa suits . . .

become 13 thrill-crazed Santa lookalikes.

let of similar trade secrets, which Jenny Zink
has updated over the years. 'A career elf,' as
she describes herself, Zink, 40, has been running Western's Santa division since 1977, when
the supply of part-time 'helpers' struggled to
keep pace with the suburban shopping malls
being built throughout the country. 'I became
obsessed with the character of Santa,' says
Zink. 'So much work goes into making him be-
lievable. The cumulative research I've done to
that end reflects our changing society—especially the relationship between child and
parent.'

"Because a large percentage of today's kids
are not living with both original parents, students are advised not to use words like mommy
or daddy or parents. 'Many children will ask
you to help get their moms and dads back together again,' Zink points out to the class. And

THE RED ARMY

How's business? Don't ask. Just look
around the retail stores at Christmastime and count the Santas. If you see
lots of little round men in red, you can
be sure that the national economy is in
a steep downdraft.

Merchants are not in business to entertain your holiday fantasies and they
will not employ any more Old St. Nicks
at $10 and up an hour than they abso-
lutely *have* to. But when the goods
aren't moving, a well-placed chorus of
Ho! Ho! Ho! can help keep sales in the
pink and ledger books out of the red.

In case of emergency it is—as ever —
Santa Claus, in multiples, to the rescue.

WORTH MORE DEAD THAN ALIVE

Insuring Santa Claus, or a reasonable facsimile, against accident and loss is a relatively new concept, acted upon in the main by owners of shopping malls. According to the trade magazines in this field, your everyday shopping mall owner will want your everyday Santa to carry about $500,000 in liability coverage.

Some companies—the Hartford, notably—will also insure a reindeer, but Lloyd's of London will not. That is not to say, however, that they *would* not. "I can't say that I have ever been *asked* to insure a reindeer," said a Lloyd's spokesman. If someone had and Lloyd's agreed to do it, the going rate today on premiums for animals is about 7 percent of the insured value.

Santa's clean record—nobody has yet filed a claim against him in any of his multitudinous commercial appearances—is attributed to the rigorous training programs that are set for incipient Santas, which involve instructions on personal appearance, attitude toward tots and their parents, and the strict avoidance on the job of alcohol and all controlled substances.

"—Who's *the jolliest of them all?*"

of every major toy, all the season's biggest sellers, *in the first 15 minutes.*' Rimelis doesn't mind the commercial aspect of Christmas, but he notes, 'It's refreshing to meet a kid who asks me for a bike instead of, say, Big Wheels.'

"By 11:00 the students are eager to try on the beloved red suit. Each Santa is handed the appropriate wardrobe, as well as a beard, wig, granny glasses and grease pencil for whitening the eyebrows. Over the years, some Santas have had their wallets lifted, so the suit has a secret pocket sewn into the pants lining as a deterrent to would-be muggers.

"As they finish dressing, Jenny Zink suggests that they wash their beards nightly. 'But never in hot water, or you'll lose that natural curl. Just take a look at Dennis . . .' she says, pointing to a Santa sporting resplendent Smith Brothers whiskers.

"'I'm Anthony,' a voice warbles from behind identical clouds of pearl-white curls.

"'I didn't recognize you, Anthony,' she apologizes.

"By noon, the Santas are beginning to get a bit edgy. Some are fighting to remove flecks of beard from between their teeth.

every fifth girl can be expected to ask for a baby brother. 'In those cases you should say, "That's clear out of my department, but Santa will be thinking very hard about it for you." Then steer conversation back to their major concern: toys and other gifts.'

"'The first day on the job you learn the power of TV advertising,' says Dave Rimelis, 31, who as Santa has been discussing toys since 1972, when kids asked him for Silly Putty and Slinkys. 'You wind up knowing the brand name

"Jenny Zink senses their discomfort and lines them up for commencement exercises. It is a graduation right out of *The Twilight Zone*, as 20 Santas in full dress file down the aisle to receive their diplomas. 'Pomp and Circumstance' blares over the PA system. Hotel guests pause to gawk through the open door at the bizarre processional.

"As each Santa approaches the podium, a 'school official' flips a tassel to the left side of Santa's red cap. 'Santa Mark!' the commencement speaker booms as the first graduate steps forward to claim his degree. 'Santa Dave. . . .'

"Thunderous applause tears through the room as the Santas clap for one another. They are jubilant, but no one lingers for any small talk. 'There's no time,' Al Clogston says, trading in his seasonal garb for a pair of faded jeans. 'Think of all the kids I've gotta see.'

"Edging toward the door, Clogston stops precipitously, then wheels around to face a near empty room. 'Ho! Ho! Ho!' he roars, breaking a cardinal rule of the University of Santa Claus. 'I couldn't help myself,' he shrugs, before disappearing onto the street."

If They Could See Me Now

Some of us dream of being movie stars, rock stars, stars of stage and screen. Some of us dream of being astronauts, aquanauts, nauts of every sort. And some of us—quite a large number of us, actually—dream of being Santa Claus.

It's not so strange. Santa is a big star with boffo annual ratings. He flies through the skies with more flair than Superman and more geniality than Captain Marvel, and he has more adoring fans than all the other stars rolled into one. If you are secretly envious of Santa Claus and wish that you, too, could slip into a cunning red suit and don a silky white beard, get stared at with love and regarded with awe, dispense joy and good will to all and sundry, and get credited for philanthropies which are actually administered by others, don't wait another minute. Call Western Temporary Services, because Western Temporary Services wants *you*.

Western claims to be the largest source of trained Santas in the country. Working from 240 offices dotted across the land, they have trained more than 3,000 Santas and launched them on brief but merry careers in stores and showrooms—anyplace where a Santa is required. A lot of Western's Santas are in it strictly for the money, of course, but a clear majority—more than 60 percent, in fact—do it because they *want* to, fitting it in around their full-time regular jobs or taking their annual vacations at Christmastime in order to be Santas every day during the season.

There is no end, it seems, to what some people will do for a little love.

And you can do it, too.

Yes, Virginia

We take pleasure in answering at once and thus prominently the communication below, expressing at the same time our great gratification that its faithful author is numbered among the friends of *The Sun*:

> Dear Editor—I am 8 years old.
> Some of my little friends say there is no Santa Claus.
> Papa says, "If you see it in *The Sun* it's so." Please tell me the truth, is there a Santa Claus? Virginia O'Hanlon 115 West ninety-fifth street.

Virginia, your little friends are wrong. They have been affected by the skepticism of a skeptical age. They do not believe except they see. They think that nothing can be which is not comprehensible by their little minds. All minds, Virginia, whether they be men's or children's, are little. In this great universe of ours man is a mere insect, an ant, in his intellect, as compared with the boundless world about him, as measured by the intelligence capable of grasping the whole of truth and knowledge.

Yes, Virginia, there is a SANTA CLAUS. He exists as certainly as love and generosity and devotion exist, and you know that they abound and give to your life its highest beauty and joy. Alas! how dreary would be the world if there were no SANTA CLAUS! It would be as dreary as if there were no Virginias. There would be no child-like faith then, no poetry, no romance

Contemporary kids and customary lore are combined in crayon Christmas concepts.

to make tolerable this existence. We should have no enjoyment, except in sense and sight. The eternal light with which childhood fills the world would be extinguished.

Not believe in SANTA CLAUS! You might as well not believe in fairies! You might get your papa to hire men to watch in all the chimneys on Christmas Eve to catch SANTA CLAUS, but even if they did not see SANTA CLAUS coming down, what would that prove? Nobody sees SANTA CLAUS, but that is no sign there is no SANTA CLAUS. The most real

things in the world are those that neither children nor men can see. Did you ever see fairies dancing on the lawn? Of course not, but that's no proof that they are not there. Nobody can conceive or imagine all the wonders there are unseen and unseeable in the world.

You tear apart a baby's rattle and see what makes the noise inside, but there is a veil covering the unseen world which not the strongest man, nor even the united strength of all the strongest men that ever lived, could tear apart. Only faith, fancy, poetry, love, romance, can push aside that curtain and view and picture the supernal beauty and glory beyond. Is it all real? Ah, Virginia, in all this world there is nothing else real and abiding.

No SANTA CLAUS! Thank GOD! he lives, and he lives forever. A thousand years from now, Virginia, nay, ten times ten thousand years from now, he will continue to make glad the heart of childhood.

(Editorial in the New York *Sun*, Sept. 21, 1897, by Francis P. Church)

TWO BELIEVERS

"After he leaves the presents, he goes back to his reindeer and gives them the candy canes I leave for them."

CHRISTINA RIESEBECK, 4, VERONA, NJ

"He wears a red hat and he wears very red shoes. He lives on the moon. He comes in a sleigh driven by reindeers. I have seen him."

KANISHA MEHTA, 7, ELMHURST, NY

ONE SKEPTIC

"Last year I stopped believing in Santa Claus because I saw my father eating the cookies I left for Santa Claus."

PETER FERNANDEZ, 9, WEST BABYLON, NY

Getting Through to Santa

As Christmas Eve approaches, many children in America are seized with a compelling need to be in personal touch with Santa Claus. They want to remind him to be *sure* to drop by on the 24th, they want to assure him that they have been very, very good, and most particularly they want to acquaint him with what's on their Christmas lists.

Most kids just scrawl "Santa Claus, North Pole" on their mail, drop it in the nearest postal slot, and hope for the best. And while this is not so vagrant an approach as you might think, there do exist in this modern age a few somewhat more sophisticated ways of getting through to the Old Gent.

For example, if you write to Santa c/o Det. 2, 11th WS, Eilson AFB, Alaska, 99702, you will get a reply. You didn't know that Santa is in the Air Force? He's not, really, but he has friends up in Alaska in an Air Force Weather Squadron, and for 30 years members of this unit have been Santa's postal representatives.

Here's how it works: (1) child writes letter to Santa; (2) sneaky parent prepares a phony reply and encloses this, along with a stamped envelope addressed to the child, with child's letter. When the missive reaches the 11th WS, (3) self-appointed gnomes there turn the mail around so that (4) child receives Santa's "reply" from the mailman. There is no fee, but you must be sure to get your letters into the mail to Det. 2 before the 10th of December if you want to be sure of a reply before Christmas.

A similar service is performed each season when you write to Santa at Santa Claus House, Santaland, North Pole, Alaska, 99705. For this one you do not have to enclose your own reply; this is provided. But you *do* have to pay for the exchange. Enclose $2 with your child's letter and a return envelope.

In the maxi-bucks category of communication with Santa, it is now possible through U.S.

Experts plot Santa's course to the eastern seaboard.

Sprint to set up a private teleconference between your child—in a viewing room reserved for you at one of the company's national offices—and Santa "in his workshop at the North Pole." This sight-and-sound communication came along in 1986 at a cost of $10 for ten minutes and $25 for a half hour. Call (800) 241-8470 for the latest developments.

While only the wealthiest of kids can afford some of these commercial contact schemes, the vast majority—tens of thousands—resort annually to the U.S. Mail at a cost of a regular postage stamp and, curiously, most are not disappointed. For 50 years the U.S. Postal Service has run a program called Operation Santa Claus, which rounds up Santa mail at general post offices around the country and distributes it to any citizens who volunteer to answer some of these letters.

Most participants reply to a child with a note and sometimes a small gift, though there are some letters that defy the resources of even the greatest good will and ingenuity. When a child asks Santa for a home, or something to eat to-morrow, there's not much a stranger can do. Every year there are pleas for lots of impossible dreams. One of the best from 1986:

"Dear Santa,

"I would like some brains and to look cute. But if you cannot make me cute, I will just take the brains."

We Sign You a Merry Christmas

There are many, many ways of giving, and many, many things to give, and Santa knows them all. On several weekends before Christmas he shows up in Madison, Connecticut, specially equipped to talk to deaf and hearing-impaired children. For the children and their

parents, it is a thrilling experience; for everyone involved, these are heartwarming occasions.

The signing Santa is Robert Smith, a translator for the state's Commission on the Deaf and Hearing Impaired, and the happy meetings are set up each year with the enthusiastic assistance of the Madison Chamber of Commerce.

When the program first began, in 1984, one nine-year-old child, Tina Geer, from the American School for the Deaf in West Hartford, travelled some 30 miles to meet Santa Claus. Now children come from all over the state to converse with Santa, shown here seated on a wicker chair on the porch of a white colonial building in downtown Madison.

Little girls cradle their arms to show him that they want dolls for Christmas; little boys sign for toy cars and trucks. Parents and family members sign to each other excitedly about what a good time it is for everyone.

And one mother, on her way out with her ecstatic child, had a special message for Santa. "You're a good Santa," she signed to him.

"Merry Christmas."

Real joy: A deaf child signs to Santa for the first time.

Christmas, 1988

Dear Stephanie,

Christmas is coming! Isn't that exciting?
Things sure are humming here at the workshop, and
I'm sure everyone's busy getting ready for the
holidays at your home, too, Stephanie.

Let's see, how old are you now? My goodness!
You're 4 years old already! You know, Stephanie,
you'll be all grown up before you know it. Won't
that be fun?

Last week I spoke with Chris, who told me that
you've been a good girl this year. Being good all
the time isn't easy. It makes us very happy and
proud when you try so hard.

When I make my deliveries to Springfield, I
really look forward to stopping off at the Meyers
home to bring a very special gift just for you,
Stephanie. No, I can't tell you what it is yet.

Well, Stephanie, I have to get busy packing toys
and taking care of the reindeer. Keep being a good
girl, and Christmas will be here before you can say
"Ho! Ho! Ho!"

Merry Christmas with love,

Santa

Personalizing Santa's Mail

Like so many of us, it seems, Santa has turned to the computer for help with his correspondence. About 700,000 children write letters to Santa each year, and Hallmark has now found a way for the old gentleman to write personal notes to at least *some* of them.

When information about a child is put into the computers in most major Hallmark card shops, it generates a letter from Santa printed on special Santa's Workshop stationery, ready to be popped into the mail in an envelope postmarked "The North Pole."

It seems that Americans like to imagine Santa as a member of their society, and for children who are increasingly being brought up with computers, it is perfectly natural to imagine Santa using one too.

"Getting a letter from Santa is a tangible symbol of the concept that good behavior gets good rewards," explains R. Chris Martin, a motivational psychologist who acts as consultant to Hallmark Cards. "It's part of the American ideal of fair play, and that's emotionally healthy."

The "personalizing" process can include not only the person's name, but also information about a pet, a special friend, and the recipient's city. And Santa's computer can generate 729 different letter formats to make quite sure that if Santa writes to more than one member of a family, he will not repeat himself.

A surprising twist on the Letter from Santa is that adults want to get into the act, too, and are requesting letters for friends and relatives as a humorous holiday greeting.

"Looking for humor in holiday traditions becomes important as people feel pressure associated with the hustle and bustle of the holiday season," Martin believes. "Giving someone a laugh reminds us that we are supposed to be enjoying ourselves."

ALL I WANT IS . . .

The wish being confided to that jolly person with the whiskers? Whether it's for contact lenses or pierced ears, it's new every year.

"Contact lenses for me and my dog."

After early-morning muster, Santa's Helpers hit the pavements of Times Square.

Conversation with a Sidewalk Santa

Contrary to widespread misapprehension, it is not the Salvation Army who puts all those Santas on the busy sidewalks of New York in the pre-Christmas season. It is the Volunteers of America who do that and they have been doing it, according to dated photos, since 1917.

The 45 to 75 red-clad men who hit the streets at Thanksgiving are drawn from the Men's Rehabilitation Center, which the Volunteers operate. The money they raise—about $75,000 annually—supports the operation and funds Thanksgiving and Christmas meals for some 1,500 people on each holiday.

Each Santa gets $15 a day plus room and board and a 15 percent commission on his daily take. Says one staff member, "It helps them to be really jolly St. Nicks."

For Mike Welky, in his sixth season as Santa's Helper on Fifth Avenue at Rockefeller Plaza—a prime position—the adulation of children is all in a day's work.

ALMANAC (*poking his belly*): Is that all you in there?
MIKE: Every bit of it. I don't need any padding.
ALMANAC: How old are you?
MIKE (*to children*): Hi! God bless you! Merry Christmas! What?
ALMANAC: How old are you?
MIKE: I'm 40.
ALMANAC: How do you keep warm out here?
MIKE: Thermal underwear. God bless you! It's a long day, cold and long, but I love it. Hi!
ALMANAC: Is this typical . . .
MIKE: I do a lot of posing during the day.

ALMANAC: If you've been doing it for five years now, you must like it.

MIKE: Hi! I *love* it. I get to see the best people. I get to see them loving their children. How're you? Wonderful!

(A woman shoves her infant at Mike.)

WOMAN: Could you just . . .

MIKE: How're *you*, sweetheart?

INFANT: Sannasanna . . .

(Mike hands the infant back to its mother.)

MIKE *(waving to departing mother and child)*: It's amazing to see the Christmas spirit developing. I don't have any children of my own, so it's very rewarding for me to make children happy.

ALMANAC: How are you doing with contributions?

MIKE: It's up every year. This year, at this location, which is the best location in the city,

I'm doing $200 to $300 a day. Used to be I was lucky to do $100 in a day.

(A large group of Japanese tourists approaches with cameras.)

MIKE: Hi! Hi!

TOURISTS: Hai! Hai!

MIKE: No, no.

(Mike indicates his chimney collecting boxes and the tourists thrust cash into the slots.)

A TOURIST: Thank you very much.

MIKE: Thank *you* very much. *Arigato!*

(Japanese tourists depart, waving and bowing. Mike bows to them.)

ALMANAC: That's very nice.

MIKE: It's wonderful to see people so happy to see you standing there. No matter how tight and stingy people might be, they all have a basic need to give. That's where I come in.

A few children pause along the tracks to retrieve flung trinkets, but most race after the Santa Claus Express.

He'll Be Comin' Round the Mountain When He Comes

For 43 years now, up in the hills and hollers of Appalachia, Santa has made his first seasonal appearance on the back end of a train—the Santa Claus Express. And for all too many of the little children up there who put their ears to the rail to hear if he's coming and run along the rails behind him as he passes, it's the only visit from St. Nick that they are going to have.

This is mountain country, raw and rough. Unemployment is always high, sometimes over 20 percent, and all along a ragged line of track from Pikeville, Kentucky, and across Virginia

into Kingsport, Tennessee, whole families camp in the poplar forests by the tracks on the Friday night preceding Thanksgiving weekend, waiting for Santa's train whistle early Saturday morning.

When Santa's engineer spots crowds of people down the line, he slows the train to a halting chug and Santa and his helpers, mostly Kingsport businessmen, fling great handfuls of candy and little toys—decks of cards, comic books, Frisbees, and baby dolls—out across the receding track to the children who run to keep up.

The experience is enough, say men who have done it, to make grown men cry. But it also is enough, as they well know, to insure that a lot of very poor children are touched by the spirit of Christmas. And there are some businessmen on the train today, who in their childhood were themselves running behind the train with paper sacks. They know exactly what it feels like to hear the whistle of the Santa Express on a cold and frosty morning, and to see the jolly Old Gent in the flesh and hear him call them "darlin'" over the public address system as he choo-choos by.

Officials of CSX Transportation, which donates the locomotive cars and crews, will not say what it costs to put Santa on the observation platform of a train for a day. "It's a permanent part of life in these mountains" is the only official statement.

Santa Claus is just a myth. He cannot relieve the grinding poverty of the Appalachian mountain people. He cannot reopen and revitalize the coal mines that provide the major employment in those parts. But, thanks to his friends and helpers, he *can* get on a train at Pikeville once a year, and chug along through the 32 tunnels on his twisty route, and come round the bend for a thousand eager children . . . and he *does* call everybody "darlin'."

WAY TO GO

A special railroad train is not the only unusual form of transportation for the Christmas gift-giver.

In Czechoslovakia, Santa slides down from heaven on a golden cord. He is *Svaty Mikulas*, patron saint of children, and he is led by an angel and an evil spirit called *Cert*.

Children in Italy wait for a kindly old witch called *Befana*, who flies through the air on a broom. She leaves a gift for every child whose home she passes, hoping that one of them will be the Christ Child, for whom she has searched for centuries. *Befana* has a counterpart in Russia known as *Baboushka*.

In parts of France, the gift-bringer is Mother Air, called *Tante Aria*, who rides through the countryside on a donkey, accompanied by Father Star.

The Dutch *Sinterklaas*, on the other hand, arrives on a splendid white horse, wearing a bishop's robe, miter, and white gloves. His helper, *Swarte Piet* (Black Peter), walks beside him carrying switches, ostensibly to punish bad children.

In Germany, the *Weihnachtsman* has no form of transportation. He trudges along on foot, all by himself, heavily laden with a sack of gifts on his back and carrying sticks in one hand and a Christmas tree in the other.

And in some far-off desert lands, children wait for the Gentle Camel of Jesus, the youngest of the three camels who brought the Wise Men to Bethlehem. He doesn't carry a Santa—he himself is the gift-giver.

Halted at a whistlestop, Santa distributes gifts.

Just a Bunch of Overgrown Kids

In most of the department stores and malls where Santa holds court today, children stand in line for long stretches of time in order to sit on Santa's knee and whisper to him what they want for Christmas. In all those places, patient parents stand together with the children, then hold their coats and look on admiringly as the kiddies ascend to the golden throne.

That's not how they do it in Stateline, Nevada, reports *USA Today*, where Santa is enthroned in the lobby of Harvey's Casino and a good quarter or more of his starry-eyed lap-sitters are fully grown high rollers who will do anything for luck. Stateline Santa Bill Horning

broke these gambling folks into three categories. "The younger adults ask for fancy cars and money," he confided. "Middle-agers usually want happiness or diamonds."

The Golden Oldies seem to be a little more focused, he said. "They just ask to hit a jackpot or two."

Hark!
The Hell's Angels Sing

It's a little-known fact that America's bikers—Hell's Angels and the like, who love to travel in roaring packs and whose mere menacing pres-

Why Santa was late.

In Portland, Santa is a wild one.

ence can unhinge most local constabularies—have more to them than a lot of tattoos and a tendency to crush empty beer cans in their naked fists. They have a sentimental streak a yard wide, especially at Christmastime, and have come to be noted for their generosity toward children during the season.

So it seems that Santa comes on a motorcycle sometimes, bearing lots of toys for girls and boys, gathered from the donations of retailers. These particular "angels" in disguise drop off their collection of packages at the Shriners' Hospital for Crippled Children in Portland, Oregon. Then, without pausing for thanks and with barely a backward glance, they rev up their engines and roar off into the night.

Santa Goes to the Dogs

It cannot be said that animals have no place on the Christmas scene. The ox and the ass and masses of sheep all have their parts in the Nativity story. And on the Santa front, we've got white goats, a white horse, eight tiny reindeer, and yet again a ninth with a red nose. But chihuahuas?

In Rockville, Maryland, at the Rockville Pet Hotel, Santa comes annually before Christmas to greyhounds, danes, and collies, to poodles, dachshunds, hunting hounds—and every kind of pet, even gerbils. Doting owners beam as their petty-poos are photographed on Santa's knee; a canine Christmas party follows, with dog lollipops stuffed into red stockings embroidered with the witty legend: "Have A Dawg-Gone Merry Christmas." The zenith of the afternoon is the giving of the gifts, with a gaily wrapped present for every pooch. Says one pet-lover: "They do love to unwrap presents."

The event is in its fifth season and grows in popularity and attendance every year. "It appeals to me," says hotel owner Linda Buel, "because I enjoy people who enjoy their animals. Pets are part of the family, and families are part of Christmas and that's about all there is to it."

Exactly.

In Key West, Santa is a tired one.

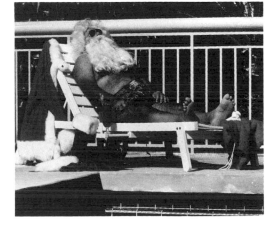

Modernizing the Myth

When today's adults were children, it was perfectly easy to believe in a fat, jolly Santa, bulging in an ermine-trimmed red suit, who arrived out of the starry night on Christmas Eve in a sleigh drawn by tiny reindeer. Perfectly feasible, we all agreed, 30 and 40 and 50 years before the even more preposterous fantasies of Steven Spielberg found credence in this decade. It was also, then, OK to accept that the aforesaid Santa would land his rather spindly Victorian spaceship on the roof of the house, take up a bundle of presents, and slip all sooty down the chimney *right into our living rooms* and there deposit the swag. Most of us left cookies and a glass of milk for the benevolent housebreaker and, sure enough, on the magic morning of Christmas Day we found—in the cookie crumbs and drained glass on the table by the fireplace—*irrefutable proof* that, in fact, there is a Santa Claus.

"The token liberal, madam."

But today, how fares the myth? What forces fly in the face of willing gullibility? Well, one thing is the almost coast-to-coast disappearance of the chimney. In the race to cover the land with condos and tract houses, the chimney has flown away with the storks who used to sit on it, leaving Santa with no means of access and egress on his annual mission of supply and demand.

And what of little ones who live in 40-story skyscrapers? There's not even a proper roof on most of those things, current architectural fashion lying as it does. Where will tiny reindeer park their tiny feet? And how will Santa descend to the 14th floor? Children think of these things.

One city child, pondering the matter in her heart, decided that Santa would have to come via the garbage chute. Other high-rise kiddies have come up with the magic idea of Santa as a kind of ghostly presence, able to slip through sealed glass windows at high altitudes, able to materialize and vanish like the smoke from his jolly old pipe.

But one Park Avenue youngster with a highly practical mind never gave that a thought; he was concerned merely with the probability that the snooty doorman in his building would never admit such a curiously dressed old gentleman to the premises. When his mother heard about the problem, she arranged for her little boy and the doorman to have a word together, and the child got the assurances he needed.

Another mother, recently confronted by her suspicious daughter, found necessity the mother of wild invention: "Now, darling," she cooed, "you don't need to worry that we don't have a fireplace. Santa doesn't come by sleigh anymore because, you see, he's so old and so tired that he rarely travels. But his elves are busy all year and he sends lots and lots of lovely presents to all the boys and girls in the world by overnight UPS."

THE
MAGIC TREE

THE BEST TREE
WE EVER HAD

O h, yes. I've read all those stories about the near-mystical joys of choosing the tree. That one tree that grew just for us—the one that is just the right height, its perfectly formed branches reaching out to us like the trees in *Better Homes and Gardens*. And I know how every family in America gathers around its tree and covers it with exquisite ornaments; I even have visions of Victorian ladies simpering around their tree, casting fond glances at dapper husbands who eternally lean with one elbow on the mantel over the blazing fireplace. And I wonder why it is never quite like that for us.

It never has been, and I am resigned to the fact that it never will be.

To begin with, we can hardly ever settle on a time when we are going to *get the tree*, and stick to it. Someone always has to go somewhere else at the last minute and one person is left thinking the unthinkable—"Let's not have a tree this year."

But we always do have a tree and we almost always buy it at the last minute. Often only straggly trees are left by that time, but we console ourselves by saying that we can turn the sparse branches toward the wall and no one will ever know.

This year it will be just the same.

We have learned, though, to measure the opening in the tree stand so that the bottom of the tree fits easily between the three screws that are supposed to keep it from toppling over.

We always do this.

And always, after we carry the tree up the three flights of stairs into our brownstone apartment, it doesn't fit into the stand.

I always protest that we mustn't use the best, sharpest knife in the kitchen to whittle down the base so that it will fit into the stand—and each year that is exactly what

Late 19th-century cast-iron stands supported the tree with two brackets and a screw underneath (left) or in a ring with three clamps (right).

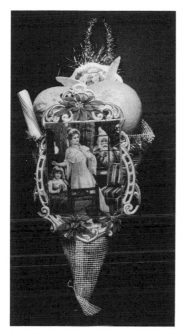

Lavishly decorated cornucopias of sweets were early tree ornaments made popular by German settlers.

we do because we don't have anything else to use. Eventually we do get the tree wedged into the stand, but it usually keeps falling over even though it is not supposed to and no one else's ever does. Last year we tied the tree around a table and the table fell over too. Nothing was broken, but things didn't start off quite the way they say they should in the magazines.

We don't have what you might describe as a theme tree—the kind designers and celebrities have. We never have a tree that is all white, for instance—two hundred white doves and dainty bows of white velvet ribbon—that sort of thing. Instead, we have a motley assortment of what could loosely be described as "objects"—things that we have acquired over the years.

And as we unwrap each ornament from its nesting of tissue paper, we exclaim over it and remember when we got it and who was there and how pretty—or how awful—it is and we hang it on a branch no matter what it looks like because each ornament "belongs," simply because it is ours.

Among these treasures are six eggshell halves trimmed with tinsel, now sadly faded, that the children made in kindergarten. Each precious one cradles a darling little ornament bought with loving pennies from a long-vanished Woolworth's. There are a few tin angels from a long-ago holiday in Mexico and a silver bell with our name on it, when our family had a different name from the one we have now. There is a Mickey Mouse on a bicycle with a red "fur" hat and some really quite beautiful little ornaments that we have bought over time, as we acquired what passes for "taste." All this assembly of remembrances finds a home somewhere on the tree. At first we hang the ornaments carefully but there are so many that, after an hour or so, we just put them wherever there is a space.

We play old records while we are decorating. It is all part of the ritual. And every year we play the same music—nothing uplifting like the *Messiah*, but more along the lines of that song (maybe you remember it) "All I Want for Christmas Is My Two Front Teeth."

Finally, when everything is finished and the tree is twinkling with fairy lights and surrounded by far too many packages—because we always fear that we have not bought enough presents for each other—we step back and declare that this is *absolutely the best tree* we have ever had.

And it always is.

And later in the night when we come downstairs to take another look, we are as happy as can be that our tree is still standing.

And it always is.

OF TREES AND PRESIDENTS

Andrew Jackson loved Christmas and made a great feast of it. In 1835, his French chef made him a sugar-frosted pine tree and surrounded it with toy animals made out of flavored ices, in the French style.

In 1856, Franklin Pierce, who was a native of New Hampshire, had the first Christmas tree set up in the White House.

In 1895, Grover Cleveland became the first President to use electric lights on the White House tree.

In 1923, Calvin Coolidge began the tradition of lighting a tree on the White House lawn.

Teddy Roosevelt was such a gung-ho conservationist that, in 1902, he forbade his children to have a Christmas tree. But his attitude softened when he was approached on the question by Gifford Pinchot, a Cabinet member and the founder of the Yale School of Forestry. Pinchot assured the President

that thinning the forest by cutting down Christmas trees actually helped the trees survive; persuaded, Roosevelt gave in to his children.

Will the *First* American Christmas Tree Please Stand Up?

BY NANCY KIPPER

If the first American Christmas tree were *really* asked to stand up, there would be a lot of pushing and shoving to claim the honor of that distinction. Between 1832 and 1851, and perhaps even earlier, many "first" American Christmas trees began to appear all across our country—from Philadelphia, Pennsylvania, to Pasadena, California—each with an eventual claim to the title.

One such tree was decorated in 1832 by a German political refugee, Charles Follen of Boston, for his young son. The following description comes from memoirs published by his wife in 1842:

Every Christmas since Charles was two years old, his father had dressed a Christmas-tree for him, after the fashion of his own country. This was always the happiest day in the year to him. He spared no pains, no time, in adorning the tree, and making it as beautiful as possible. . . .

Every one in the family contributed to its decoration. Then he placed wax tapers on every branch, carefully, so as to light the tree perfectly, but not to set fire to anything. All the children of our acquaintance were invited to see it; after tea, at the ringing of a bell, the door of the room where the tree was placed was opened, and the children entered. . . . "It was in their eyes," he used to say, "that he loved best to see the Christmas-tree." After the lights were burned out, and the baskets of sugarplums that hung on the tree were distributed, the children danced or played games the rest of the evening.

Harriet Martineau, a guest of the Follens that particular Christmas, expressed her impressions as well:

I was present at the introduction into the new country of the spectacle of the German Christmas-tree. My little friend Charley and three companions had been long preparing for this pretty show. The cook had broken her eggs carefully in the middle for some weeks past, that Charley might have the shells for cups; and these cups were gilded and coloured very prettily. . . . We were all engaged in sticking on the last of the seven dozen of wax-tapers, and in filling the gilded egg-cups and gay paper cornucopiae with comfits, lozenges and barley-sugar. The tree was the top of a young fir, planted in a tub, which was ornamented with moss. Smart dolls and other whimsies glittered in the evergreen, and there was not a twig which had not something sparkling upon it. . . .

It really looked beautiful; the room seemed in a blaze, and the ornaments were so well hung on that no accident happened, except that one doll's petticoat caught fire. There was a sponge tied to the end of a stick to put out any supernumerary blaze, and no harm ensued. I mounted the steps behind the tree to see the effect of opening the doors. It was delightful. The children poured in, but in a moment every voice was hushed. Their faces were upturned to the blaze, all eyes wide open, all lips parted, all steps arrested. Nobody spoke only Charley leaped for joy. The first symptom of recovery was the children's wandering round the tree. At last a quick pair of eyes discovered that it bore something eatable, and from that moment the babble began again. . . . I have little doubt the Christmas-tree will become one of the most flourishing exotics of New-England.

Historians generally agree that Americans were first exposed to the Christmas tree by Hessian soldiers staying in the American colonies during the Revolutionary War. But what is not generally known is the fact that the original

Know Your Trees

Balsam Fir
Symmetrical in shape, with irregular spaces between branches. Dark green short, flat, glossy needles that grow at right angles to the branches. Smooth bark, either gray or brown in color. Easy to decorate. Good needle retention. Strong, very pleasant fragrance.

Colorado Blue Spruce
Almost perfectly symmetrical. Short, lush, sharp, silver-blue to blue-green needles. Pale gray and sometimes reddish bark. Very poor needle retention. Mild fragrance.

Douglas Fir
A very symmetrical member of the hemlock family. Short, yellow-green to deep green needles, flexible and soft to touch. Easy to decorate. Reddish or dark brown bark. Very good needle retention. Pungent, aromatic fragrance.

German trees were little tabletop models and that the fashion for luxurious floor-to-ceiling Christmas trees was an innovation possible only in timber-rich America.

A German political refugee, Charles F. E. Minnegrode, is credited with introducing the Christmas-tree tradition to Williamsburg, Virginia. In 1842, Minnegrode, a teacher of Greek and Latin at William and Mary College, cut down an evergreen in the woods near the home of Judge Nathaniel B. Tucker. He and the Tucker children decorated the tree with strings of popcorn and gilded nuts. They wired candles to the tree and neighbors and children flocked to see it. Judge Tucker continued this tree-trimming custom until his death. Today, when Williamsburg recreates the Christmas of colonial days, a tree is placed near the Tucker house, and it could very well be that this tradi-

tion was the beginning of the custom of lighting a "community tree" in cities and towns across America.

An immigrant tailor in Wooster, Ohio, is believed to have brought the Christmas tree to that town. In 1847, August Imgard, away from his homeland of Hesse for the first time, decided to show his niece and nephew how Christmas was celebrated in the old country. His story goes as follows:

> I walked up Apple Creek, taking the North side to where Spruce Dam now is. (About the place where the present distillery stands.) When I got to where the trees were I found the water so high I could not get across. So I walked along until I found a tree fallen from bank to bank and crossed on that. I cut a tree and carried it to the fallen log. But to get across this time I had to tie the tree to my neck and crawl on hands and feet. People looked at me

Eastern Red Cedar
Bushy and symmetrical in shape. Flattened, scalelike, dark blue-green needles that are extremely short, ⅛ to ½ inch in length. Reddish-brown bark. Good needle retention. Mild fragrance.

Eastern White Pine
Conical and symmetrical in shape. Silvery, thin, flexible blue-green needles, 2 to 5 inches in length, five to a cluster. Branches are dense and horizontal. Grayish to dark green bark. Good needle retention. Mild fragrance.

Fraser Fir
Symmetrical in shape, with irregular spaces between branches. Dark green, short needles, ½ to 1¼ inches long. Brownish gray bark. Excellent needle retention. Very pleasant fragrance.

with considerable curiosity when I walked through town with my tree.

He decorated the tree with paper ornaments, and a local tinsmith hammered a star for its top; the locals loved it and August Imgard is honored in Wooster each Christmas by the placing of a tree at the entrance to his tomb.

By the middle of the 19th century, Christmas trees were turning up throughout the Deep South. Included among them was a tree that was decorated in 1851 for the Swedish singer Jenny Lind by the hospitable ladies of Charleston, South Carolina. Miss Lind was in town to give a concert at the invitation of P. T. Barnum. The following account of her arrival was reported in the Charleston *Courier*:

As she landed, hundreds of enthusiastic citizens

jammed sidewalks and streets to see her ushered triumphantly to the Charleston Hotel where the ladies of the town had erected a brilliant Christmas tree in front of her window.

Jenny Lind was known for her deep attachments to the customs of her Swedish homeland, and she loved Christmas especially, so she must have been very touched by the Southern hospitality shown to her.

The diary of Mrs. James Roach, a niece of Jefferson Davis, documents the appearance of the first tree in Mississippi in 1851. She writes:

The children had such a number of gifts that I made a Christmas tree for them; Mother, Aunt and Liz came down to see it; all said it was something new to them. I never saw one but learned from some of the German stories I had been reading.

Norway Spruce
Very full and symmetrical. Short, dark green, single needles, ½ to ¾ inch long. Reddish brown bark. Slightly drooping branches that make it difficult to decorate. Somewhat poor needle retention, especially if allowed to dry out. Mild fragrance.

Scotch Pine
Bushy and pyramidal in shape. Dark blue-green needles, 1½ to 3 inches in length, that cluster in pairs. Bright orange-red bark. Excellent needle retention. Remains green even after the tree is dry. Mild fragrance.

Virginia Pine
Asymmetrical, with branches markedly separated. Grayish to yellowish green needles, two to a cluster, 1½ to 3 inches long. Purplish bark. Good needle retention. Mild fragrance.

THE NATION'S "OTHER" CHRISTMAS TREE

The oldest living thing in the world is the "Nation's Christmas Tree," a giant Sequoia so designated in 1926. This most giant of redwoods stands in King's Canyon National Park, near Sanger, California. It stands 267 feet high, has a circumference of 107 feet, and is believed to be about 4,000 years old. As has been often observed during Christmas services at its base, this tree was already 2,000 years old when Christ was born, and was no negligible shrub in the days of Abraham. The Nation's Tree is far too big to decorate—its lowest limb extends 130 feet above the ground—but a wreath is laid at its base every Christmas by a member of the National Park Service. Since 1867, it has been called "The General Grant."

The entry in her Christmas diary the next year states that the tree was improved and verifies the beginning of the holiday tradition for one family in Vicksburg, Mississippi.

While it was not the very first one in the City of Brotherly Love, another documented early appearance of a Christmas tree was that of Dr. Constantin Hering of Philadelphia. In 1852, Dr. Hering, originally from Leipzig, crossed the Delaware River to New Jersey, where he and a friend, Friedrich Knorr, cut down a tree. Hauling it back through the streets, they gained considerable notice and excitement from the children of the neighborhood, who waited in anticipation for the finished product. The good doctor did not let them down, and on designated nights he allowed patients and friends in to see his creation. He carried on the custom for at least 50 years.

Also in 1851—this time in Cleveland, Ohio—Pastor Henry Schwan, a Lutheran, attempted to decorate a Christmas tree in his parish. This act created quite a scandal and Pastor Schwan almost lost his pulpit because of it. The pastor and some of his parishioners were called idolatrous, while the boughs, ornaments, candles, and pageantry of it all were declared pagan and unnatural. Threats were made on the poor pastor's life. Undaunted, he collected the facts and evidence in his favor. One strong piece of support was a letter from Pope Gregory I to Augustine of Canterbury in 597, encouraging the adaptation of the pagan reverence for the fir tree, along with other rituals, into Christian worship as a means of converting the English to Christianity. Schwan must have been convincing in his argument, as the following year he and his congregation decorated and enjoyed their evergreen without incident.

The first Christmas-tree lot was set up in 1851 in New York City by Mark Carr, a woodsman from the Catskill Mountains. His wife laughed at his idea, but in spite of her he loaded two ox-sleds with balsam firs and took them into the city, where he rented a strip of sidewalk for one silver dollar. The "sophisticated" New Yorkers exhausted his stock in no time. The next season he returned, bringing even more trees, and this time had to pay $100 in rental for his sidewalk lot. Not to worry. Mr. Carr still made an excellent profit! Thus started the evergreen trade, and by the 1890s the Catskills alone provided 200,000 trees each Christmas season.

While a few of the early trees were put outdoors for the community to admire, the "community tree" as we know it today is a quite recent phenomenon. And why do those Christmas trees now twinkle at us from every town in the nation? For a peculiarly American reason: because of electric lights. Colored lights first appeared on the scene in the early 1900s, complete with all-weather wiring, and the new technology took America by storm. In 1904, San Diego lighted a pine tree. In 1909, Pasadenans hiked themselves up Mount Wilson and decorated a tall evergreen. In 1912, trees were set up in New York, Boston, and Cleveland. In 1914, Philadelphia followed suit.

Now, in the fourth quarter of the 20th century, Christmas trees are everywhere: in the mail, by the church, set out like seasonal hydrants along Main Street U.S.A., all of them wired to glow through the night (and daytime, too). By the first week of December, every township has installed its Christmas trees in such profusion that you cannot imagine what you pay taxes for . . . until you see the right tree. An evergreen set out on a town green, with plenty of open space around it, or in a quiet triangle where two streets diverge, with just enough lights to make you sniff the winter air for the smell of pine, and maybe one or two children staring at it. *That* is the tree that makes you think of an American Christmas, and *that* moment makes it all worthwhile.

Nancy Kipper's work focuses mainly on American family and country life.

Fresh = Safe

A fresh tree is a safe tree, say the National Safety Council and the National Christmas Tree Association. A fresh tree will not sustain a flame, but a dried-out one will. So before buying your tree, check for the following features that indicate freshness:

- A trunk that is sticky with sap
- Branches that bend easily without snapping (unless the tree is really frozen)
- Needles that are green and flexible and do not pull off easily (a few dead needles usually drop off when you bounce a fresh tree on the ground a few times, but a tree that "snows" needles is too dry)

Once indoors, a tree needs water, water, and more water to stay fresh. A six-foot tree can drink up to two quarts of water a day; larger trees will drink even more. A tree will stop trying and start dying if the water is not there. Unless a cut tree gets its daily water requirement, it is more of an incendiary device than an ornament.

When you first bring your tree home, cut off a 1-inch slice straight across the bottom of the trunk and keep it upright in a pail of water in the garage or a sheltered place. Before setting it up indoors, cut another straight slice off the trunk. Set the tree in a stand that can hold at least a gallon of water, and refill the stand *every* day.

In addition, prevent your tree from drying prematurely by positioning it away from radiators, fireplaces, televisions, or other heat sources. Make sure tree lights and connections are in good condition, and don't leave lights on overnight or when you leave home. Jack Frost is not supposed to be nipping at your nose while you wait for the fire engines to arrive.

One, two, three! Assemble a tree.

Constant Companions: Trees That Don't Die

Somewhere among the expense, the effort, the sense of waste, the mess of needles, and the bare patch you didn't see in the store, a decision has been gradually taking shape in your mind: no more needle-dropping hulks—next time you're going to get a tree that *lasts*.

Is It Fir Real?

The first alternative that occurs to you is an artificial tree. If you have visions of a bottle-brush-and-broomstick construction in garbage-bag green, you have a pleasant surprise in store. Artificial trees have come a long way from their goose-feather beginnings, and the good ones are now very close to the real thing. However, if you feel the switch is going to save you money, beware! You may have to follow the lead of the apocryphal couple who decorated their tree with cutlery the first year to get their budget back in line.

Nowadays consumers seem to be interested enough in natural-looking trees to spend up to $175 or $200 for a convincing replica. The Barcana Colorado Classic, the Georgian, and Mr. Christmas's deluxe seven-foot Noble fir are all big sellers in that price range. Silvestri's hit, the seven-foot "slim silhouette" American fir at a little under $100, has spawned a whole new line of somewhat less expensive trees available in slim models. All of these are made of polyvinyl chloride, or PVC. First introduced in 1963, PVC captured between 80 and 90 percent of the artificial tree market by 1970. Aluminum and paper still have a place on the artificial tree floor, but PVC trees definitely hold sway.

Assembly is not a problem—artificial trees may be made of a series of branch "wreaths" that stack onto the central trunk, or the branches may be hinged in the center so all you have to do is open them up like a crepe-paper ornament. And there is no need to worry that your neighbor will have the same tree. Artificial trees come in a variety of species, heights, and colors, from forest green to blue-green to frosted white to two-tone (also called "snow-storm") and even red-tip, not to mention "decorator" colors. And to evoke the smell of the forest, you can spray on a dose of "Christmas Tree Mist," "Bayberry Mist," or "Cranberry Mist" from a little four-ounce container.

If this doesn't work for you, however, there is another alternative: a completely real, replantable tree.

A Real Tree That Doesn't Shed?

If you are going to get a living Christmas tree, it is quite important to make your decision early for at least two reasons.

First, nurseries do run out. The best tubbed or replantable trees are gone by the first week in December. Second, if you live in any part of the United States where the ground freezes and you haven't already dug the tree's hole and set aside its nice blanket of dirt, you're going to be facing the undiggable come the New Year.

Remember that most Christmas trees grow to be very large and provide an overwhelming amount of shade; take care to select a planting site accordingly.

Some species will thrive better in certain parts of the country than others (ask your nurseryman), but the only universal requirement for a living Christmas tree is that it be able to withstand a week or so of dry, warm conditions inside the house. Spruces, Fraser firs, Douglas firs, and most pines are among the species that can cope fairly well, but you cannot keep a living tree in the house much longer than a week. Two weeks will drastically reduce its chances of survival.

Some tips for success with a live tree: When you go to buy the tree, check the root ball carefully. It should be full, firm, and well attached to the tree. Inspection will not reveal everything about the condition of the tree, so try to get some information about the nursery before you buy.

Once you get the tree home, don't rush it into the house. You need to sneak the temperature up gradually so the tree will stay dormant. Cover the root and put the tree in the garage, on the porch, or in the basement for a day or two.

Decide how best to water a huge ball of earth in your living room and consider investing in a washtub.

Ease your tree out of the house in the same stages you did when you eased it in; don't shock it awake with a change in temperature. And if the temperature is below 20 degrees Fahrenheit, delay planting.

Once you get the tree into its hole, cut away the root ball wrapping and fill the hole with soil and mulch. Water it slowly with two or three gallons and stake the tree if it looks at all wobbly.

Tree Hunting We Go!

For many city dwellers and their children, the Christmas season really starts with a nostalgic walk through an evergreen "plantation," the new term for choose-and-cut tree farms. Armed with a tape measure, warm boots, and soup in a thermos, these people are on a quest for a fresh, specially selected tree at something of a bargain price.

Some bring a saw to cut down their choice; others carry a spade, burlap, and twine to dig up and bag their tree. In either case, they are benefiting the environment: Two or three new trees will be planted in the space vacated by one, and these young trees give off far more oxygen than older ones.

Cut-your-own operations are booming, providing 20 percent of the 35 million trees Americans take home every Christmas. There are more than 2,000 such farms, in every state except Hawaii and, surprisingly, Alaska—and California leads: annual sales $30 million.

A Salute to the Noble Christmas-Tree Growers

The variety of Christmas trees being grown right now is as startling as their numbers. Scotch pine is the big seller of the 1980s. There is also the prototypical balsam fir—the tree everybody wanted in the '40s, right up to the mid-'50s—and Virginia pine, and Eastern pine. Colorado blue spruce has many faithful adherents, too, as does Norway spruce. And there are so many more.

As to numbers, would you believe that there are close to 700 million trees in the ground right now—more than we could ever see except in our mind's eye, when we rove in imaginary bliss over miles of forested hills and valleys and smell the sweet sap? For the growers, though, there is not much romance in it; they spend all their time guarding against such ravages of nature as needle cast, balsam twig, woolly aphids, weevils, fungus, and pine-shoot moths.

Christmas trees are a $650 million business—and not an easy one, either. It is a business characterized by an unbelievably short selling season, a crop in which harvested leftovers have to be thrown away, and lots of work in cold weather in the big three Christmas-tree states of Michigan, Wisconsin, and Minnesota. In addition, it takes about ten years for most crops to reach maturity (although Virginia pine grown in the South can be marketed in under five years).

Today there is not as much profit in Christmas trees as there used to be. Equipment costs are higher, hourly wages for shearers and balers are rising, and educated consumers will no longer accept so-called "forest thinnings." High-quality trees are in demand and high-quality trees take high-quality land, fertilizer, and farming techniques. A Christmas farmer has to absorb all these costs. More than 95 percent of the cut trees sold in New York City, for

Outside Monroe, Oregon, a Monroe Tree Farms helicopter drops its maximum load of 36 trees at a shipping point. Three helicopters are airborne every working day during the season.

example, have traveled over 1,200 miles and freight charges have increased four times since 1974.

In addition to these difficulties, a Christmas-tree glut may loom on the horizon, although the industry trade group—the National Christmas Tree Association—vigorously defends against the notion. Sixty million trees were planted in 1983, 84 million in 1984, and 90 million in 1986, a number that those in the know believe will remain stable until a probable decline in the 1990s. Christmas-tree sales only run about 35 million trees a year. So even if only half of the seedlings make it to treedom, there are still an awful lot of trees in the ground, considering the fact that only some

40 percent of United States households buy cut trees at Christmastime.

However, the National Christmas Tree Association is undaunted. It plans to move those trees out of the ground and into homes. In 1982 the trade spent only about $50,000 to support its industry. Now the Association asks growers as well as retailers to contribute five cents for every tree sold to an advertising fund called Operation Real Tree, which intends to encourage families to buy two trees a year—or more—as they would televisions. A tree in every room.

Operation Real Tree has also targeted those Americans who are hanging their tinsel on something no better than tinsel itself (according to a politicized tree grower). About half of the country's tree-decorating households get their trees out of the basement each year, and if these families were to come back into the real-tree fold, every live young tree in the supposed glut would be a joyous source of profit to its grower.

Somewhat glossed over by the Christmas-tree growers is the fact that new marketing ideas are needed now because the tax laws have changed. The business of Christmas trees owes its existence not just to holiday sentiment but in a large part to the tax laws enacted in 1954, which protected Christmas trees over six years old under the same provision that protects conventional timber. As of 1987, however, Christmas-tree profits are no longer exempt in any way.

Nonetheless, it's on with business for those who are dedicated to their work. Even though almost 80 percent of growers work part-time, competition is fierce. A grower needs patience and a reliable income to help him through the lean years—as well as a plot of deep, well-drained sandy loam high in organic matter, many pairs of mittens, and a love of trees. If he or she has all (or at least most) of the above, Christmas-tree growing can provide a constant challenge, a feeling of accomplishment, and a way to have Christmas all year round.

PRICKLY PAGEANT

Here they come, the American trees. Tall, lean, and beautiful, although at this pageant legginess is a flaw. It's the annual National Christmas Tree Association pageant: Hourglass figures are out, conical ones are in. An ideal tree has a 66 percent taper, meaning that the width at the base, or bottommost branches, is two-thirds the height of the tree. (For a six-foot tree, the bottom spread should therefore be four feet.)

The pageant is held in August and trees travel at their growers' expense from all over the country to compete. Already winners of their state competitions, they must conform to the very highest standards: straight trunks, no drooping branches, definitely no fungus, and only one branch at the top, for the star.

The national winner gets a blue ribbon, industry fame, and the chance to select the tree for the Blue Room at the White House. Imagine having your picture taken next to your own tree and your own President. It's almost worth cutting down your best tree in August. *Timber!*

All over the country (as here, in Pennsylvania) the Christmas-tree harvest starts well before Thanksgiving.

Conversation with a Christmas-Tree Grower

Mark Courchaine, 31, is a Christmas-tree grower who lives in Wolcott, Vermont, in a house he has built mostly out of trees cleared from the surrounding land. As we sit at the kitchen table—also a product of his own workmanship, borne on delicate Queen Anne legs—the snow falls for the fourth straight day onto five-foot drifts, filling the room with a chilly bright light that is softly reflected by the golden pine counters and beams.

ALMANAC: How did you get into the Christmas-tree business?

MARK: I guess it all started with logging and cutting timber. I studied immensely, because when I like a topic I do become obsessed, and so for a couple of years that's all I would read, books on forestry and the trees of the world. I spent a lot of time arguing with the loggers around here, too. Even my Dad was of the old school and didn't feel the need to save any trees. The hardest thing to get through the heads of those guys was that, just like in farming, the problem really is one of genetics, and the tree you leave should be the best one there is. At one logging job in

· 164 ·

THE EARLY LIFE OF A TREE

Trees have had an important role in religious rites long before the Christmas tree—borrowed deliberately and quite frankly from earlier pre-Christian practices—came upon the scene. From earliest times, all over the world man has admired the endurance of the noble tree through every season, has sought to emulate it, and even worshiped it. Some notes from the mists of time:

- When wandering tribes made clearings in the primeval forests of northern Europe, they would leave a "mother tree" in the center and all worship took place beside it.
- Ancient mythologies all around the Mediterranean held that trees were spirits or places where spirits could find protection; "tree worship" developed, and continues to this day in parts of Asia.
- The age-old ceremony of "wassailing" fruit trees was traditionally performed in England to insure a good crop by drinking to the trees' good health in the year ahead.
- Ancient Egyptians brought green date palms into their homes to celebrate the winter's solstice; the trees were considered symbols of life triumphant over death.
- During the mid-December celebration of Saturnalia, the ancient Romans carried trees lit with candles, symbolizing the return of the sun in the spring.
- Early Scandinavians, who worshiped the oak tree as an embodiment of their god Woden, were persuaded by Christian missionaries to transfer their homage to the fir tree.

Elmore I left trees the size of this table, and the old loggers were going crazy; but I felt a lot of pride in the way I left that place. Some of those trees were the same age as trees half their size, they were that much better, and those were the ones that I left. That got me thinking about seeds.

Those trees were from my great-grandfather's time. They linked me to the past, and I felt very strange cutting them down. Then I got the feeling that I wanted to leave something for my kids, well, I guess for my grandchildren, so I went and bought 50 walnut seedlings even though I was broke. Then I bought 200 little butternuts. I felt so incredibly good about planting them instead of cutting them down! Then I bought a thousand blue spruce, and I really felt great. The next year I bought another thousand. . . .

ALMANAC: How long does it take for a Christmas tree to get to marketable size?

MARK: About 10 to 12 years from seed. But you can make a pretty good tree out of a wild or neglected "Charlie Brown" in a few years with careful pruning.

ALMANAC: How do you prune a Christmas tree?

MARK: Most Christmas trees are pruned once a year, usually in the spring. The top bud is cut off, which makes two shoots grow out. The next spring one of those will be cut short while just the bud will be trimmed on the other, stimulating two more shoots, and so forth. That slows the upward growth. Then the outside buds are cut so that the tree has good shape. The 6- or 7-foot trees have the root growth and energy of 15- to 18-foot trees now because of their age, and they are so bound and determined to get to the light that they will fill in every little space that's left if you keep cutting them back. If you never pruned them they would look naked by comparison.

Of course, millions of Christmas trees are being raised down South for the first time now. They grow in half the time there and have to be pruned twice a year so they don't get out of hand. They are something like clones, though, because they are shaped by these pruning machines, big cones that set down over the trees with knives whirling all around, so every tree is going to be almost identical. There is a fear that they will cause a glut on the market.

ALMANAC: Are you worried about that?

MARK: Well, the ones I saw were young and looked fine from a distance, except that they were pines, which I'm not even considering growing anymore. They have good needle retention because of all the pitch, but they have no smell, they're very bristly, the trimming deforms them more so they don't fit easily into stands, and they look pretty much like pruned-up bushes. I don't know, maybe that market will go South.

ALMANAC: What is your own favorite Christmas tree?

MARK: All the firs are good: Douglas fir, Fraser fir (a gorgeous tree, but very expensive), and balsam fir, the most common. White pine can be picture perfect, but it's too weak for

the old-fashioned ornaments. I wouldn't recommend any of the spruces except for Colorado blue, because most of them just don't last. I do think that Colorado blue spruce makes the best live Christmas tree, too, if you're willing to put the effort into helping it survive.

ALMANAC: How can you identify a fresh Christmas tree?

MARK: Most trees are cut toward the end of October or the beginning of November. I myself don't usually start cutting until the second week in November; but since the trees are dormant in any case, the way a tree is handled between the time it is cut and the time it is taken inside is actually more important than when it is cut. The thing to look for is vibrant, rich color. Forget any tree that looks yellowish. Forget that stupid test of bending the needles or branch-tips, too. If it is 20 degrees out, any needle is going to break when you bend it in half!

ALMANAC: Can you offer any special advice about choosing a tree?

"If Rockefeller Center says No, I'm afraid we're stuck."

MARK: Don't wait until the last minute. The selection I take down to Avon, Connecticut, to open "Santa's Trees" on December 1st each year is the best I can give you unless you special-order while I am there. The longer you wait, the less you will have to choose from. Take your tree home, cut a little off the end if the stump is long enough, and leave it outside in a bucket of water. Then cut it again before you take it inside. Don't be embarrassed to ask what kind of tree it is, and be sure to remember how you liked it. Everyone has preferences, and a little attention to what you liked or didn't like will help you get just what you want for next Christmas.

After Christmas: Making the Most of Your Tree

- Put your tree outside with suet, peanut butter, seeds, and orange slices all over it to serve as a gigantic Christmas feeder for the birds. A couple of trees stacked together will make a whole grove for the birds, and protect them against the cold and wind while they eat.

- Place small whole trees or very big branches along the sides and on the tops of beds of perennials, roses, and other plants to protect them from the sun and wind.

- Break off some branch tips and shake off their needles for use in sachets.

- Trim the trunk and big branches down to use in your fireplace, a couple of logs at a time.

- Use trimmed trunks for stakes, tripods, and trellises in your garden.

- Put cut branches in a window box. Or use them as decorative mulch around street trees. An added plus to whole-branch mulch

is the fact that the tree branches will keep fly-away loose mulch in place.

- Spread trees along beaches to encourage the development of sand dunes.

- Use whole or cut-up trees as filler in gullies. They will control natural erosion by holding in all kinds of organic debris.

COLOR ME UGLY

Contrary to the Christmas spirit though it may be, tree poaching is a problem for those who have evergreens on their property; starting in mid-November, many trees seem to be able to sever their trunks and wander off by themselves during the night.

To ensure that no thief will be able to enjoy a lovely evergreen that does not belong to him, Cornell University has developed this sure-fire formula to turn evergreens an unholiday pink.

UGLY MIX

20 ounces hydrated lime
4 ounces "Wilt-Pruf" anti-desiccant liquid
2 gallons water, 63 degrees Fahrenheit
2 bottles pink food coloring

Mix the lime and "Wilt-Pruf" until a smooth paste is formed. Fold the paste slowly into the water. When the mixture is smooth, light, and milky, stir in the pink coloring.

Apply the mix to the tree with a broom, a paint roller, or rags tied to the end of a stick.

NOTE: Rain will gradually wash the color off.

TREASURES FOR THE TREE

S ome people like to think that the custom of hanging treasured objects on a tree started in primitive times with the very sensible instinct to hang precious food up high where wild animals could not reach it. The tradition can certainly be dated more accurately to medieval times, when evergreen trees were hung with red apples on December 24, which was celebrated as Adam and Eve Day. The earliest account of a tree decorated with cookies and candies comes from the diary of a traveler to Strasbourg, in Alsace, written in 1605.

Tree lights also have their share of legends. An old manuscript in a Sicilian monastery tells the following tale: When Christ was born, all the creatures of the earth, including the trees, went to Bethlehem to give him gifts. Some trees, like the fruit-bearing ones, had plenty to give the child and they pushed the little fir tree, which had nothing but its evergreen leaves, into the background. An angel, seeing its plight, asked some stars to come down and rest on the fir tree's dark boughs. When Jesus saw the shining tree, he blessed it, and the custom of Christmas ornaments was born.

In the past, legend attributed the first indoor lighted tree to Martin Luther. Supposedly, he dragged a fir tree home one Christmas and decorated it with lighted candles to show his children the beauty of the twinkling stars above the night forest—a beauty that, for him, was comparable to the light of God. However, this story is probably apocryphal because there is no further mention of lighted Christmas trees until scattered accounts appeared well over a century later.

Lighted Christmas trees with non-edible ornaments, as we know them today, did not become popular until the latter half of the 19th century. Beginning in Germany, cottage industries sprang up which soon occupied whole towns, as well as the working lives of men, women, and children, in what was to become a huge Christmas-tree ornament business. Every one of those early ornaments sold in stores was individual: hand-cast, hand-blown, hand-painted, and hand-assembled.

Today, those who relegate their old family ornaments to the attic, keeping them only for sentimental reasons, may find that they have been saving treasures which have much more than sentimental value in a newly competitive collector's market.

Ornaments

1870s: The earliest ornaments to appear in the stores were flat geometric shapes, cast in lead: various stars, crosses, butterflies, and diamonds. They were first produced by the toy-makers of Nuremberg, Germany, and became popular in the United States between 1870 and 1890.

The first blown-glass ornaments went on sale in the United States. These ornaments, originally heavy-walled and known as *Kugel*, were made in the German town of Lauscha, where glassmakers used to entertain themselves by

competing to blow the largest ball. Then, with the introduction of the Bunsen burner, they were gradually able to blow lighter and lighter paper-thin bubbles.

Flying angels, animals, and miniature replicas of the Christ Child were being made of wax cast in molds. Gilded cardboard often served as angel wings and clothing was made from tinsel or ribbon garlands.

1875: Although they were considered a hazard because they caught on fire so easily, celluloid toys became very popular and were joined on American Christmas trees by all kinds of miniature wooden toys, including soldiers, dolls, and birdhouses.

1880: Reluctantly at first, Frank Woolworth began to sell blown-glass ornaments in his 14 stores. Within a decade, he would be ordering 200,000 annually.

1880–1910: "Dresden Christmas-tree ornaments" were introduced—small gold or three-dimensional cardboard ornaments, embossed in gold or silver. These realistic wonders came in a fantastic array of shapes, from camels, storks, and peacocks to pianos, sailboats, and opera glasses, each amazingly detailed.

A new kind of glass ornament was introduced by Czechoslovakian glass-bead makers. Geometric shapes were made with beads and hollow glass tubing that had been strung on wire, in a variety of colors and designs.

1890s: Cotton-batting ornaments were added to the range of decorations available to Americans. The cotton was folded and glued over wire or cardboard shapes, which were given paper faces and covered with powdered glass to make them shine. Most popular were big fluffy Santas in cotton-wool furs and cloud-like angels with gilt buttons down their robes.

Japanese lanterns, colored parasols, and miniature fans were popular items to hang on the Christmas tree. These "ornaments" reflected the increasing interest in the Orient—Japanese styles in particular.

1892: Christmas-tree hooks were invented and advertised in a wholesaler's catalog.

1900: Glassblowers were now producing not only the standard Christmas-tree ball but all

kinds of figurative ornaments, including story-book characters, vegetables, fruit, and fish.

1908: The first red honeycombed paper bells, 3 inches in diameter, were made by the Paper Novelty Products Company of New York. The larger version of this bell is still a Christmas classic.

1910: Sears began advertising and selling glass ornaments by mail.

1918: The first American-made ornaments became available in toy stores. Because of the wartime embargo on all German products, Americans had to manufacture their own. Round balls were the only ornaments available

and a far cry from the high quality of the German versions.

1938: The first hand-blown ornaments were made by glassblowers in Brooklyn, New York. Again, in comparison with the German ornaments, the glass was heavy and crudely formed.

1939: Corning became the first company to mass produce machine-made Christmas-tree balls. After much experimentation, the method was perfected and a year later Corning's workers were producing more ornaments in one minute then the German glassblowers could in one day.

1940s: World War II made it hard for Corning to obtain silvering for their ornaments, but production continued nonetheless. Characteristic of this period were clear glass bulbs painted with stripes. By the end of the war, cardboard caps had replaced metal ones.

1940s–50s: Max Eckardt, an importer of German ornaments in the early 1900s, expanded his Shiny Brite ornament company to be the premier producer in the world.

1960: Corning resumed decorating its own ornaments and is still producing most of the glass ornaments made in America today.

A Collector's Advice to Collectors

Back in the 1950s, when I wandered into antique stores in hopes of finding old Christmas-tree ornaments, the dealers appeared amused. "Nobody asks for them," they would say. Today the responses are completely different. "You're the fifth person this month to ask for them," one man said to me. "What is it with old Christmas-tree ornaments?"

There are two answers. One is simply the nostalgia we feel for an old-fashioned Christmas. The other is more complicated. People are beginning to appreciate anew the artistry that went into the making of the various little figures and objects that decorated Christmas trees around the turn of the century.

Ornaments are valued for their age and rarity, but these particular characteristics can be very difficult to determine. Some of the designs were produced for only a single season by a single glassblower. Of course, such pieces are rare. But other designs were produced for five decades or longer. I am always wary of any dealer who guarantees the antiquity of an ornament, because the molds can be used over and over again, and a quite recent piece can come out of a venerable mold. In addition, no matter what the original production figures were, orna-ments from the 19th century tend to be in short supply. Chemical imbalances in much of the paper-thin glass that was used then can cause the ornaments to self-destruct eventually. And cats' paws, dogs' tails, and children's elbows have also taken their toll.

The antiquity of one kind of ornament, the original *Kugel*, can be guaranteed. The *Kugels* are immediately identified by their thick glass, heavy weight, and dull sheen. They made their first appearance in America in the 1860s, mixed in with the household treasures of immigrants from Germany. Because their heavy construction made the ornaments sufficiently sturdy to withstand accidents, many of them survived and can still be discovered in attics and antique shops. And since they were no longer produced after the turn of the century, a *Kugel* is definitely a product of the 19th century—though beyond that, dating is speculative.

Perhaps the most reliable indications of age in a thin-walled glass ornament are to be found in its design and construction, and in the mellowing process. Any ball that is decorated with wire tinsel, cotton batting, or silk tassels is very likely to have been made between about 1890 and 1910, when designs such as these were popular. And if you come across an ornament whose top is finished with a round metal cap pierced by a hole, it almost certainly pre-

Though made of glass, some of the earliest Christmas ornaments were molded like chocolate Easter bunnies.

dates World War I. Before the appearance of the spring-clip fastener commonly used today, many ornaments were fastened to the tree with a piece of string that was passed through the hole in these rounded caps. Other fastening devices found on ornaments from this period include glass hooks that are integral parts of the ornament and metal spring clamps such as those used for Christmas-tree candles.

Patina as a sign of age is perhaps the most certain method of determining the date of an ornament's manufacture. In the very oldest pieces, both the lacquered surface and the silvered lining are softly mellowed. In addition, you may find that the silvering is cracked, similar to the silvering that backs an old mirror. Sometimes this cracking occurs in a pattern of horizontal rings, although ring cracks are not to be considered an infallible sign of age; they also are found in some improperly silvered post-World War II ornaments.

As the value of antique Christmas-tree ornaments escalates, they paradoxically become easier for collectors to find. Dealers buying estates now consider it well worth their while to hold on to objects that they would formerly have discarded as being too fragile to bother with. And owners wishing to sell their ornaments now find it advantageous to advertise them in the classified columns of collectors' magazines. However, if you plan to purchase ornaments through the mail, be sure to ask the seller to wrap them carefully in tissue paper, pack them in metal cookie or coffee cans, and place the containers inside corrugated boxes. Also, caution the seller not to attempt to wash his old ornaments. Any sort of water or dampness will cause the lacquer on an old ornament to peel right off; they should only be wiped with a soft, dry cloth.

Lest these precautionary measures make it sound as though collecting fragile Christmas-tree ornaments is a pastime meant only for brain surgeons, let me hasten to add that my own ornament collection is in use every year. It

---

THE GLITTER

1878: "Icicles," first made and sold in Nuremberg, Germany, were thin strips of silver foil. They became a huge success in America, even though they tarnished quickly.

1880: "Angel hair," made of spun glass, was first used to make garlands in Germany. In America, strands would be scattered separately over the whole tree to give the illusion of shimmering cobwebs.

1890s: Garlands of "tinsel" became popular. They were made of silver-plated copper wire—the wire was produced by a "secret" process originally developed in France for decorating military uniforms—bunched and clipped to give a bushy effect.

1920s: American manufacturers developed lead-foil icicles that did not tarnish.

1960s: Lead-foil icicles were replaced by mylar because of the danger of lead poisoning.

---

seems somehow alien to the spirit of Christmas to lock away even admittedly fragile ornaments from the hands of children, when a little common sense and discretion can keep these valuable items perfectly intact. The appropriate place for Christmas-tree ornaments is, after all, on the Christmas tree.

Phillip V. Snyder
The Encyclopedia of Collectibles
Time-Life Books

Though it may look ever
so humble now, the very
first lighted tree was
a real turn on.

The Lights

1882: The world's first electrically lighted
Christmas tree was decorated in the New York
City home of Edward Johnson, a colleague of
Thomas Edison at the then newly formed Edi-
son Electric Company.

1890s: General Electric, which had bought Edison's rights and his light bulb factory, began to
promote Christmas-tree lights. These were individual bulbs shaped like the standard light
bulbs of the time, which were smaller than
those of today and had pointed tips. The services of a "wireman" (the electrician of the era)
were needed to add the electrical wiring.

1903: The Ever-Ready Company of New York began manufacturing and marketing strings of lights, calling them "festoons."

1907: Ever-Ready issued a standard series-wired set with eight light sockets that could be joined to make a set of 16, 24, or 32 lights.

1909: The first figurative miniature light bulbs were handmade and hand-painted in Austria by the Kremenetzky Electric Company of Vienna. They were made of clear glass delicately shaped and colored to look like fruits, flowers, birds, and animals. Efforts by American and Japanese craftsmen to copy them were crude by comparison.

1910: General Electric changed its miniature Christmas lights from standard light-bulb shape to ball shape and added color by dipping them into transparent lacquer.

1920s: General Electric introduced the corrugated cone-shaped bulb.

1920–1950s: Japan produced handmade, mouth-blown versions of the original Austrian light-bulb ornaments in quantity, having switched from clear glass to translucent white milk glass in 1917. Shapes included characters such as Popeye, Little Orphan Annie, Andy and Min Gump, and Dick Tracy. An indefinable Ori-

ental flavor crept into the Japanese mold and painting. Even Santa Claus bore a distinct resemblance to Buddha.

1927: General Electric replaced the old series wiring with parallel wiring, which meant the entire chain would not go dark if one light failed.

1930s: Christmas lights that flashed on and off became available.

1936: Under a license from Walt Disney Productions, NOMA Lights produced strings of standard-series bulbs dressed up with colored plastic "lampshades." Each little shade was decorated with a decal of a Disney character, and Mickey Mouse, Donald Duck, Pluto, and Snow White made their first appearance on the American Christmas tree.

1945–1950s: "BubbleLites" were launched with much fanfare—and for a few years in the mid-50s, sales were spectacular. Invented by Carl Otis, an accountant for Montgomery Ward, the bulbs contained methylene chloride, a liquid that will boil at the low temperature of a tree light.

1970s: Flashing midget lights, marketed as "twinkle lights," became the biggest sellers in the history of tree lights.

A Peanut-Butter Christmas

BY RICHARD ATCHESON

When I was a child, my younger brother ate a Christmas ornament that was dangling from our tree. He bled a lot from the mouth, and had to be snatched away and repaired. He was not spanked because it was Christmas morning, but I was aware that all the adults were unsettled by what he had done.

It made near-perfect sense to me then and does now. Nothing looks more delicious to a child, nothing says "Eat Me!" half so yummity smackeroo as the sumptuous *Tannenbaum*. The Germans, who invented it, well know it.

The best tree I ever saw was in Germany, a long time ago, when I was bleakly in the Army there and went to stay for Christmas with friends in Rothenburg. They were desperately poor and hungry in the war's aftermath and were just barely getting by in their 15th-century stone-cold house on the Herrngasse. I used to ship them canned goods and peanut butter from the PX, and they declared that the peanut butter, which they had never encountered before, was the best food that they had ever tasted. It was also, of course, a rare and invaluable source of protein for their two small children.

On Christmas Eve I drove to Rothenburg on icy roads, over miles of flinty, open fields, through the medieval gates of tiny, lightless villages, through miles of white, sepulchral forests, more brilliant than the night, until at last my carload of American excess rattled on the cobbles of the Herrngasse.

In their main receiving room, a room rarely used and then barely heated by an antique porcelain stove, they had put up a tree the likes of which I had never seen, loaded with ornaments and decked on every branch with a fat white candle in a silvery holder. Near midnight, just before they woke Angelika and Mattias, they

lighted all the candles and brought the children in to see.

I understood in those tiny children's faces what the magic of Christmas really is. The astonishment of the golden candlelight transformed the room and all of us in it; the warm, quivering flames cast a glow from the fresh green boughs that was holy, hopeful, wildly improbable with promise in a time of little, of almost nothing, of potatoes and peanut butter. That is the tree. That is Christmas. Or at least that is what it was, then, in that long-ago time, in that very ancient house, when Christmas lunch tomorrow would feature, I knew, peanut butter soup.

As I live and weary of those who weary of our lives and our riches, I think back to that Christmas Eve and can weep again at the sight of the faces of Angelika and Mattias—children dependent upon me, an occupying soldier, for much of their protein—who saw beauty in the magic tree. I was embarrassed then and I am embarrassed now at my relative wealth.

We grown-ups watched the tree with them, and had a glass of wine, of which there was still enough. Then we put the candles out and went to our cold beds, where there were hot bricks in flannel waiting.

I put my sock-feet close around my hot brick and in the dark I thanked God that I could give something to those children, in that year of such desperate want; that I was allowed, in my time, to be more than a taker, with—at least—peanut butter.

Once upon a time my brother ate a Christmas ornament because he loved it. I understand. Today, I could eat the whole tree.

THE HOLIDAY HOME

SLOUCHING DOWN
HOLLYHOCK LANE

I have been browsing in the gardening columns of great American magazines in years past, and it seems to me that it can't have been very much fun to read them then, unless you really liked being told what to do all the time. The worthy women who wrote this kind of thing were providing, I assume, what their readers expected—and enjoyed. But, at the distance of decades, their exhortations arouse all kinds of guilty feelings—in me, at any rate. They seem to have spied out our propensity for letting the days slip by, allowing sloth and indolence to overcome our positive *duty* to festoon our homes with garlands of greenery.

Take this from the woman writing in the December 1895 issue of the *Ladies' Home Journal*: "I would impress upon the minds of the committee on decoration," she begins— and I am already cowed, though all the members of that committee must long since have joined the chorus of angels in the sky, "the importance of thoroughly planning the decorative scheme before anything is done about trimming the church. Unless this is done the result is almost sure to be unsatisfactory." Oh, dear. And you see, I hadn't even *thought* of the church yet.

Here is Hester M. Poole, writing for the December 1899 issue of *Good Housekeeping*: "While we rejoice, let us forgive all shortcomings in others." Right on! But she goes on to complain: "House decorations for Christmas are usually too hackneyed. A stiff round wreath hung in the center of a window sash, even enlivened with holly or crude red immortelles [what on earth are immortelles?], cannot be pronounced artistic." Her exciting alternative suggestion is to use pine boughs. "Pine boughs," she intones, "still bear their fruitage of cones and are decorative. Nothing can be brighter than groups of these, attached to the walls, while between them is draped the flag of our country." Well, it's a thought.

By the 1930s, gardening writers have lightened up some and it seems to be OK to have a certain amount of fun with Christmas decorations, but it is arresting to realize that in 1930 large numbers of homes in America had neither hot and cold running water nor electricity. Again and again in magazines of

A gift-wrapped house topped with a jaunty bow of red oilcloth mounted on a wooden frame won a prize in Des Moines in 1939.

Streamers of White Crepe Paper No. 2 W 1, ending in festooned balls, were Dennison's recommendation for a 1923 Christmas staircase. To complete the scene: a crepe-paper snowman built around the newel post.

"Cunning ideas" and "snappy new decorative stunts" for the 1940s from *Better Homes and Gardens*. "Turn the offspring loose . . ." exhorts the magazine.

THE YULE LOG

Spare a thought for the Druids while you fork up that delicious chocolate-covered Christmas Yule log; without them, you might have had to eat fruitcake.

For all the ancient northern peoples, winter's long gloom caused distress, so they lit fires to encourage the sun to return. The word "Yule," in fact, probably comes from the Gothic word for wheel, because the sun was thought of as being a turning wheel that alternately cast its light toward the earth and away from it again.

It was natural, then, for the Druid priests to celebrate the season of the winter solstice by choosing a huge log that would be ceremonially burned and then saved to rekindle the fire for the next year. The custom continued all over medieval Europe, where all kinds of rituals grew up around the Yule log. One, transported to the American South, held that no one should work while the log still burned, so the slaves would sprinkle it discreetly with water to keep the fire going as long as possible.

that vintage you will find references like this one, in *Good Housekeeping*: "Whether or not your home is equipped with electric lighting . . . " The piece goes on to advise the reader how to hook up the Christmas-tree lights to dry-cell or storage batteries.

Also from 1930 comes this irresistible snippet from the December issue of *Better Homes and Gardens*, addressed to the Junior Garden Clubbers:

"*Greetings*, Junior Gardeners," gayly calls Cousin Marion as she stands at the open door to the Hollyhock Lane Garden House.

From here, there, and everywhere appear members of our merry troop of Junior Gardeners. Red cheeked and eyes a-sparkle, their happy voices fill the garden house with merry clamor, "What have we in Hollyhock Lane on this early December morn?"

It turns out that they have the fixings for the Santa Apple illustrated here.

Christmas Candles

The noble candle has been called upon to cast its glow on all our important occasions for thousands of years, and today it is just as necessary and as evocative to us as it ever was.

In the ancient world, candles were known in Egypt and in Crete, at least from the year 3000 B.C., and ceremonies associated with candlelight are traced back into the mists of time. During the Roman Saturnalia, merrymakers used to exchange glowing tapers as expressions of good will and affection.

At about the same period, the Jews commemorated religious freedom with a Feast of Lights. The joyful festival was later adopted by the Christian world to celebrate the Nativity, when Pope Gelasius established February 2 as Candlemas Day. This feast honored the purification of the Virgin Mary 40 days after the birth of Christ, the occasion when his parents presented Jesus in the Temple at Jerusalem and the aged Simeon proclaimed the child as "a light to lighten the Gentiles" (Luke 2:32).

By medieval times, it was customary to light a candle on Christmas Day that would be carefully tended and made to last until Twelfth Night.

Candlelight, then, naturally came to symbolize the banishment of the darkness of paganism, and alongside this religious significance the superstition lingered that a long-burning candle would be a sure guarantee of long life.

The single candle was also often viewed as representing the star of Bethlehem. This may have been why, in 1741, Count Nikolaus von Zinzendorf led his Moravian followers with a lighted candle to a cabin in the wilds of Pennsylvania, where they named their new settlement Bethlehem to celebrate the birth of Christ in a manger.

In the next century, immigrants from Ireland brought with them the tradition of leaving their front doors open on Christmas night and placing lighted candles in the window to welcome the priest and passers-by.

Antique candle holders cradle the glowing lights.

Even today, the holiday season opens on December 20 in Williamsburg, Virginia, with the children walking in a "White Light" procession, led by a fife and drum band playing ruffles and flourishes. As many as 2,000 candles are lighted and displayed in shop windows, homes, and public buildings for this re-creation of a colonial Christmas.

Candles are so integral a part of our modern celebration of Christmas that more than 100 American companies are still manufacturing them, though today computers often control part of the manufacturing process and the candle-cutting equipment may be laser-operated. In this efficient, multimillion-dollar business, candles now take on every kind of shape, color, and fragrance, from vanilla, bayberry, and cranberry to strawberry, lemon, and spice, with names such as English Lavender, Evening Romance, Pina Colada, and Wine and Roses.

The kindly light that began in the Dark Ages with rush dips burning in tallow or oil has moved right along through beeswax into the petroleum wax of modern times without ever losing its honored place in our lives—as esteemed by fashion as by affection.

For Christmas, though, it will always be the simplest, pure white candles that prove the most enduring and win our hearts without fail, every year.

THE RE·GREENING
OF AMERICA

The idea of decking our halls with evergreens at Christmastime is as old as our pleasure at seeing green growing things amid the winter's snow. In the days before the mass production of ornaments, tinsel, and paper chains changed our habits entirely, conifer boughs and branches of holly, ivy, and mistletoe used to festoon all the rooms where guests would be welcomed and children would compete for the honor of crowning each picture on the parlor wall with its spray of evergreen.

Alongside all the manmade decorations, however, fresh, natural elements have been making a steady comeback. Now we are using more kinds of greenery than ever, and re-learning, too, the old skills of cutting and drying summer flowers and fall berries to delight us afresh with their subtle colors and graceful shapes. City florists stock a whole host of attractions fresh from the country—and free beauty waits for us in the dried grasses and seed pods by the roadside, or in the green leaves lurking in our very own backyards.

Conversation with a Naturalist-Designer

"Christmas to me is not red and green," summarizes Thomas Southard, whose business card reads:

> WILD, EXOTIC FLOWERS, BRANCHES,
> GRASSES, MOSSES, AND DESIGNS IN VINE
> FOR THE DISCERNING.

The "discerning" are some of New York's top designers, and his natural harvests embellish storefront windows and movie sets. He specializes in discovering, reintroducing, and supplying native greenery to the floral market: his

version of a Victorian Christmas tree, studded with dried flowers and berries, makes our standard tinsel and lights seem like the neon signs of Times Square.

As sole Victorian greenery designer for Cape May, New Jersey, Tom Southard harvests the land of his native Pine Barrens, where his ancestors have lived for more than 200 years. On a typical day of preparation for Christmas, he begins work at 4:30 A.M. and finishes around 1:00 the following morning, making vine wreaths, baskets, tree stands, and decorative swags. This 38-year-old self-proclaimed "corporate dropout" and former actor combines an academic knowledge of Victoriana and family-taught botanical information with a tremendous affection for his homeland. The result is a Christmas that sparkles with the unpretentious beauty of nature.

ALMANAC: What greenery do you recommend for a jubilant holiday decoration that requires minimal attention?

TOM: In terms of needle shedding and keeping its color, the Colorado blue spruce holds better than anything, and so does white pine.

ALMANAC How can you tell if the greenery you purchase is fresh?

TOM: Shake the damn thing! Basically, it's just like spaghetti. Before it's cooked, spaghetti will break, but when it has moisture in it it's nice and *al dente*. If the greenery is old or tired, look for droppage.

ALMANAC: What can be done to make greenery decorations last?

TOM: A tree will seal itself off. You have to cut it back so there's a little bit of sap running, and put the trunk in warm water—at least 100 degrees. Let it sit in warm water for the whole first day. If you want your water aerated so you don't get that skunky smell, use a little bit of bleach to keep the oxygen going. Aspirin or vinegar can be good, too, because certain evergreens like acidity—it keeps the pores open so they can suck water longer before sealing. If you don't want to deal with that, Floralife is available at any floral shop.

ALMANAC: What can be done about the problem of indoor heat?

TOM: A humidifier is the easiest way to keep things from falling apart as far as external drying goes. Even if you have baseboard heat, you should put a tub of water down so there's steam coming up and a little humidity.

ALMANAC: What tips can you offer for securing arrangements?

TOM: I've reintroduced sphagnum moss as a medium that can be used. It works better than floral foams, Oasis, and things like that. Oasis breaks up, whereas you can pack sphagnum moss as tight as you want and it

WHY WE KISS UNDER THE MISTLETOE

We may be approaching the 21st century, but we still believe that mistletoe is the kissing-bough. Apparently, if it was good enough for the Norsemen, it is good enough for us.

Legend has it that Freyja, the Norse version of Venus, goddess of love, arranged to have her son, Balder, the Norse Apollo, protected forever against anything derived from fire, water, air, and earth.

But Freyja forgot about mistletoe, a parasitic plant that grows on trees without ever touching the ground, and is therefore not *of* the earth. Sure enough, a clever but evil foe made an arrow from a branch of mistletoe and felled poor Balder.

With considerable help from the local pantheon, Freyja revived her son. Afterwards, she made the then-remorseful mistletoe promise never to cause harm again, and since that time the plant has become a symbol of peace between enemies and love between friends.

In more recent times, Washington Irving wrote in his *Sketch Book* of "one berry, one kiss." A man could kiss a woman under the mistletoe if he picked a berry each time he puckered up. Once all the berries were plucked, the kissing stopped.

And if you believe that one, you probably believe in Santa Claus, too.

will breathe and come back again. Once you've broken up Oasis it's gone. However, if you are making a vase arrangement, Oasis is the easiest thing to get.

ALMANAC: What material is best for making a wreath?

TOM: I mount mine and make all my rings by hand. Don't use wire rings because when the evergreen dries the wire just falls loose. I use vines for all mine and they keep their body and shape. One lady keeps hers until August! I use honeysuckle, snake vines, Virginia creeper, porcelain vines, red huckleberry, and dogwood branches. For greenery, white pine is very good; and so is spruce in terms of using the least amount of branches, because it's wide. I don't recommend balsam at all. It's the most popular because it's cheap, but when you buy wreaths for three, maybe four dollars and bring them home,

they fall apart on you. I deal in the unusual—I even make garlands out of cattails.

ALMANAC: What about swags?

TOM: A Christmas swag is simply three or four branches tied together with wire—it comes out like a fan. I recommend using 20- to 23-gauge florist's wire. Anything finer than that breaks; the lower you go, the heavier your wire. If you stick some holly or red alder twigs in, it's really very pretty. The more interesting evergreens can be simple, yet still just as effective and dramatic.

ALMANAC: Some greeneries are more aromatic than others. Can you suggest which are best for scenting the Christmas home?

TOM: Our native juniper, which is red cedar, smells wonderful. It doesn't drip sap, has short needles, and even when it dries out it doesn't drop. Bayberry is really nice. Its spicy, fragrant branches blend well with evergreens.

ALMANAC: What are some unusual mediums to use as alternatives to traditional greenery?

TOM: I've reintroduced *Ilex glabra*, which is a kind of holly that holds three weeks out of water, five weeks in. It keeps its color year round and doesn't drop like American holly. Bittersweet is not always allowed to be harvested—it's on some protected species lists—but there are states that permit it. It's beautiful and looks great wrapped around a Christmas tree; it also dries very nicely.

I also like to use dried rose hips. Ivy's neat; doesn't shed; seems to hold better in wintertime. I use laurel a little—it's like the American holly in that it dries out and blackens. It's a very popular and cheap roping medium, but it doesn't hold well unless it's in water. Swamp magnolia is good. I like white mistletoe, but it's not native to this area. Privet is good, too, and rhododendron leaves (which hold like laurel). Yews are nice.

Douglas fir, Scotch pine, and blue spruce are good. Although the spruce's needles fall off a little faster than the Scotch pine's, it keeps its color a little better. White pine is

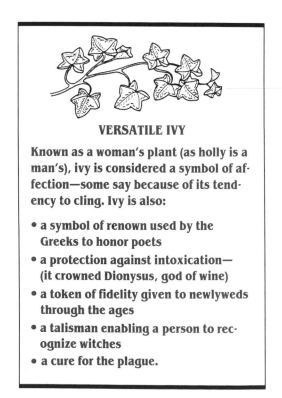

VERSATILE IVY

Known as a woman's plant (as holly is a man's), ivy is considered a symbol of affection—some say because of its tendency to cling. Ivy is also:

- a symbol of renown used by the Greeks to honor poets
- a protection against intoxication—(it crowned Dionysus, god of wine)
- a token of fidelity given to newlyweds through the ages
- a talisman enabling a person to recognize witches
- a cure for the plague.

the superior pine of all pines. I love blueberry juniper. When using juniper, the male is your choice because you don't want needles to drop. It has no berries, but it can have pretty little yellow pollen sacs because it pollinates in the winter.

Mosses not only look beautiful, but in arrangements they retain moisture without using a lot of water, and they'll keep things aerated. I also collect 250 varieties of wildflowers which I dry over the summer and fall.

ALMANAC: What is an example of an unusual Christmas decoration that you make?

TOM: One thing people don't know much about is decorations that you can put on graves at Christmastime. They're called grave blankets—sprays placed on the grave in memory of someone. For example, my grandmother loved birds. So each year I make an all-natural birdseed grave blanket with holly, winterberry, dried bayberry, blueberry juniper, and dried sumac. It makes an attractive decoration, and serves a purpose in feeding the birds, which she would have liked.

ALMANAC: Describe your version of a Victorian Christmas.

TOM: The Victorians were very naturalistic. So I make Christmas-tree stands out of vines and decorate the tree with dried flowers. For colors, subtler mauves were their choice. One of my most effective designs is the red-on-red-on-red of red rose hips, black alder, and American holly. Wild rose hips grow up to six feet, so I use tall vases. It looks like a big spray of red with just a few sprigs of green.

Oriental motifs were popular then, so I do Ikebana designs. Teardrop-shaped, open wreaths were also popular in Victorian times; I'm the only one that makes them now. Of the flowers I dry, over 75 percent are wild. I like coxcombs—they have a nice, deep maroon color. Immortelles, or pearly everlastings, are white. Sea lavender, or statice, is a subtle violet; I mass a whole tree with it to make a veil.

HOLY HOLLY

Some people like to think that the word "holly" is related to the word "holy," but in fact the name we use for the plant today is believed by linguistic experts to be directly derived from its Old English name, spelled *holegn* or *holen*. However, holly has long had a symbolic association with Christ: the white flowers are his purity, the red berries his blood, the leaves his crown of thorns, and the bitter bark his sorrow.

Long before Christ, the ancient Druids believed that holly was sacred, probably because it was evergreen and therefore favored by the sun. And since being sacred meant being inhabited by spirits, the Druids brought holly branches indoors in winter to give the spirits shelter from the hardships outside.

Centuries later, when holly had become an integral part of Christmas festivities in the north, it was believed that fairies and gnomes who lived in holly trees came indoors with the cut branches and gleefully stayed to enjoy the twelve days of Christmas—unobserved.

My favorites are what we call cats'-paws or cottontails—cotton grasses that grow wild in cranberry bogs and look like rabbit tails. They're a subtle brown. Dried pampas grass is beautiful, lacy, and really fills in a tree. Cattails are great. I've cut close to half a million in my time and I still love them.

CHRISTMAS IN FLOWER

I n the millennia before blooms from the other side of the world could be airlifted to brighten our bleak midwinters, the presence of a colorful, living, growing plant in dark December seemed positively miraculous. This is surely why so many Christmas flowers have wonderful tales connected with their origins.

Today, the most miraculous thing about gift plants may be the success of the industry in providing us each season with a bigger and better selection of plants to choose from. Christmas-flowering plants are produced on a massive scale, under rigidly controlled conditions, for the failure of a crop to blossom in time for the Christmas market can mean instant financial disaster. With our Christmases guaranteed to be banked with color, we are groomed along with the plants so that we will be ready to buy exactly when the flowers are there to be sold. In this case, fortunately, just about everyone benefits.

A Treasury of Christmas Plants

AMARYLLIS *(Hippeastrum)*

Blush-pink "Apple Blossom," salmon-orange "Beautiful Lady," bright red "Fire Dance," ruby-red "Scarlet Admiral," and "Snowy White Giant" are the varietal names of the full trumpet-like blossoms, nodding atop this plant's tall, slender stalk—to be anthropomorphic, picture Audrey Hepburn sneaking glances at her feet. The perennial bulb, which hails from South America, usually produces two stems, each with two to four flowers that last up to six weeks. They make lovely cut-

tings for arrangements, or can remain on the plants.

SELECTION AND CARE: Make sure the bulb feels firm and full. In a started plant, check to see that the blossom stalk has begun to develop. Water, following the directions that come with the bulb.

ARDISIA

A deep green, bushy top starred with clusters of bright berries makes this a true Christmas plant, one that can carry Yuletide sentiments throughout the year because the fruits last for many

months and even accompany the opening of tiny, fragrant blossoms.

SELECTION AND CARE: Look for full, leafy plants with rich color. Because Ardisia is of Asian origin, it enjoys day temperatures of about 70 degrees with bright, indirect light and nights cooling down to 50 to 55 degrees. Keep the soil evenly moist and mist around the plant but not directly on the blossoms. Cut back to 2 inches in early spring and withhold water until new shoots appear, then remove all but the three or four strongest shoots, repot in new soil, and resume feeding a month later.

AZALEA (Rhododendron species and hybrids)

Clouds of brilliant pink, white, yellow, or mauve flowers conjure up the pastel sunsets in their native lands of Japan, China, and the Himalayas, while red azaleas evoke images of Christmas.

SELECTION AND CARE: Look for large buds just beginning to open and bright foliage. Full sunlight and cool nights, about 60 degrees, are ideal (move plants to the floor or a cool windowsill at night if house temperatures are warmer). Mist regularly and water thoroughly as the peat-moss soil, if allowed to dry out, becomes impenetrable to water. Well-grown plants can be summered outdoors and brought inside just *after* a light frost; if you keep them in a cool (40 degrees), sunny room, they may rebloom.

BEGONIA (Rieger hybrids)

Tropical, flashy begonias come in all kinds of colors—red, white, pink, yellow, and orange—with flowers that are like bees buzzing around a woman's bonnet above large, light green leaves. They will bloom freely for months.

SELECTION AND CARE: Choose stocky, well-branched plants with multiple buds and no brown edges or signs of fungus. Begonias do well in bright, indirect light and night temperatures around 50 degrees, and should be placed on a tray of moist pebbles to maintain a humid environment. When all the

---

CRADLE PLANTS

Legend tells us that Joseph gathered heaps of grasses to provide a resting place for Mary, and upon that soft bed Jesus was born. Wild thyme, symbolizing strength and activity, and sweet woodruff, a sign of humility, both gently supported the new mother and child. The white flowers of Our-Lady's-bedstraw turned to brilliant gold and burst open, it is said, when the baby was laid upon them and sweet-smelling sainfoin bloomed to form a wreath of pink flowers around the Christ Child's head.

Outside the stable, the light that had guided the Wise Men broke up into the masses of tiny flowers we now call star of Bethlehem.

flowers have faded and no buds remain, allow the soil to dry completely for ten days, then water when the top half feels dry. Prune back to 3 inches with a sharp knife, and remove the dead leaves. When new growth appears, water and fertilize regularly, being sure the plants get four hours of direct sunlight until they resume flowering.

CHRISTMAS CACTUS
(Schlumbergera, formerly called Zygocactus)

In the rain forests of Brazil these cactuses hang from trees, where they struggle to find light, their segmented stems falling like a daddy longlegs tipped by fuchsia-colored, satiny-petaled flowers. Outside such exotic environments, they look great in hanging baskets or clay pots.

SELECTION AND CARE: Buy plants with large, ready-to-open buds on firm, green stems. Be sure the plant gets plenty of air circulation and even temperatures of approximately 70 degrees during the day and 60 degrees at night, but keep it out of direct sunlight. It summers well outdoors in a shady spot or in a bright window. Two or three months before Christmas it should get little or no light between 5:00 P.M. and 8:00 A.M., until the first bud has opened.

CHRISTMAS PEPPER
(Capsicum annuum)

The fiestas and piñatas of a Mexican Christmas are called to mind by this plant's oblong chili peppers, which start out green, then turn white, yellow, purple, and finally an orange-red in time for the holiday season.

SELECTION AND CARE: Buy plants that have fruit and flowers at all stages of development, and check carefully for whiteflies. Mist frequently and keep in bright sunshine, with night temperatures in the 60s, but protect from extreme heat. Once the fruit starts to wither, discard the plant.

CHRYSANTHEMUM

Feathery, pungent leaves back up a rich variety of flower shapes: big, bushy pompoms; sprightly daisies; spindly "spiders"; and miniature buttons in spun-sugar pink, lemon yellow, snow white, dusty gold, burnt orange-brown, and many shades more. A special favorite of Japanese horticulturists, these long-lasting plants are now raised to bloom at Christmastime as well as in the fall.

SELECTION AND CARE: Choose plants that have healthy foliage and many buds, with at least a few beginning to open. Keep well watered and in cool témperatures of 65 to 70 degrees by day and 55 degrees by night. Most plants from the florist do not winter well, but try bringing a plant through to the next season by cutting it back after flowering, repotting in the spring and setting it outdoors, then bringing it back inside again in the fall.

CITRUS (all species)

Fragrant white flowers and bright orange tangerines, yellow lemons, or pale green limes bring a welcome promise of warmer days to any winter. Fruits and flowers often appear simultaneously, and will be produced intermittently over many months.

SELECTION AND CARE: Look for abundant, shiny leaves and at least a few open flowers. Citrus plants thrive in direct sunlight at 68 to 72 degrees and require at least four hours of sun daily, with night temperatures of 50 to 55 degrees.

POINSETTIA: THE AMERICAN CHRISTMAS FLOWER

Most flowers, herbs, and plants used at Christmas are associated with very ancient celebrations. But the poinsettia is an addition of a much later date, the New World's contribution to Christmas.

In 1825 Joel Roberts Poinsett of South Carolina, a diplomat who was the first American minister to Mexico, became intrigued with the brilliant red "flowers" topping spindly shrubs all over the countryside. The local people called them "flame flowers" or "flowers of the Holy Night" because they were used as decorations in Mexican Nativity processions.

Dr. Poinsett, an enthusiastic botanist, sent cuttings home for his greenhouse and shared them with friends.

About a century later, Paul Ecke of California saw these plants and began to cultivate, interbreed, and experiment with them. Today the Ecke family has a thriving business supplying 5,000 growers around the world with cuttings that produce millions of holiday plants each year—an American success story that has become another Christmas legend.

The flowers may need to be shaken or hand fertilized with a paintbrush to encourage fruit to form. Pinch off new growth to control the plant's size.

CYCLAMEN (*Cyclamen persicum*)

Originally from the Middle East, cyclamen is the most dramatic of seasonal plants. The delicate white, pink, or red flowers balance like butterflies atop long stalks; heart-shaped, dark green leaves are highlighted by splashes of silver and light green.

SELECTION AND CARE: Buy plants with rich, succulent foliage and buds at all stages of development beneath the leaves in the center of the plant. Be particularly careful of cyclamen mites. Provide as much light as possible but be sure of cool temperatures, less than 68 degrees by day, 40 to 50 degrees at night. Water thoroughly from below. Once flowering ceases, allow to dry out, and let the corm rest for at least a month before resuming watering. Plant the pot outdoors during the summer in a shady spot, then repot it in acid soil and bring it indoors for the winter.

GLOXINIA

If flowers could make a sound, these would surely ring out "Joy to the World." Flaring trumpet shapes of pink, lavender-blue, and white rise on thin stalks above large, velvety, dark green leaves.

SELECTION AND CARE: Look for good foliage color and avoid leaves with crisp edges. The flowers will last four to six weeks if fading ones are removed and the plant is kept in direct sunlight at 60 to 65 degrees. Do not overwater. Once flowering ends and the leaves begin to yellow, stop watering until the plant goes completely dormant. Remove the dry rhizome from the soil and store it in a plastic bag. New sprouts will appear in approximately three months. Repot with fresh soil and peat moss, placing the flat top of the rhizome even with the soil surface. Keep the mixture just moist, and do not feed until stem growth begins.

JERUSALEM CHERRY

(Solanum pseudocapsicum, also called Christmas cherry, Cleveland cherry)

This plant's brilliant red-orange fruits are so wickedly enticing that one could imagine them part of a children's fairy tale, tempting a princess with their poisonous charm. So long as they are not eaten, they make the Jerusalem cherry a merry ornamental plant—for an all-adult household. SELECTION AND CARE: Obtain healthy, bright plants with no yellowing or whiteflies. They prefer cool nighttime temperatures, 50 to 55 degrees, and need four hours of direct sunlight each day. Treat them as annuals and discard them once the fruits die.

KALANCHOE *(Kalanchoe blossfeldiana*, also called panda plant, velvetleaf)

Kalanchoes come from the sultry island of Madagascar and sport tight scarlet-red flowers clustering above succulent foliage, in shapes that resemble the bouffant hairstyles of the 1950s. SELECTION AND CARE: Buy compact plants with plump, unwrinkled leaves and buds that are mostly unopened. They require a minimum of four hours of good sunlight with daytime temperatures of 70 to 75 degrees, going down to 60 degrees at night. Water only when the soil is dry. To ensure blossoms for next Christmas, summer plants outdoors, pinching them back to keep the foliage busy, or start new ones from cuttings. From mid-September to early October, keep plants in darkness for 15 hours a day.

POINSETTIA *(Euphorbia pulcherrima)*

An emblem of Christmas from south of the border, the poinsettia's brilliant "flowers" (they are actually brightly colored bracts which attract pollinating insects to the hidden, tiny green flowers) burst forth in red, pink, white, and marbled colors amid handsome green leaves. Poinsettias range from miniatures to six-foot trees, and for best effect they should be clustered, as their growth can be straggly.

SELECTION AND CARE: Plants need three to four hours of bright, filtered sun with daytime temperatures of 65 to 70 degrees and 55 to 60 degrees at night. They are sensitive to temperature changes, so avoid placing them in drafts or near heat ducts. Water only when the surface soil is dry to the touch and remove any excess water in the saucer. A plant may continue to bloom through July if you keep it in total darkness at night, feed it soluble fertilizer, and place it outside in warm weather. Most people find keeping poinsettias year round too time-consuming, but it can be done with proper care. Consult a botanical guide for specifics.

STREPTOCARPUS (Cape primrose)

Native to Cape Province, South Africa, this plant has become a welcome Christmas immigrant, with its pink, blue-purple, white, or red flowers nodding like sleepy heads on "throats" painted with contrasting colors above circles of stemless, quilted leaves. SELECTION AND CARE: Buy plants with vigorous foliage and erect stems. They do well in warm daytime temperatures of up to 80 degrees, and 70 degrees at night. With indirect light, moist soil, and regular removal of dead flowers, they will flower for months.

OUR CHRISTMAS FOLK ART HERITAGE

OUR CHRISTMAS
FOLK ART HERITAGE

A s the bells rang out to announce the birth of the new nation, the young country had already begun to establish a new and distinctively American art form. Well before 1776 and for fully another hundred years, people up and down the eastern seaboard delighted in decorating the everyday objects they used in their living and working space. Their work reflects the spirit of the times. Utility came first, beauty followed. Samplers were not only for decoration; they taught young girls their letters and numbers. Sewing was no hobby in those early days but a necessity, for all the clothes had to be produced at home and people made quilts and rugs to keep themselves warm, with no inkling that they were creating fine art.

These men and women were artisans, using whatever materials they had at hand: metal and wood, tin and pewter, rags and scraps of cloth. Neither fancy nor frivolous, their work is filled with the exuberance of experimentation. It is naive, but its very innocence is the essence of its charm. Small wonder, then, that the many objects that have endured have become part of every American's heritage.

It is fascinating to discover how many of the subjects beloved by folk artists—angels and mermaids, stencil designs, flowers and stars—had their origins in medieval images and the naive art of many cultures. Adopting them as if they were the first to use them, early Americans made these images their own. Maybe the images that we pass along in our time will be computer-generated, but we can still adapt them to our individual liking. Then we can begin to create heirlooms for our own children and great-grandchildren and know that in a century or two our art will be cherished every bit as much as we cherish the work of our ancestors. Like them, we can get by with little or no formal training. The important thing is to continue to respect the making of things by hand, for each then bears our own unique signature. And if it makes someone else laugh, so much the better.

The colorful portfolio that follows expressed all the warmth and lovingness of working people's art. The objects have been chosen with great affection from museums and private collections; to them we have added some examples of contemporary craftsmen's skill. Many of these artists delight in using the same materials and methods as those through whose work we can literally touch the time when America itself was just beginning.

Handmade copper sculpture by Jacque Tatum, 1987.

Pieties quilt
Maria Cadman Hubbard. Probably New England, 1848. Cotton, 88½ × 81½ inches. Collection of the Museum of American Folk Art, New York: Gift of Cyril Nelson in loving memory of his parents, Cyril Arthur and Elise Macy Nelson, 1984.

Wood carvings by Nancy Thomas, 1986.

Virginia lily quilt
Maker unknown, c. 1870. Cotton, 91½ × 89¾ inches. Collection of the Shelburne Museum, Shelburne, Vermont.

Poinsettia design appliquéd quilt
Maker unknown, 1830. Cotton, 70 × 72 inches. The William A. Farnsworth Library and Art Museum, Rockland, Maine: Gift of Mr. and Mrs. Rufus Foshee in dedication to Louise Nevelson, 1978.

Baltimore album quilt
Elizabeth Miller, S.A. Mules, Margaret Head and others, 1847. Cotton, 100 × 102 inches. Collection of the Shelburne Museum, Shelburne, Vermont.

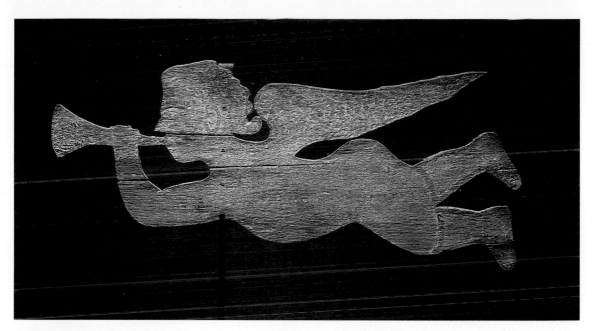

Angel Gabriel weather vane
Artist unknown, 1800. Polychromed
wood, 33½ × 13 inches. Collection of
the Shelburne Museum, Shelburne,
Vermont.

Wood carvings by Nancy Thomas, 1987.

Detail from sampler
Mary Ann Hall, 1826. Silk on wool, 14¾ × 11¾
inches. Collection of the Museum of American Folk
Art, New York: Gift of Alfred Rosenthal.

Christmas hooked rug
Artist unknown, c. 1930. Wool on burlap, 37 × 42
inches. Collection of the Shelburne Museum,
Shelburne, Vermont: Gift of Fred MacMurray.

**Wood carvings by Nancy Thomas,
1983–1987.**

Deer (one of a pair)
Artist unknown, 1860–1900. Chalkware, 10⅝ × 8½ × 4⅛ inches. Collection of the Museum of American
Folk Art, New York: Gift of Effie Thixton Arthur.

GREETINGS!

SHOUT WITH JOY YE MORTALS PRAY
FOR CHRIST IS BORN ON CHRISTMAS DAY

SENTIMENTS OF THE SEASON

Christmas cards in America today are a billion-dollar annual business, a bonanza for the Postal Service, a sentimental pleasure for millions, and a source of guilt for nearly everybody. For while it is nice to be remembered by friends, it is appalling to be remembered by somone we forgot to remember, and it happens to all of us, every year.

When we make up our Christmas-card lists we do a kind of ingathering of our tribe, of all those who populate the mental village of our recall and recognition. Our cards *really* say "I know you. You are in my club." So it's awful when you get a card from someone whose card says you are part of his life, while your omission has said, more or less, that in your world he doesn't exist.

People in business don't like this, because in that world the sending of cards is a signal of intent to continue doing business. A single glitch in the computerized mailing list can shake corporate empires and make the sweetest sweetheart deal turn sour. Heads can roll, from the mail boy to the big boss, when some captain of industry and valued client/supplier/financial backer doesn't get his card and takes offense. There are no excuses in this game. It is almost as bad as forgetting your great-aunt Agatha, who is loaded and from whom you have great expectations.

Christmas cards are sent in many parts of the Western world, but only in America does the tradition have so firm a grip on national behavior at every level of society. Only in America can you buy plastic card racks which enable you to turn your own living room into a facsimile of a card shop. Only in America are cards as intrinsic to the holiday decor as the tree, the ornaments, and the twinkling lights.

A hundred years ago, people wrote letters to each other all the time, by hand, on notepaper. For major holidays, some shops would offer stationery with holiday trim, and calling cards with—for Christmas—sprigs of holly or mistletoe. Technology intervened first in 1874, when a Boston lithographer named Louis Prang offered a selection of cards bearing art reproductions with as many as 20 colors, from original work by contemporary painters found in prize competitions. Prang quickly developed a following among the English, who liked his delicate reproductions of flowers. Americans, on the other hand, came to show a preference for tranquil Madonnas, floating golden cherubim, and quaint children in night-

Louis Prang's concern with quality led him to inaugurate open competitions with generous prizes. He published the winning designs as cards printed by lithography in as many as 20 colors. The design above won Rosina Emmett first prize and $1,000 in 1880; other winners are shown overleaf. A century has not dimmed their charm.

dresses waiting for St. Nick. Particularly appreciated, too, were the printed sentiments that adorned the reverse side.

In the 1890s, the penny postcard hit the market, and Prang and other quality manufacturers were forced out of business by German card-makers whose price was right. The penny Christmas card reigned until American declared war on Germany in 1917 and blocked all imports—at which point American makers came on the scene again to meet demand with a product of superior quality. An integral element in the packaging of the new cards was the pre-composed message inside, which made it no longer necessary to write a regular letter.

And so began the steady emergence of second-hand sentiment in America.

The front and back of 1888's "Fourth Popular Prize" winner appear at left and above.

A card decorated with cherubim, right, was placed third and won $300 in 1880.

In 1882, Dora Wheeler was awarded the second prize of $500 for this grand design.

TO CHRISTMAS WITH LOVE: THE HALLMARK STORY

T he story is so like the Horatio Alger myth that you might doubt it happened.

A plucky, determined youth with lots of salt and the requisite dose of protective innocence departs home and school at age 18, takes on the world, and wins. Wins big, too, leaving at his death in 1982 a $1.5 billion corporation, friendships with people like Churchill, Eisenhower, and Truman, and enough honors and awards to adorn three lifetimes.

But Joyce C. Hall, founder of the business that would become Hallmark Cards, was no Horatio Alger character. The hero of an Alger book succeeded by pleasing a powerful patron. Hall didn't ride on anyone's star wagon, and the motive that drove him was as basic as the alphabet. "All I was trying to do," he once said, "was make a living. In those days if you didn't work , you didn't eat. And I like to eat."

The story begins on January 10, 1910, with Joyce Hall's arrival in Kansas City from his Norfolk, Nebraska, home. Picture postcards were big then, and he had two shoe boxes full and a scheme for distributing them. With the same kind of marketing audacity that would one day send Hallmark cards into more than 100 countries, he dispatched packets of cards to dealers throughout the Midwest.

Perseverance paid off with modest success, and several years later Hall's two brothers, Rollie and William, joined him in the postcard business.

Even in those early years Hall, with his keen nose for new market directions, sensed the

The "Christmas-card tree" opposite was given by the Hallmark staff to their founder-president, Joyce C. Hall. Right, Hall as a young man.

MAKING THE CARD

What's up-to-date in Kansas City? Everything, according to the song, and nowhere is this more evident than at Hallmark Cards, where 2,500 Christmas-card designs are issued each year. About 3,000 people, executing up to 300 steps, may be involved in conceiving, creating, and manufacturing a single card—a cycle that runs from 18 to 24 months.

Before the card comes the idea. And before the idea comes research, conducted by 100 professional demographic analysts, to determine what designs and sentiments will best meet public attitudes this year. The information guides the work of a consortium of professionals, ranging from the artists who work on the outside of the card, and the writers and calligraphers who work on the inside, to the graphic designers who put the whole card together.

Behind the scenes, technicians are using laser and holograph technology to create intricate cutouts and shimmering effects, or manufacturing paper and ink that cannot be purchased commercially. Finally, the card must pass relentless scrutiny at no fewer than 30 testing points before being shipped to the stores.

A woman of words, Hallmark writer Linda Elrod, writes messages for millions.

Long ago, neat rows of artists toiled to create the cards that were displayed in neat rows of racks.

business potential of Valentines and Christmas cards mailed in envelopes—an added touch greatly favored by the carriage trade.

Trusting his instinct, Joyce Hall abandoned postcards in 1914 and replaced his stock with greeting cards, with a special focus on the Christmas season that has continued throughout the company's history. That was the real birthdate of Hallmark Cards.

A number of landmark events and decisions influenced the company's growth over the years. Probably the most important was the fire early in 1915 that destroyed the firm's entire inventory of cards from its suppliers.

"We were $17,000 in the hole," Hall later recalled. "If you want to quit, that's a good time."

Refusing to quit, the Halls floated a loan to buy an engraving firm. This first small step toward creating their own cards climaxed in today's Hallmark Cards, where some 700 writers, artists, and technicians annually create more than 14,000 greeting card designs, making a total of 11 million cards published every day in 20 languages.

At first, one staff artist did all the designing, but by 1925 a dozen artists were at work and the number soon became hundreds. The Hallmark lines also included many reproductions of works by Old Masters and such contemporary artists as Picasso, Dali, Buffet, Georgia O'Keeffe, Saul Steinberg, Norman Rockwell, and Grandma Moses.

Hallmark's first addition to the card business was the production of specially designed gift-wrap paper. This had its beginnings at Christmas 1917, when the Hall brothers ran out of tissue wrapping paper and tried offering imported envelope lining papers from their warehouse at 10 cents a sheet. Customers snapped them up so fast that the company soon realized a new business had been born and started manufacturing its own designs.

Since then, Hallmark has diversified into a range of products, from Christmas ornaments and party goods to puzzles and picture frames. Regular productions in the "Hallmark Hall of Fame" series remind us that there *can* be classy shows on television. The most conspicuous milestone yet is the $500 million Crown Center complex financed and developed by Hallmark around its Kansas City headquarters.

And that is how Joyce Hall's way of making a living changed the American way of celebrating Christmas—and a multibillion-dollar business was founded on a house of cards.

Steinberg's Christmas card has Santa riding into town on his own toy train.

Joyce Hall regularly discussed ideas with Norman Rockwell (left), whose humorous, heart-warming designs, such as the card shown here, headed Hallmark's lists each year.

Trends in Cards

You need only a couple of hours in the Hallmark archives to realize that greeting cards are a mirror of their times, reflecting the public events, fashions and fads, beliefs and behavior that were dominant when the cards were published. It's all there, as in a miniature encyclopedia: the Great Depression, World War II, "flower power," changes in clothing styles, our obsessions with science and technology. Public trends become card trends.

This is particularly evident in Christmas cards of the last two decades, when American attitudes, manners, morals, and concerns began to change at jet speed. The language, art, and sentiment say "today" in unequivocal terms.

A 1971 Hallmark card shows Santa, gas mask in place, driving his sleigh through a murky sky. The words: "Silent Night, Holy Night, All Is Calm, And Visibility Is Poor."

Ecology, pollution, peace, and hippies were the popular "now" themes.

A couple of years later, it became trendy to poke fun at poor Santa. On one card Santa flashes the peace sign, but in this case it means, "Two beers, please." Nor was Mrs. Claus exempt from some gentle ribbing. "Yes, Mrs. Claus," a card announced, "there is a Virginia." Inside a generously endowed young girl in a short skirt is perched on Santa's knee.

Gathering momentum, the Christmas humor

1932

Greetings

OF COURSE I'D LIKE TO SEE YOU
AND HAVE YOU "PUT 'ER THERE"
TO WISH YOUR CHRISTMAS MERRY
AND NEW YEAR JOYS TO SPARE

BUT IT CAN'T BE DONE OLD TIMER
FOR I'M FAR AWAY YOU SEE
BUT NOT TOO FAR AWAY FOR YOU
TO HAVE A SMOKE ON ME

No more bustles, no more stays,
No more petticoats these days,
No more puffs and no more rats,
No more Merry Widow hats,
But though the styles have changed, it's true,
And lots of other things have, too.
This good old wish for Christmas cheer
Remains unchanged, year after year—
MERRY CHRISTMAS

1929

1917-1919

trend then took off in new directions. Defying the axiom that you don't make fun of a very good thing, barbs in the form of verses soon took on the most cherished Christmas traditions—including fruitcake. One of a whole series of such cards depicted a disappointed character opening a gift and sighing, "Oh, how nice! A fruitcake." The punch line: "Nobody likes getting food that will outlive them."

A card that aims straight at the bull's-eye, Christmas itself, expressed the view: "Christ-

1940s

Merry Christmas from a Poor Working Girl

*Don't spend my hard-earned money
On just anyone, it's true,*

1945

1959

1971

THE COMPLETE CHRISTMAS CARD

The circumstances were, I wanted the family to do something really old-fashioned. Make our own Christmas card. Carve one of those linoleum blocks, then roll red ink off a piece of window glass, and stamp the cards out on rice paper by leaning hard on the back of the block with both hands, or, if you're careful, even standing on it.

But a very simple card. Don't want too many curlicues, or you lose the image in the ink stains. So my wife, the artist, sketched out this snowfall—more an ice storm, really—and then I added the shortest Xmas word I could think of, at the bottom of the block. NOEL. I carved all around each letter—N, O, E, then L—so they would be raised in red, not sunken in white.

We let the kids do the inking, out in the kitchen, while we addressed envelopes. Let them stomp on them, with newspaper under the rice paper, and they were doing them up like Hallmark until Number One Son came in and asked, "Why are you sending them all to this one guy?"

"What guy?" I said.

"Leon."

"Who's Leon?" I said. "Are you messing up out there?"

"No way. It says 'Leon' on all of them. See for yourself."

So I rushed out to the kitchen and, sure enough, all the imprints said "LEON," raggedly backward, because I had forgotten to do the letters in reverse on the block—L, E, O, then N—so they would print out "NOEL." Instead, we had who knows how much personalized stationery for anybody answering to "Leon," and I made haste, midst merry laughter, to place an order with UNICEF.

Brock Brower
Harper's
December, 1985

---

mas is just plain weird. What other time of the year do you sit in front of a dead tree in the living room and eat candy out of your socks?"

Perhaps the most striking current trend in Christmas cards, given the common view that ours is a secular society, is the resurgence of greetings that play up the basic religious significance of Christmas. Christmas is Christ's birthday, these cards say, and they salute it with traditional anthems: "Rejoice! Hallelujah!

However, in many cases the presentation is totally contemporary. Bright, bold designs and almost frivolous images predominate. A cat may balance precariously atop a Christmas tree, polishing a star in the sky, but the language is unambiguously religious: "May the light of His love always shine on you."

Another consistent theme is world peace, the preoccupation of the 1960s. It took on new relevance with efforts for famine relief (cards from 1985 featured doves and the lion and lamb lying down in harmony), and current concerns about global ecology are reflected in a spate of cards celebrating earth's natural beauty in photographs and fine art.

But while fads appear and disappear with passing fancies, sales records show that most people still prefer the familiar Christmas sentiments and symbols—Madonna and Child, Santa, evergreens, Wise Men, snowmen, peace on earth. The hearth that burns the warmest and means the most is located in the family living room.

Some trends are forever.

MERRY CHRISTMAS

1961

As winter comes
and
Christmastime
draws near,
I make this wish
for those I love--
good times,
good friends,
good health,
good cheer.

1987

1987

Emily Post, Meet the Christmas Card

Dominant signs of the times—couples living together informally, divorce and remarriage, career women, blended families—call for some new rules to direct the giving of Christmas cards. Hallmark Cards, the world's largest greeting card company, has been monitoring demographic and social trends since 1910 and offers these card-sending tips:

- When sending a card to a couple with different last names, address the envelope to "Mary Smith and John Jones." If there are children, use "Mary Smith, John Jones, and family."

- Divorced women frequently reclaim their maiden names. Make sure you know which last name and courtesy title the lady prefers.

- If there are children in the household you are "carding," include their names, too, if the card is for personal friends. Traditionally, family signatures begin with the father's name, followed by the mother's, then the children's. An acceptable alternative is "John, Mary, and children."

- If a card is from more than one person, the person who signs it should write his or her name last, out of courtesy.

- Write a personal note, if possible, and always sign the card, even if your name is imprinted.

- Signatures should be informal. No courtesy titles, and, to close friends and relatives, no last names either. A return address on the envelope will tell the recipient who "Bob" is.

- Don't be afraid to send cards to people who follow a faith other than Christian. Non-Jewish people, for example, may send holiday greetings to Jewish friends and vice versa, since Christmas and Hanukkah are celebrated close together. Best to respect the religious convictions of the recipient and choose a card with neutral messages such as "Happy Holidays" or "Season's Greetings."

- Take special care when there has been a death in the family and select one of the cards that offers condolences. If the card is sent to a recent widow, address her as "Mrs. John Jones."

- Avoid holiday pressures by mailing early. Any time after Thanksgiving and before New Year's Day is appropriate.

- Use first-class postage so your cards will be forwarded or, if the addressee cannot be located, returned to you. Using first-class mail also allows you to write a personal message on your cards.

"I've got it! Instead of sending cards, I'll sing 'O Holy Night' on the answering machine with you accompanying me on the harmonica."

THIS COMPUTER CAN RHYME . . . FOR THREE BUCKS EACH TIME

If you can't find just the right verse in a greeting card and your own talent doesn't rise above "I'm not a poet, and I know it," you might turn to the Computer Poet.

The invention, developed by a computer programmer and a poet using Apple's Macintosh microcomputer, composes a personalized three-verse limerick for the object of your attention. You'll find the Computer Poet in more than 300 card and gift shops and military post exchanges across the country. The computer asks you for the name of the person you'll send the verse to, the person's home town, the occasion for the poem, and a description of the recipient (artistic, sexy or bossy, for example).

The computer will display appropriate limericks. You can attach the printed poem to one of 80 colorful card fronts. You owe nothing unless you select a poem for printing.

Changing Times
January, 1986

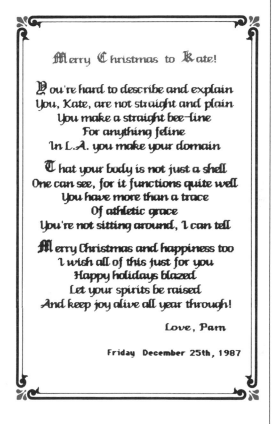

Merry Christmas to Kate!

You're hard to describe and explain
You, Kate, are not straight and plain
You make a straight bee-line
For anything feline
In L.A. you make your domain

That your body is not just a shell
One can see, for it functions quite well
You have more than a trace
Of athletic grace
You're not sitting around, I can tell

Merry Christmas and happiness too
I wish all of this just for you
Happy holidays blazed
Let your spirits be raised
And keep joy alive all year through!

Love, Pam

Friday December 25th, 1987

- Include your return address on the envelope. Not only does this comply with the U.S. Postal Service's request, it will help your friends keep their mailing lists current.

Business Christmas cards have an etiquette all their own. Some pointers:

- They should be more tailored and formal than cards directed to family and personal friends. Keep the messages brief and, usually, secular.

- As a general rule, mail cards to clients or business associates at the office. But, if you are socially acquainted or have met the person's spouse, send the card to the home.

- When sending the card to a colleague, send the card to the home and, if the recipient is married, address it to "Mr. and Mrs."

- When sending a card to a married woman who uses her maiden name only at work, address the card to "Mr. and Mrs. John Smith" at home. If the lady's preference is to use that name for all occasions, address the card to "Mr. John Smith and Ms. Susan Jones."

- Your spouse should not sign a business card unless he or she has met the recipient.

Something Special in the Air

Time was, and not too long ago, either, when a "special" Christmas card was a card that was flocked, flittered, coated, dyed, engraved, embossed, or treated to look like leather, wood, satin, or cloth, or able to pop up into a three-dimensional greeting. It might even have been fitted with a microchip and a miniature speaker and battery in order to play Christmas tunes in harmonies, flash on lights, or even send the recipient "season's greetings" in a scratchy voice. But today the word "special" has taken on a larger dimension. According to Hallmark, peo-ple are becoming increasingly discriminating in their card selection and want cards that reflect their individual relationships—all part of the trend toward more personalized communication.

Ever think of sending a card from your pet to the pet next door? Perhaps it is only another way, amusingly disguised, of course, for good neighbors to pay the compliments of the season to each other, but it's now possible. The cards are there, if you're so inclined. Do the cats and dogs smile at their cards? Probably not. But their owners do. And spreading good cheer at Christmas is what the season's all about.

Better include your babysitter among the beneficiaries of the good cheer—especially if your household has one of the more than 20

MY BROTHER

Usually looking for trouble

Always sticking it where it doesn't belong

Gives you a hand now and then

Always has little surprises

Has a big heart (whether he knows it or not)

Bottomless pit

PATTERSON

Nobody else could fill 'em

million working American mothers. Cards aimed at this huge audience are available. And, who knows—perhaps letting Suzy or Jane or Joe know that you think she or he is really special will make it easier to deal with Junior's tantrums the next time around.

The most popular of the special Christmas cards is the one aimed at the biggest of all gangs of "specials"—kids. Now available in boxed sets for the first time—in response to research indicating that schoolchildren are increasingly exchanging cards—they are inexpensive, with designs ranging from storybook classics to coloring cards with Crayolas. More kids' cards are sent, and received, than any other "niche" card.

UNICEF: CARDS THAT DO GOOD, TOO

When you buy cards from UNICEF, the United Nations Children's Fund, you touch more lives than you know.

• One pack of cards buys enough oral rehydration salts to treat ten children suffering from serious dehydration, a death-dealer in third-world countries.

• Two packs buys an illustrated teaching guide describing treatment and preventive measures to be taken against dehydration.

• Three packs cover the cost of immunizing one child against the six major child-killer diseases: diphtheria, measles, whooping cough, polio, tetanus, and tuberculosis.

UNICEF's first card was a Czechoslovakian child's painting, given in thanks for help to her village after World War II. Below, it is re-created at Lincoln Center by New York children under the direction of copyist Sidewalk Sam.

Since 1949, artists from around the world have contributed designs and some $200 million from card sales has been spent on projects benefiting children in 119 developing countries. UNICEF's toll-free number—800-553-1200—receives orders and provides information.

Collectible Cards

If your old Christmas cards are piling up—tied with ribbons, stashed in shoe boxes, locked away in trunks, or stuffed in desk drawers—it may be time to take your collecting instinct seriously and develop a strategy for future efforts. Cards, it turns out, can be more valuable than you may have thought.

Old or rare cards can be worth hundreds of dollars. You may not have in your collection Christmas cards by 19th-century artists and publishers such as Kate Greenaway, Esther Howland, Jonathan King, or Louis Prang. But remember those cards that Grandma left behind? They may well contain such treasures.

Other cards have value because they refer to significant events or turning points in American experience, according to Hallmark Cards. They are a contemporary record, for example, of wars, Prohibition, the Depression, the sexual revolution, the opening of the Space Age, women's lib, and much more.

Here are some suggestions from Hallmark to guide your future collecting and help organize the cards you already have.

The first ground rule is to save those cards with deep personal meaning; they will provide a road map of your past. In some distant time, you can turn to these cards as you would to a photograph album and find out what your life was like in "the good old days."

In addition, save cards that reflect:

- Social milieu—fashions, cars, computers, slang, TV shows, sports, and celebrities.

- Crazes and fads—break dancing, streaking, hula-hoops, skateboards, nerds, "Valley" talk, hairstyles, popular songs—that are not likely to have a long shelf life.

THE ANTICIPATED PRE-HOLIDAY BEHAVIORAL UPSWING

- Lifestyle changes—male/female roles, dating, mating, divorce, stepfamilies, dieting.

- Controversial social issues—war, nuclear energy, smoking, drinking, drug use, sex, chauvinism.

- Your other collections and special interests—matchbooks, license plates, cars, needlework, movie and TV stars, aerobics, etc.—that are often shown on cards.

- New card materials and processes—musical cards, laser-cut and movable cards, pop-ups, fold-outs, cloth and plastic cards, cards with add-ons or produced in unusual shapes and sizes.

- Firsts—like Hallmark's à la mode cards with coupons you could redeem for Baskin-Robbins ice cream, the first cards to offer food coupons.

- Postcards—a collecting fad at the turn of the century, they are back, reflecting signs of our times.

Oh, give me an old-fashioned
  Christmas card,
With mistletoe galore, and holly by
  the yard,
With galumptious greens and
  gorgeous scarlets,
With crackling logs and apple-
  cheeked varlets,
With horses prancing down a frosty
  road,
And a stagecoach laden with a festive
  load,
And the light from the wayside
  windows streaming,
And a white moon rising and one star
  gleaming.

Oh, give me an old-fashioned
  Christmas card,
With hostlers hostling on an old inn
  yard,
With church bells chiming their silver
  notes,
And jolly red squires in their jolly red
  coats,
And a good fat goose by the fire that
  dangles,
And a few more angels and a few less
  angles.
Turn backward, Time, to please this
  bard,
And give me an old-fashioned
  Christmas card.

Ogden Nash

CHRISTMAS
1941

A MERRY CHRISTMAS

from

THE PRESIDENT

and MRS. ROOSEVELT

Roosevelt 1941

Greetings from the White House

When Dwight D. Eisenhower decided to send the first official presidential Christmas card in 1953, he turned to an old friend for help. That "old friend" was Joyce C. Hall, founder of Hallmark Cards Inc. Since that time, Hallmark has published official presidential Christmas cards for every President. And though it is considered a huge honor to receive a card from the White House, it is not one reserved for a few close friends. LBJ set a record by ordering 40,000 and no President has sent fewer cards since.

The art has varied according to presidential fancy. For example, Presidents Nixon and Ford selected early prints of the White House. Jimmy Carter gave the nod to a Georgia artist named Harvey Moriarty, who drew the White House's south entrance. And the Ronald Reagans chose

Christmas 1945

A Merry Christmas

from

The President and Mrs. Truman

Truman 1945

Season's Greetings
1958

Eisenhower 1958

Kennedy 1962

Johnson 1966

With all best wishes for a
Merry Christmas
and a Happy New Year

The President and Mrs. Nixon

Nixon 1973

Jamie Wyeth in 1981 and 1984 to reprise snowy scenes of the White House at Christmas.

Two of the Presidents' cards provide poignant footnotes to history. In 1945, the card was in readiness for Franklin and Eleanor Roosevelt, but the President died before the holiday season. For this reason, President Truman's official card bears the same date of 1945.

In 1962, President Kennedy used a family photograph of Mrs. Kennedy and the couple's two children riding in a sleigh drawn by the family's pet pony, Macaroni. The Kennedys' third Christmas card was never mailed; the President was assassinated the day Hallmark shipped the cards to Washington and they were destroyed upon arrival.

In 1982, Hallmark donated its presidential Christmas card collection to the National Museum of American History, a part of the Smithsonian Institution.

Ford 1974

Carter 1977

Reagan 1983

Mailing Christmas Cards

Use first-class mail to send greeting cards in envelopes or holiday greeting postcards. If your card is not letter size, make sure it is marked "First Class."

Cards must be at least "minimum size" or they will be returned to the sender. The U.S. Postal Service defines minimum size as follows:

Pieces that are ¼ inch or less in thickness will be mailable only if they are:

- rectangular in shape
- at least 3½ inches high
- at least 5 inches long
- at least .007 inch thick (about the thickness of a postcard)

Cards that exceed the standard-size range will be accepted by the post office but at an extra charge. Nonstandard-size first-class mail is

mail weighing 1 ounce or less which exceeds any of the following:

- 6⅛ inches in height
- 11½ inches in length
- ¼ inch in thickness

In addition, the card's "aspect ratio" must fall between 1.3 and 2.5 to qualify as standard.

> ## CHRISTMAS SEALS
>
> **The first Christmas seal in America was created in 1907 by Emily Bissel, then State Secretary of the Wilmington, Delaware, Red Cross to raise funds to fight tuberculosis. Today, Christmas seals are sold by more than 100 medical research and charitable organizations.**

To determine aspect ratio, divide the length of the card by its height.

Stamps and Postmarks

Special Christmas stamps have been issued by the U.S. Post Office since 1962. A sampling of both religious and secular designs is shown on these pages.

Stamps can be bought by mail by using a Stamps by Mail Order Form, available from post offices or letter carriers. A personal check or postal money order made payable to U.S. Postal Service or Postmaster can be used to pay for the stamps.

If you would like your Christmas cards to be postmarked from a city or town with a holiday name, instead of from your own home town, make a package of your *stamped* envelopes and send them to the postmaster of the post office of your choice. Your cards will be individually postmarked there and mailed out.

In 1962 the U.S. Post Office started issuing a specially designed Christmas stamp each year, and since 1970 there has been a choice of traditional or secular subjects. This sampling of designs also shows the mounting cost of first-class postage.

CHRISTMAS CARD POSTMARKS

The sampling of place-name possibilities that follows is drawn from all 50 states. To select your own favorites, check whether their post offices can accept cards for mailing, and add appropriate zipcodes, consult the Zip Code Directory in your local post office or library.

Advent, WV
Angel Fire, NM
Antlers, OK
Arctic Village, AK
Bear, DE
Bethlehem, CT; GA; IN; KY; MD; NH; NC; PA; SD
Big Bow, KS
Brilliant, AL
Christmas, FL; MI
Christmas Valley, OR
Concord, MA; VT
Emblem, WY
Evergreen, LA; MT
Friend, NE
Frost, MN
Happy Kauaian, HI
Harmony, CA; ME
Holly, CO; MI

Hope, ND; RI
Ivy, VA
Joy, IL
Mistletoe, KY
Noel, MO
North Pole, AK; CO; NY
Prosperity, SC
Rudolph, OH; WI
Santa, ID
Santa Claus, IN
Silver City, IA; NV
Snowflake, AZ
Snowville, UT
Spangle, WA
Star, MS
Star City, AR
Sunbright, TN
Tranquility, NJ
Turkey, KY; NC; TX

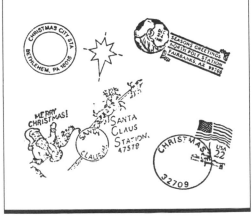

And May All Your Christmases Be Blight

Dear Alice and Bud,

Got your wonderful, warm Xeroxed letter in lieu of a Christmas card and just loved getting caught up on your family doings. Your annual letter is always a bright spot among the usual Christmas cards, and you needn't apologize that you have so many friends it seems the only way. We just adore knowing we're on that list of dear friends.

I was sorry to hear that the appliances weren't working well and that the cat had been sick. Bud's operation sounds grim, but I'm glad he's up on crutches. Harry says it's lucky the back didn't act up until you got back from Mexico. I was sorry to hear Alice didn't find the shopping opportunities up to her hopes, but I'm sure glad Bud found rum there at $2 a quart. And of course it always makes Christmas a little cheerier to hear that your lifestyle continues to be busy and happy. I'm sure Bud never has an idle moment, what with all that barbecue cooking and the lawn work.

Harry and I were sorry to hear that your nephew's wife, Dodie, had a miscarriage and that Allen—of course I remember his skin problems—has quit his job in the arts and crafts department of the senior citizens hall. But I know he'll enjoy white water rafting while he sorts out his priorities. I always say what's money for if you can't support your children. Tell Allen Happy New Year for us.

I was astounded to hear Bud found vanilla for only $1 a pint across the border in Nogales. One does use up vanilla so fast, and it's handy to be able to lay in a supply. The devaluation of the peso must have been a real boon when you stumbled on that bargain.

Bud's high school reunion in June sounds like a real blast. Too bad he had laryngitis and couldn't tell them about some of the unique experiences you put in your Christmas letter every year. I know they would have loved hearing about the new way you have of keeping your pool clean. We couldn't tell, by the way, which one of you it was who fell in fully clothed at your Thanksgiving cocktail party. Sometimes the "we" you use in your letters gets confusing.

We have been thinking for years that we should pop in on you out there in sunny Arizona. Every Christmas when you invite us in your letter, we tell ourselves we should go. You sound so cordial and your life sounds so much fun. Would it be okay if we brought the kids and Harry's mother? And maybe the dog? I'll give you a day or two's notice.

Well, I guess I'd better sign off, but I just felt I had to sit right down and write to you when your letter came. And the handwritten note at the end made us feel so special.

A Merry Christmas and Happy New Year to you, too.

Love,
Elizabeth and Harry

Elizabeth C. Mooney
The Washington Post
December 25, 1983

HOME ENTERTAINMENT

CHRISTMAS IN PRINT
Recalling a Pleasure of Christmases Past

O nce upon a time, before the coming of television changed our Christmas habits permanently, the greatest entertainment of the holiday season was the advent of the Christmas annual. Families would eagerly await publication of each year's volume, crammed with uplifting contributions from eminent authors and illustrators of the period, and gather together to read it aloud to each other. The idea persisted for quite a while in the "bumper books" for children that used to be published each Christmas, but we have little time these days for reading aloud and the annual has become—almost a fairy story.

The Christmas Annual

An unidentified elderly gentleman wrote in the *Dublin University Magazine* in 1847 that:

> . . . of all the many attractions which Christmas possesses in our old eyes . . . there are few to be compared to a quiet hour in our easy chair by the fireside, while, spread out upon the table before us lie, in all the gorgeous array of their crimson and gold binding, the Christmas Books.

The "gorgeous array of their crimson and gold binding" and the moralizing uplift of their contents aptly recall the contemporary efflorescence of the Christmas annual.

A Christmas annual was a special book, usually an anthology of poetry, prose, and pictures, issued in November or early December in time to be bought and presented as a Christmas gift. In Great Britain and the United States, in the five decades of the 1820s through the 1860s, the Christmas annual was so popular a gift that thousands upon thousands of copies of nearly a hundred competing titles were issued, sold, wrapped, and given as presents. Many of these were bound in gold-stamped red leather or red boards; others, not so elaborately decorated, were still found wrappered in intense colors of gold and blue or turquoise and black.

The origins and predecessors of these annuals have been debated. One surmise is that they were extensions of the special Christmas numbers of magazines, especially children's magazines popular in the 18th century. The *Juvenile Magazine*, a monthly which last published in 1788, offered each December an issue with a special title page that was produced far more elegantly than usual. Similarly, *The Youth's Magazine* (1816) added to its December number extra engravings in the spirit of holiday festivities.

Another suggestion is that the Christmas annual is related to two familiar and popular English publications, the pocket diary and the almanac. Some pocket diaries included poems, stories, and essays devoted to such subjects as country dances or prominent persons in the news. The almanacs frequently included engravings meant to symbolize each month, and they also offered pages filled with information on such various subjects as royalty charts of Europe and lists of members of Parliament.

Despite such cloudy origins, however, it is clear that in November of 1822 Rudolf Acker-

mann, the London publisher, offered for sale a book "expressly designed to serve as tokens of remembrance, friendship or affection, at that season of the year which ancient custom has particularly consecrated to the interchange of such memorials." Ackermann's gift book was called *Forget Me Not, A Christmas and New Year's Present for 1823*, and with its publication he started a vogue that was quickly to sweep through Britain and into the United States.

For 1823 there was only one annual, but for 1824 we find at least three, and for 1825 there were at least nine. For 1826 there were at least nine English and four American titles, and by 1829 there were at least 24 English and 17 American Christmas books. And each was almost unabashedly an imitation of Ackermann's original.

Virtually all of the great names of early 19th-century English literature contributed at one time or another to Christmas books, including Wordsworth, Coleridge, Scott, Tennyson, Mary Shelley, and Macaulay. In the United States the competition for contributions from the famous authors of the day was just as keen. Irving, Cooper, Whittier, Bryant, and Holmes each contributed to Christmas annuals. Younger writers, whose reputations were still to be made, also contributed. Nathaniel Hawthorne's first publication was in *The Token* of 1830, and Poe's "Manuscript Found in a Bottle" appears in *The Gift* of 1836.

For a vogue, Christmas annuals had a surprisingly long life: *Forget Me Not* did not cease publication until 25 issues had come out, *Friendship's Offering* ended after 21 years, and *The Keepsake* lasted 30 years, until 1857. In the United States the record holder is *The Rose of Sharon*, with 18 annual publications, and *The Token* is second with 15. Between 1846 and 1852 there were nearly 60 annuals published, but by 1860 the American literary Christmas gift was virtually extinct.

Patrick McGuire
American Book Collector
November/December, 1985

CHRISTMAS FOR VOICES RAISED

Rejoicing in the Music of Christmas

T he first Noel, starlit and miraculous, was probably orchestrated by a shepherd's flute, a baby's cry, and the bleats of barnyard animals. From then on—at least in recorded history—Christmas has been a feast for the ear as musicians have sought to capture every aspect of the holiday's spirit: the mystical reverence attending the virgin birth, the austere beauties of the winter solstice, the warmth and jollity of modern celebrations. The music of Christmas, in nearly 2,000 years of evolution, is one of the season's greatest gifts.

Heavenly Music: Bach to Bop

It's not just a handful of carols. Soon after Thanksgiving, we're bombarded with two dozen or so songs that everyone in America associates with Christmas: "Silent Night," "God Rest Ye Merry, Gentlemen," "Good King Wenceslas," "Jingle Bells," and the rest. Yet the occasion has inspired far more works by some of the greatest classical, pop, and jazz composers, in large forms and small, devoted to sacred and secular themes.

Throughout the history of Yuletide music, there is a sense of gathering together, from ancient community celebrations to our modern family reunions. Composers reached out to incorporate popular tunes of the day, melodies

that would give their works a feeling of homey familiarity. At the same time, Christmas songs initially written for religious services made their way into the public domain. The music embraces its listeners, and they respond.

Carols and Choirs

Europeans in medieval days observed the season with Christmas plays, special masses that had somber dramatic interludes—dialogues between shepherds and midwives or confrontations between the Magi and King Herod. Like most of the music that has survived from that time, these plays were in the style of plainchant, a single melodic line following the Latin text—music that still sounds best echoing along the aisles of stone cathedrals. Even in those ascetic times, the celebratory character of Christmas came through; a play might well include a bit of secular melody, its origins now long lost.

We can also trace Christmas carols back to the Middle Ages. The French *carole* was a 12th-century dance form; even then, there was plenty of cultural traffic across the English Channel. In Britain, the early carols were popular songs on religious themes, probably sung, at first, in non-Christian ceremonies. Some of the first carols were doubtless written by the same churchmen who wrote Christmas plays. They were sung (and even danced to) in cathedrals, at court, and at great feasts.

Similar traditions of popular-style pieces for the season grew up all around Europe, such as Germany's *Weihnachtslied*, Italy's *ninna* and the Central European *pastorella*; later, classical composers would borrow from these "vernacular" favorites.

Through the Renaissance and baroque eras, the leading musicians of the day were employed by the church or the royal courts. For those in the church, the liturgical calendar became their composing schedule, and the largest works were written for Christmas and Easter. With the Renaissance, church music became more elaborate; instead of the single line of plainchant, counterpoint came into style.

In the 15th and early 16th centuries, composers built elaborate counterpoint above a traditional plainchant melody; voices interweave and overlap in long, long lines that are almost otherworldly.

The next generation wrote less serene music. The 17th-century master Claudio Monteverdi, generally considered the father of modern opera, brought moment-to-moment drama—a sense of individual character—to his sacred music. (At about the same time in painting, the madonnas and saints of liturgical art begin to look more like ordinary people, showing emotion.) The *Monteverdi Vespers* of 1610 is a monumental collection, with some pieces that revert to the contrapuntal style, others that are almost operatic, with a single melody rather than a web of counterpoint.

Celebrating the Sublime

Even grander works were to come: Christmas oratorios, including Johann Sebastian Bach's *Christmas Oratorio* of 1734. This is a set of six connected cantatas for choir, soloists, and orchestra, to be performed on six days of the 13-day observance. An "evangelist" narrates the story in Biblical language, and soloists and the chorus personalize the action, expressing jubilation and awe.

Then, in 1742, came the oratorio that just about everyone in the English-speaking world associates with Christmas: George Frideric Handel's *Messiah,* which actually celebrates both Christmas and Easter. It begins with the Nativity and continues with the Passion, or the story of the Crucifixion, and the Redemption. The famous "Hallelujah" chorus is in part two, but that doesn't prevent groups everywhere from performing *Messiah* at Christmastime.

Sacred Christmas music is about to be sung by the choirboys of St. Thomas's Church in New York.

Its robust choruses, as well as its marvelously hushed solo arias, continue to inspire devotion among both musicians and listeners.

By the mid-18th century, however, classical music was moving from church and court to concert hall—and the repertory, by and large, grew secular. With the exception of Saint-Saëns' 1858 *Christmas Oratorio* and Tchaikovsky's well-loved ballet *The Nutcracker*, very few wrote big important works specifically for this holiday. But that didn't mean people stopped singing Christmas songs. On Christmas Eve, 1818, an obscure German organist named Franz Xaver Gruber came up with a song for midnight mass called *Stille Nacht*: it spread around the world, translated (and with its original melody slightly altered) as "Silent Night." British hymns with Christmas texts, such as "O Come All Ye Faithful" and "Joy to the World," left the church to be sung universally. Meanwhile, many of the carols we know now were collected, published, and popularized in 19th-century England, when people began to worry about folk traditions dying out.

The purely religious aspects of Christmas have grown diluted in our own century, but its central role as a family holiday—an occasion for reuniting and rejoicing—has grown ever stronger. And far from dying out, Yuletide music has soared. In the classical world, there have been at least two Christmas operas, Gian-Carlo Menotti's hugely popular *Amahl and the Night Visitors* and Thea Musgrave's adaptation of Dickens's *A Christmas Carol*. The British composers Ralph Vaughan Williams, with *Fantasia on Christmas Carols*, and Benjamin Britten, with *A Ceremony of Carols*, paid tribute to their heritage of folk songs.

The Pop Explosion

Popular music also got into the act. Besides such classics as "God Rest Ye Merry, Gentlemen," Americans now sing Irving Berlin's "White Christmas," Mel Torme's "The Christmas Song," and Johnny Marks's "Rudolph, the Red-Nosed Reindeer"—secular songs, without a religious message that some might take amiss. There's an album of jazzed-up Christmas songs called *Jingle Bell Jazz* and innumerable country and pop Christmas albums, such as Willie Nelson's *Pretty Paper* and Joan Baez's *Noel*. John Fahey, solo folk guitarist and notorious iconoclast, put out a wonderfully understated collection of Christmas tunes called *The New Possibility*. Phil Spector, symphonic-pop architect of the 1960s, gathered the Ronettes, the Crystals, and his other groups to belt out favorites on the thunderous *Phil Spector's Christmas Album*. Christmas songs are so familiar to us that a creative musician can stretch them in all sorts of directions.

What the modern musician sees in Christmas music has been there for centuries—warmth, coziness, a sense of continuity. Whether it's been around for 600 years or just one, the music basks in the generosity of the season. The best draws us in, lifts our hearts, maybe even invites us to sing along. It gives our own finest impulses back to us in song.

Jon Pareles
Harper's Bazaar
December, 1985

DO YOU HEAR WHAT I HEAR?

"After the Sunday school class had sung 'Silent Night' and been told the Christmas story, the teacher suggested that her pupils draw the Nativity scene. A little boy finished first. The teacher praised his drawing of the manger, of Joseph, of Mary and the Infant. But she was puzzled by a roly-poly figure off to one side and asked who it was.

'Oh,' explained the youngster, 'that's Round John Virgin.'"

Reader's Digest
December, 1958

From Angels, Saints, and Simple Folk

They gave us the Christmas carols we love the most, and unloose with greatest glee upon the eager ear when the much-awaited time comes, every year, to sing out loud the glad news: "Glory to God in the highest, and on earth peace, good will toward men." That was the lyric of St. Luke's "multitude of the heavenly host," and it has never been improved upon, but we try. When St. Francis of Assisi staged the first manger scene, with live donkeys and statue stand-ins for Mary, Joseph, and the Christ Child, he was so thrilled that he burst into song, "caroling" spontaneously.

The carol is not liturgical; it belongs to the people, often originates in a popular ditty, is adapted, and sticks. Is "White Christmas" a carol? Not yet. But in a couple of hundred years, its secular source forgotten, it could become one. (After all, how liturgical is "God Rest Ye Merry, Gentlemen?") It's true that many carols began as hymns, seriously composed for Christmas occasions, but they have been swept into common possession, away from the church and the concert hall into the hearts of the people. How can you tell a carol? It's the song that everyone knows and everyone sings, from aged grannies to babes in arms and all together, thanks to angels, saints, and simple folk.

Carols selected for inclusion in this section are either entirely or partly American in origin.

Away in a Manger

This much-loved carol was certainly not written by Martin Luther, though many have attributed it to him for at least a century. It was first published in Philadelphia in 1885 as a nursery hymn but not with the familiar music. Two years later it appeared again in *Dainty Songs for Little Lads and Lasses for Use in the Kindergarten, School and Home* under the title,

"Luther's Cradle Hymn (composed by Martin Luther for his children, and still sung by German mothers to their little ones)," and with the tune that has come down to us. It is *probable* that this melody was composed by the compiler of *Dainty Songs*, James R. Murray of Cincinnati.

Deck the Hall with Boughs of Holly

Nobody denies that his hearty carol, which deals not with piety, but entirely with celebration, is a Welsh air. Indeed it was first published with Welsh lyrics in London, in 1784, under the title *Nos Galan*, meaning "New Year's Night." A darker whisper from one authority has it that the melody is traceable to Druidic celebrations of 3,000 years ago; certainly the pre-Christian observance of the winter solstice is referred to in "the blazing Yule" cited by the lyrics. The tune was instantly popular—even Mozart picked it up and incorporated it in a

The Yuppie Days of Christmas

On the twelfth day of Christmas,
    my true love gave to me ...

twelve lunches doing,
  eleven banks foreclosing,
    ten "k's" a-jogging,
      nine pairs a-wingtips,
        eight Volvos revving,
          seven lawyers suing,
    six condos leasing,
      five Krugerrands!
        four calling cards,
          three trench coats,
            two savings bonds,

              and a
              tax-deferred
              annuity!

composition. The lyrics are certifiably American; they appear for the first time, without attribution, in *The Franklin Square Song Collection*, published in New York in 1881. The use of fa-la-la's echoes the style of medieval minstrels who used the form when they did not know or like a song's words, or to complete a musical phrase. But this is no more than wishful thinking, for we know that all these fa-la-la's are American-born.

It Came Upon the Midnight Clear

The lyrics to this work were initially a poem, written by the Reverend Edmund Hamilton Sears, a Unitarian minister of Wayland, Massachusetts. The poem was first published by the *Christian Register* in Boston in 1849. The music, composed by Richard S. Willis, was originally written to accompany another poem,

"See Israel's Gentle Shepherd Stand," and was printed in 1850 in Willis's *Church Chorals and Choir Studies*. It was not until 1910 that the carol was published with Sears's words and Willis's music in *Christmas Carols and Hymns for School and Choir* by Hollis Dann. This is the only Christmas carol by a Unitarian ever to gain popularity. Students of theology will note that the lyrics Unitarianly avoid any reference to the birth of Christ or the actuality of any such event. Those of us ignorant of these fine points have sung the carol very happily for generations.

Jingle Bells

The most popular of secular American carols must surely be "Jingle Bells," which was composed by Bostonian James Pierpont in 1857, for a Sunday-school presentation. Technically speaking, the lyrics of "Jingle Bells" will suit any winter occasion, but for over 100 years Americans have associated them closely with Christmas. Incidentally, though most of us don't know it, "jingle" in this lyric is something we are supposed to *do*, as in "ring." At least it was Pierpont's intent that we jingle those bells as we ride along in a one-horse open sleigh.

Joy to the World

However improbable it may seem to those familiar with the Old Testament, the lyrics to this hymn-turned-popular-carol are, or, in any case, were intended to be an altered version of the Ninetieth Psalm. The author, an Anglican priest, sought in this undertaking to put the psalms into modern English verse in order to show Christian symbolism. He published the result in 1719 under the respectful title of *The Psalms of David, Imitated*. The lyricist was Isaac Watts and among pieces of his still being used as hymns is the impressive "O God, Our Help in Ages Past." Watts's original "Joy to the World" was sung to a tune unknown to us.

The melody we use in America today was created in Boston in 1839 by American composer Lowell Mason, who embroidered upon a theme from the *Messiah* and published the results as a hymn at that time called "Antioch."

O Holy Night

In many ways, this carol is a steal, an English lyric tacked onto a French melody composed by Adolphe Charles Adam, a prolific composer of the 19th century, whose chief claim to fame today is his frequently performed ballet "Giselle." The English verses are the work of an American clergyman, John S. Dwight, loosely based on the French version of Adam's *Cantique de Noel*. Dwight's version is neither a translation nor a gloss, but a fresh undertaking altogether, and it has become the most popular American carol for solo performance.

O Little Town of Bethlehem

The story goes that the music for this carol came to its composer in a dream. The words that inspired him were the work of Phillips

---

CHRISTMAS BELLS

I heard the bells on Christmas Day
Their old, familiar carols play,
And wild and sweet
The words repeat
Of peace on earth, good-will to men!

And thought how, as the day had
    come,
The belfries of all Christendom
Had rolled along
The unbroken song
Of peace on earth, good-will to men!

Till, ringing, swinging on its way,
The world revolved from night to day,
A voice, a chime,
A chant sublime
Of peace on earth, good-will to men!

Then from each black, accursèd
    mouth
The cannon thundered in the South,
And with the sound
The carols drowned
Of peace on earth, good-will to men!

It was as if an earthquake rent
The hearth-stones of a continent,
And made forlorn
The households born
Of peace on earth, good-will to men!

And in despair I bowed my head;
"There is no peace on earth," I said;
"For hate is strong,
And mocks the song
Of peace on earth, good-will to men!"

Then pealed the bells more loud and
    deep:
"God is not dead; nor doth He sleep!
The Wrong shall fail,
The Right prevail,
With peace on earth, good-will to
    men!"

Henry Wadsworth Longfellow

Brooks, who in 1868 was prompted to recall his visit to the Holy Land three years before, when he had journeyed on horseback from Jerusalem to Bethlehem and stood on Christmas Eve on the Field of the Shepherds, gazing down on the birthplace of Jesus. Brooks was then rector of the Church of the Holy Trinity in Philadelphia and he went to Lewis Redner, his church organist, to ask him to write a tune the Sunday School class could sing. Redner is supposed to have dreamed his dream on Christmas Eve and completed the carol in time for the Christmas Day service. The music and lyrics were first published in *The Church Porch* in 1874, under the title "St. Louis," a play on Redner's first name. Phillips subsequently became the Episcopal bishop of Massachusetts, and this lovely American carol appeared in the Episcopal hymnal in 1892, one year before its author's death.

We Three Kings of Orient Are

The melodic line of this carol has been said to move like the step of a plodding camel, each verse describing one of the three kings, Caspar, Melchior, and Balthazar, and each king sometimes being represented by an individual voice. John Henry Hopkins, Jr. wrote both the words and the music of this exotic carol while he was rector of Christ's Church in Williamsport, Pennsylvania, about 1857. This was definitely the composer's most famous, though not his only work, and was published in his *Carols, Hymns and Songs* in 1862.

It takes leather tonsils to out-shout a New York subway train, but these carolers are undeterred.

Popular Christmas Music: Ups and Downs in a Winter Wonderland

BY RICHARD ATCHESON

Popular Christmas songs do not age in the way that other music does. We hear other popular music, we like it for a while, and then, mercifully, it goes away. Not so Christmas songs; the best of the breed pop up annually to trigger our tears. Take, for example, "All I Want for Christmas Is My Two Front Teeth." Or don't take it. Spike Jones and His City Slickers recorded it in 1948, and my Aunt Mary Belle declared that it was the funniest thing she ever heard. I was 14 at the time, and extremely sophisticated, and I thought it was the most stupid song I had ever heard. I still do. And yet I also remember my dear aunt, now long gone, giggling and laughing fit to bust over that idiotic song, and I see her happy, and want so badly to hold her and join in her laughter, and keep these arms around her always, always laughing.

When I was a little boy, which is a long time back now, my hero was Gene Autry. Once I got to see him *in person* at the Houston Fat Stock Show and my face hurt from grinning after that. Later Gene recorded some of the really institutional Christmas songs: "Frosty the Snowman," "Here Comes Santa Claus, Right Down Santa Claus Lane," and, of course, "Rudolph, the Red-Nosed Reindeer." None of those songs means as much to me as "Back in the Saddle Again," which was Gene's theme song, but that voice of his winds its way through Christmas after Christmas, laying a kind of gentle vacuum over everything.

But don't suppose that Gene Autry was the only singer I was in love with. He had to share my passion with Judy Garland. I had loved her long before she sang "Have Yourself a Merry Little Christmas" to that disgusting Margaret O'Brien in the movie *Meet Me in St. Louis*,

which made me cry. It was 1944, and I was 10 years old. I hated that dumb old O'Brien kid. She didn't even know how to cry convincingly.

The memorable songs of my adolescence, when I was doing—I thought—a quite credible imitation of Harold Teen, were the romantic ballads that enabled me to come up against buxom girls in angora sweaters without necessarily getting arrested. In the Christmas season these included "I'll Be Home for Christmas" by Bing Crosby; "Winter Wonderland" by the Andrews Sisters; and especially Mel Torme's "The Christmas Song" as oozed by Nat "King" Cole. This is the one with chestnuts roasting by an open fire, and let me tell you, it had enormous influence on girls in the '50s.

I never hear these musical chestnuts without thinking of a wintry afternoon before Christmas in 1951, over at L.G.'s house, when I was drinking Cokes and dancing dreamily with a girl whose name I can no longer recall, and smoking cigarettes, which was a particularly wicked thing to do. L.G. turned the lights down on the sun porch, and closed the shades, and the strongest light we had came from the Christmas tree, winking at us through French doors. I remember that I kissed her fingertips, and she was very moved. I don't know how such behavior came to me; perhaps I saw Ronald Colman do it in some movie.

"Santa Claus Is Comin' to Town" by Bing Crosby and the Andrews Sisters was also big in those days, as were the instrumental "It's Beginning to Look a Lot Like Christmas," and, depending on the tempo taken, "Silver Bells." But the one that still gets me shivering in my timbers is "Winter Wonderland," because of its magical promise that "later on we'll conspire, as we dream by the fire, to face unafraid the plans that we've made . . ." Imagine the blundering boy, with all his dreams locked up inside, longing to share one or two with a beautiful girl . . . well, she wouldn't have to be beautiful, just nice . . . and it *would* be great if she filled out an angora sweater, but who's making conditions? And it *is* Christmas. . . .

Many a time I go back with the music. I am tiny, the world is alive with lights and tinsel, and the song is "Jingle Bells." I am 10, and Margaret O'Brien is blasted off the face of the earth forever, and I lie weeping in Judy Garland's arms, and she sings to me. I am 16, Nat Cole's voice is like syrup, and a girl whose name I can't remember presses herself to me because . . . maybe she even *wants* to. My sweet Aunt Mary Belle laughs, and I put my arms around her at last, finally, right by the Zenith upright radio from which there quacks, "All I Want for Christmas Is My Two Front Teeth."

White Christmas: A Nostalgia Note

Back in the 1940s, Bing Crosby made a hit movie called *Holiday Inn*, and in it he sang a song which was to become the American anthem of Christmas sentiment: "White Christmas," by Irving Berlin. Everybody knows the lyrics to that song by heart; their final couplet— "May your days be merry and bright, / And may all your Christmases be white"—struck a universal emotional chord in a time when the country was at war, and tens of thousands of

American fathers and sons were fighting in tropical jungles, constantly in peril and as far from snowfall as they could possibly be. The lyrics spoke the hope of everyone in those days for an end to battle and its dangers, and a return to safety and happiness and the white snow of home in an untroubled future of Christmases to come.

Snow, then, became more important to the general Christmas scene than it had ever been before; it became *essential*. And that is why you have to have it annually in Puma, Arizona, simulated in rolls of white cotton, just as much as in parts of the country where it can be more or less counted on to come when called. Miami Beach mounts miles of artificial snow as decoration every year, and it bakes daily through the season under a relentless sun; likewise, in San Diego, make-believe snow unrolls to deck the palm-fringed avenues where sol and surf are the natural phenomena. It no longer looks incongruous to anyone; we will have our "White Christmas" no matter where we are or what the weatherman says.

The credit for this stubborn behavior on our part lies not only with the song and its evocative longings but also with the film that launched it, a film that was enormously popular in its initial release. *Holiday Inn* is the story of a harmless fellow (played by Bing, of course) who wants to own a nightclub that will be open only on the major holidays of the year. In the film, all his friends tell him he is a dope to think of such a thing. They point out to him, as we might well today, that a club open for business so infrequently will never pay. But Bing just laughs; he is determined to realize his dream.

Sure enough, everything goes wrong that could possibly go wrong; Bing has to suffer betrayals, rejections, and deep disappointments. He struggles against insuperable odds. But in the end—what do you suppose?—everything comes out all right. The club opens on New Year's Eve and all the swells from New York City motor up in their prewar Packards, dressed to the nines and aching to spend money. A beautiful girl—is it Ginger Rogers?

(no, and does it matter?)—dances herself into a fit with Fred Astaire and Bing falls in love with her.

The beautiful girl becomes vexed with Bing for some reason and takes off for Hollywood where Bing's club and the whole state of Connecticut are re-created on a sound stage. *Holiday Inn* is about to be turned into a movie without Bing.

But on Christmas Eve, Bing surprises the beautiful girl on the set and sings "White Christmas," and they make up. And what do you think happens then? It starts to snow. Hollywood knows how to do these things. That season, in movie theaters all over the country, you could hear the stifled gasping sobs from the orchestra to highest second balcony. Here was the American truth stated once again in a new context, that in this country our dreams come true. Even if you're just an amiable dope like Bing, and you have a little grit and a little fire in your belly, you can open an absurd nightclub in the back of beyond and you will end up in Hollywood. And it will snow.

Won't it?

The Truth About Rudolph

What popular Christmas song first recorded in 1949 has since been recorded by the following diverse collection of artists? Ready? Bing Crosby, Perry Como, The Temptations, John Denver, Lawrence Welk, Paul McCartney, Guy Lombardo, Michael Jackson, The Chipmunks and Conway Twitty, Willie Nelson, and Ray Charles. Got it? Of course, it's "Rudolph, the Red-Nosed Reindeer," a song which has proved such a gold mine to its original authors and first recording artist—Gene Autry—that everybody still wants to get in on the act.

The tale of Rudolph begins in 1939, when copywriter Robert L. May was assigned to write

"A little vitamin C ought to clear that up in no time."

a give-away Christmas booklet for Montgomery Ward. May conceived of a reindeer with a nose so shiny that all the other reindeer made fun of him. They had to shut up, though, when on one impenetrably foggy night Santa picked that very reindeer to guide his sleigh. That was Rudolph (or it might have been Reginald or Rollo; for a time, May wasn't sure).

The Rudolph booklet was twice given away—in 1939, when 2.5 million copies went into circulation; and in 1946, when 3.5 million copies were distributed—before May's songwriter friend Johnny Marks gave it a shot. He wrote the song we know but, as is so often the case in stories of this kind, nobody was interested, so Marks formed his own publishing company: St. Nicholas Music. As such he approached Gene Autry to record the number as a single, and Autry agreed. The result is legend: the greatest hit Autry ever had, Columbia Records' biggest seller ever.

St. Nicholas Music collects 4.5 cents everytime any recording of "Rudolph, the Red-Nosed Reindeer" is sold. Radio time is even better: 18 cents from every station every time it plays the song. And then there are residuals from the television show, which has aired well over 20 seasons.

It all just goes to show how important it is, in showbiz, to identify with the little guy. And identify. And identify.

Donna Reed, Jimmy Stewart, and movie family try to hold it all together in *It's a Wonderful Life*.

CHRISTMAS ON FILM
Recapturing Memorable Moments

Christmas hasn't been all merry on the screen in the past couple of decades. Santa was as likely as not to be Gene Hackman in costume to make a drug bust in *The French Connection*; the holiday itself became a horror in films like *Black Christmas* and *Silent Night, Bloody Night*; and there was even an extraterrestrial turkey called *Santa Claus Conquers the Martians*. So every holiday season, television late shows and repertory movie houses have to reach far back to find films suitable to the season. Of course, there are the many versions of Dickens's *A Christmas Carol*, with Alastair Sim's winning out by a wide margin. And there is the inevitable *Miracle on 34th Street*, in which Edmund Gwenn convinces Natalie Wood, a skeptical child, that there *is* a Santa.

Making Merry at the Movies

Christmas also has a way of turning up in movies that ostensibly have nothing to do with the holiday. And so, this winter, we will certainly see reruns of Judy Garland in *Meet Me in St. Louis*, chasing the hysterical Margaret O'Brien into the snow and calming her about the prospect of the family's move to New York with a song: "Have Yourself a Merry Little Christmas." Grave little Margaret went on to have other Christmas experiences on film—in *Tenth Avenue Angel* and *Our Vines Have Tender Grapes*. And Judy had had a Merry Christmas one of the first times she appeared. In *Love Finds Andy Hardy*, Mickey Rooney, in one of his customary Andy Hardy dilemmas, has invited both Ann Rutherford and Lana Turner to the big Christmas dance. He winds up with the little girl next door. And that was Judy, of course.

A diminutive Natalie Wood wins the nod from movie mom Maureen O'Hara and Macy's Santa Edmund Gwenn in *Miracle on 34th Street*.

A radically altered Scrooge, enacted by Reginald Owen, literally knocks the pin out from under Tiny Tim, played by Terry Kilburn, in *A Christmas Carol*.

No December goes by without Bing Crosby singing "White Christmas" in *Holiday Inn*, and you'll also get to see Crosby, 12 years older, singing the same number in a follow-up movie named after Irving Berlin's song. Bing was probably the movies' foremost Christmas caroler. He warbled "Silent Night" in *Going My Way*, "Adeste Fideles" in *The Bells of St. Mary's*, "It Came Upon the Midnight Clear" in *High Times*, and "The Secret of Christmas" in *Say One for Me*.

"Adeste Fideles" also provided the choral background to the scene in *Since You Went Away* in which Claudette Colbert discovers at Christmas that her missing-in-action soldier husband is alive. And, of course, "Silent Night" has been sung again and again, notably by Deanna Durbin (in *Lady on a Train*, not in the mishmash she made called *Christmas Holiday*).

You probably recall all those soldiers, sailors, airmen, and Marines, lonely in their foxholes, dreaming of a white Christmas. But in what movie? War pictures run together in the memory. Was it *Battleground* or *The Story of G.I. Joe*, *Wake Island* or *Guadalcanal Diary*, *So Proudly We Hail*, *Thirty Seconds Over Tokyo*, *Air Force*, *Destination Tokyo*? Was

Christmas in all of them—or any of them? However, one distinctly memorable war scene in an otherwise forgotten movie, *Balalaika*— not even primarily a war film—is Christmas on the Russian front. From a trench comes the voice of Nelson Eddy, singing "Silent Night." From the enemy trenches echo choruses of the carol. Then the moment passes, and the killing begins again. Some soldiers made it into the outside world for the holidays: Joseph Cotten, the shell-shocked sergeant of *I'll Be Seeing You*, not only got away from the war but also met Ginger Rogers, who had a secret of her own—she was a prison parolee.

Barbara Stanwyck was in trouble with the law, too, in *Remember the Night*, when she went back to Indiana for Christmas in the custody of the district attorney, Fred MacMur-ray. She had a wonderful holiday with MacMurray's family, particularly with the warmest of movie mothers, Beulah Bondi. (Bondi could be Scrooge, too—as she was until Christmas touched her heart in *She's a Soldier, Too*.)

Stanwyck had other movie encounters with the season. She was a bachelor-girl columnist forced to entertain a soldier on leave in *Christmas in Connecticut*. And it was Stanwyck, again as a reporter, who created "John Doe," symbol of the forgotten man of the Depression, proclaiming that he would kill himself on Christmas Eve. He materialized in the shape of Gary Cooper in Frank Capra's *Meet John Doe*.

It was Capra who was responsible for *It's a Wonderful Life*. Jimmy Stewart, the small-town boy facing disgrace and prison, turns on his family, rushes off into the night on Christmas

In between cleaning the house, getting the meals, arranging the flowers, and teaching her children to dress like Connecticut natives, Louise Beavers tells Bing Crosby where to go in *White Christmas*.

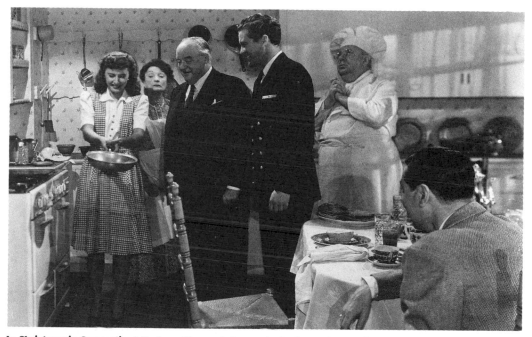

In *Christmas in Connecticut*, Barbara Stanwyck demonstrates her culinary skills to a dazed Dennis Morgan, in uniform, and Sydney Greenstreet, in mufti, as S. Z. Sakall, in toque, enlists divine intervention.

Eve, and, after wishing that he had never been born, jumps off a bridge. He is saved by his guardian angel, who shows him what would have happened if his wish had come true and he had never been born. Returning to the present to face the music, he comes home to find that the whole town of Capra types has come to his aid.

That is surely the definitive Christmas movie. But how many memorable moments there are: Myrna Loy in her Christmas mink, calmly watching William Powell taking potshots at the Christmas-tree ornaments (*The Thin Man*); first-graders putting on their own Nativity play (*The Bells of St. Mary's*); Cary Grant and Irene Dunne proudly watching their little girl in her Christmas play (*Penny Serenade*); Preston Sturges spoofing Christmas conventions as Betty Hutton gives birth to holiday quintuplets (*The Miracle of Morgan's Creek*); Monty Woolley, an out-of-work actor in a Santa Claus job, snarling at a woman startled by his tremendous alcoholic burp, "What did you expect, Madam—chimes?" (*Life Begins at 8:30*); and Woolley, in *The Man Who Came to Dinner*, in-terrupting his devastation of a suburban household for a cozy Christmas radio chat; Farley Granger and Jeanne Crain in the "Gift of the Magi" episode of *O. Henry's Full House*; Hepburn in *Little Women*, sharing Christmas dinner with a poor family; Lillian Gish and the children in the momentary respite from pursuit by the mad Robert Mitchum (*The Night of the Hunter*); Cary Grant as an elegant angel who makes everything right for David Niven and Loretta Young in *The Bishop's Wife*; Janet Leigh and Robert Mitchum in *Holiday Affair*; the love story of two lonely department store clerks (Margaret Sullavan and Jimmy Stewart) during the holiday sales in Lubitsch's *The Shop Around the Corner*; Vivien Leigh giving Leslie Howard a homemade sash in *Gone With the Wind*.

So perhaps it doesn't much matter if today's moviemakers tend to regard Christmas as *Walpurgisnacht*: We have plenty of alternatives to fall back on.

John Springer
American Heritage
December, 1983

Christmas on TV

BY MATT ROUSH

The television has long replaced the open hearth as the family gathering place—at no time more than at Yuletide. Families could chart their own children's growth by annual holiday visits to the same familiar TV clans.

As early as the 1950s, Christmas meant relying on dulcet-toned Perry Como spreading the spirit by telling the story of the first Christmas to a rapt audience: his children and the children of the crew. Then the whole gang, often with a star like Rosemary Clooney, would walk around a studo set with blowing "snow" (probably confetti) and sing carols. It was a tradition, as warm and soothing as hot cocoa.

The King family, the Crosbys, Judy Garland and her kids, the Lawrence Welk dynasty—all knew how to throw a festive Christmas party on their shows.

Through the 1960s the Osmonds were seen growing up, romping, and singing wholesome Christmas carols on Andy Williams's TV celebrations. In the 1970s, an adolescent Donny and Marie returned the favor by having Andy on the Christmas edition of their variety show. In 1986, Andy Williams took a new batch of kids—young stars of various NBC series—to Rome to meet the Pope and see the holiday sights.

As baby-boomers grew up and got more cynical about celebrity caroling, ratings for Christmas specials lost some of their luster. Only a crossover camp star like Dolly Parton could get blockbuster numbers for the likes of her 1986 "A Smoky Mountain Christmas."

"A Christmas Carol" has become a familiar tune over the years—and not just in repeats of the classic 1938 and 1951 film versions. In 1954, Basil Rathbone played Marley's Ghost to Fredric March's Scrooge in a Maxwell Anderson rewrite of the Dickens classic. Two years later, Rathbone was Scrooge in the Alcoa Hour's

Perry Como, hatted for a Christmas Special, sports holly at the chin and a holiday grin.

version of the story, "The Stingiest Man in the World," co-starring Vic Damone. In 1957, Jimmy Stewart played Jim Bowie in one of the strangest versions, a Western titled "The Trail to Christmas" on GE Theater. The narrator: Ronald Reagan!

More recently, George C. Scott gave a definitive performance as old Ebenezer in 1984, wiping out dim memories of a heavily made-up Henry Winkler in 1979's Depression-era "An American Christmas Carol."

But there were other stories to tell, too. A 1953 episode of "Dragnet" found Sgt. Joe Friday and Officer Frank Smith investigating a theft at a church. Cardinal Spellman was so taken with it that he arranged for the segment to be sent to troops in Korea. Rod Serling told a memorable Christmas story in his "Twilight Zone" series with 1960's "The Night of the Meek," in which Art Carney played an alcoholic department-store Santa. And how many sitcom families, from the Cleavers to the Huxtables, learned gentle lessons of sharing and brotherhood in time to unwrap packages madly by the holiday episode's fade-out?

Among the most memorable TV movies: "The House Without a Christmas Tree" (1972), in which sprightly Lisa Lucas warmed a brooding Jason Robards with her wishes for a tree; "The Gathering" (1977), a family drama about a dying man (Ed Asner) who brings his estranged family together for one last reunion; and, most notably, "The Homecoming" (1971), a warm-hearted mountain family drama that led directly to CBS's long-running series "The Waltons."

The tradition continues, as the creators of "Roots" gathered many of its characters together in 1987, ten years after the original miniseries, to recount a "Roots Christmas" in which the family of Kunta Kinte and Chicken George fought to free a group of slaves. Talk about a Christmas gift.

Fortunately, two of TV's more durable Christmas events show no signs of waning in popular appeal among children and their everyoung parents: "A Charlie Brown Christmas" and "How the Grinch Stole Christmas," first seen in 1965 and 1966, respectively.

Charlie Brown's yearly diatribe against the overcommercialization of Christmas is as charming and timeless as ever. And Dr. Seuss's "Grinch," with great and growly Boris Karloff pulling off a *tour de force* as narrator and villain, is pure delight. When he returns the purloined Christmas goodies to the dauntlessly happy Whos of *Who*-Ville, the heart melts.

Which is what watching TV at Christmastime is all about.

Matt Roush is the television reporter for *USA Today*.

Christmas Videos: A Selection

The Bear Who Slept Through Christmas
Dimenmark International
60 mins   Color   VHS/Beta

Animated voices of Tommy Smothers, Arte Johnson, Barbara Feldon, Kelly Lang
As Christmas approaches, all the bears are getting ready to go to sleep for the winter, except Ted E. Bear, who wants to see just what Christmas is.

> Family Home Entertainment
> 7920 Alabama Ave.
> Canoga Park, CA 91304-4991

Benji's Very Own Christmas Story
Mulberry Square Productions
60 mins   Color   VHS/Beta

Benji and his friends go on a magic trip and meet Kris Kringle and learn how Christmas is celebrated around the world. Also included: "The Phenomenon of Benji," a documentary about Benji's odyssey from animal shelter to international stardom.

> Children's Video Library
> 1011 High Ridge Road
> P.O. Box 4995
> Stamford, CT 06907

A Christmas Carol
United Artists; Renown Pictures
86 mins   Black & white   VHS/Beta

Alastair Sim, Kathleen Harrison
Dickens's classic story of how a miserly old man is brought to change on Christmas Eve.

> United Home Video
> 6535 East Skelly Drive
> Tulsa, OK 74145

The Christmas Collection
Family Films
120 mins   Color   VHS/Beta

A collection of five films including: "Glory in the Highest," a drama about the birth of Christ and "To Each a Gift," a turn-of-the-century story about the true spirit of Christmas.

> Vanguard Video
> 6525 Skelly Drive
> Tulsa, OK 74145

The Christmas Messenger
Potterton Productions
25 mins   Color   VHS/Beta

Richard Chamberlain
Brilliantly colored animation is used to portray tales of Christmas folklore. A Reader's Digest presentation.

> Pyramid Film and Video
> Box 1048
> Santa Monica, CA 90406

The Christmas Raccoons
Kevin Gillis
30 mins   Color   VHS/Beta

Animated, Rich Little narrates
The Raccoons have their very own special animated Christmas story to tell, and with a purchase of the video a wand is included.

> Embassy Home Entertainment
> 1901 Avenue of the Stars
> Los Angeles, CA 90067

A Christmas Tree/Puss-in-Boots
Rankin-Bass Production
60 mins   Color   VHS/Beta

An animated double feature: In "A Christmas Tree," two young children return a stolen Christ-

mas tree from an evil giant, and in "Puss-in-Boots," a magical cat helps his master woo a princess.

> Prism
> 1875 Century Park East
> Suite 1010
> Los Angeles, CA 90067

The Christmas Visitor
7 mins   Color   VHS/Beta

A unique visualization of Clement Moore's "A Visit from St. Nicholas."

> Sterling Educational Films
> 241 East 34th Street
> New York, NY 10016

A Currier & Ives Christmas
NTA
90 mins   Color   VHS/Beta

A video music Christmas album that sets the classic American art of Currier & Ives and other early lithographers to a continuous background of favorite Christmas music.

> Republic Pictures Home Video
> 12636 Beatrice Street
> Los Angeles, CA 90066

Decorating Your Home for Christmas
Cinema Associates-Video Tech
59 mins   Color   VHS/Beta

Learn how to make your own wreaths, swags, and centerpieces for the Christmas holidays, as well as bows, garlands, mantel decorations, and wall trees.

> RMI Media Productions
> 2807 West 47th Street
> Shawnee Mission, KS 66205

A Family Circus Christmas
Cullen Casden Production Ltd
30 mins   Color   VHS/Beta

Cartoonist Bil Keane animates the Family Circus at Christmas.

> Family Home Entertainment
> 7920 Alabama Ave.
> Canoga Park, CA 91304-4991

The First Christmas
27 mins   Color   VHS/Beta

This animated holiday program depicts the birth of Jesus.

> Paragon Video Productions
> 3529 South Valley View
> Boulevard
> Las Vegas, NV 89103

How the Animals Discovered Christmas
Coronet Films-Blackhawk Films
13 mins   Color   VHS/Beta

A delightful tale about the animals of Cozy Valley.

> Coronet Films
> 65 East South Water Street
> Chicago, IL 60601

The Little Drummer Boy
7 mins   Color   VHS/Beta

An iconographic motion picture based on the well-known Christmas song.

> Weston Woods Studio, Inc.
> Weston, CT 06883

The Little Rascals Christmas Special
Kingworld Productions
60 mins   Color   VHS/Beta

Animated, voices of Darla Hood, Mathew "Stymie" Beard

Spanky and the Little Rascals attempt to raise enough money to buy a winter coat for Spanky's mom and learn the true meaning of Christmas along the way.

> Family Home Entertainment
> 7920 Alabama Ave.
> Canoga Park, CA 91304-4991

The Night Before Christmas
Bill Turnball; Playhouse Pictures
30 mins   Color   VHS/Beta

Animated, Norman Luboff Choir

A heartwarming retelling of the charming "A Visit from St. Nicholas," with holiday music.

> Media Home Entertainment
> 5730 Buckingham Parkway
> Culver City, CA 90230
> 213-216-7900

A Walt Disney Christmas
Walt Disney Productions
45 mins   Color   VHS/Beta

Animated

Six classic cartoons with a wintry theme are combined for this program: "Pluto's Christmas Tree" (1952), "On Ice," "Donald's Snowball Fight," two Silly Symphonies from 1932–33—"Santa's Workshop" and "The Night Before Christmas," and an excerpt from the 1948 feature "Melody Time," entitled "Once Upon a Wintertime."

> Walt Disney Home Video
> 500 South Buena Vista Street
> Burbank, CA 91521

From The Video Sourcebook

A CHRISTMAS ADVENTURE

"It is Christmas Eve. The clock strikes eleven in Santa's ice-castle at the North Pole. In his office, a message flashes across the screen of his computer: Santa has disappeared! Rudolph is missing. There will be no gifts delivered this year unless someone can solve the mystery of Santa's disappearance . . . and soon!"

This is the dilemma that confronts you on your computer screen as you begin "A Christmas Adventure," the first computer game ever with a Christmas theme, by Bit Cards, Inc.

The game requires no special computer expertise and is fun, not just for small-fry computer buffs but for a group, with one person seated at the keyboard, or even a single player.

The clues aren't easy, and only Sherlock Holmes could find Santa the first time around!

CHRISTMAS IN THE PARLOR

Reviving Games of Yore

Before radio and TV, Americans made their own recreation at home, not only during holiday times but all through the year. In country settings, this could involve such gentle pastimes as taking bets on how long it would take for a pie to come out of the oven. City slickers, however, moved in the fast lane: Somebody always knew the latest parlor game and would get everybody to play it. The practice descends to us in the present day, despite the general absence of parlors and the groans of the reluctant, who forget that there is often a lot more fun in making your own fun than in having it doled out on the tube.

Your Own Christmas Fun

CHARADES

For more than 200 years, Charades has been the ruling parlor game in the English-speaking world. Players divide into two teams and one team leaves the room to agree upon a word, phrase, movie, book, or play title to act out in pantomime. The second team is told how many words are involved and, sometimes, the nature of the thing to be pantomimed. The second team throws out guesses and hunches at the acting players until the members "get" it. Sides are then reversed and the second team seeks to confound the first. In the first century of this game, only single words were guessed, broken into playable syllables. Today the terms of the game are broader, but the noise and hilarity remain the same.

BOTTICELLI

"I am a person whose last name begins with C," a player declares, and the fact that he is thinking of Julius Caesar is known only to him. The other players guess his identity by thinking of famous people or well-known characters whose names begin with C and each asking a specific identity question (say, "Are you an Egyptian ruler?"). If the original player cannot think of the name of an Egyptian ruler beginning with C in order to respond, "No, I am not Cleopatra (or Cheops)," the questioner can ask for direct information (such as "Are you alive?" "Are you a woman?"), which the original player must answer with "yes" or "no." The object is to ask tricky identity questions in order to be able to challenge the original player

directly as often as possible. "Are you an American President?" for example, could be answered two ways, but "Are you a President who got married in the White House?" has only one correct response: Grover Cleveland.

BLINDMAN'S BUFF

Understandably, most kids call this game "Blindman's *Bluff*" because it does involve a bluff of a sort. One person is blindfolded and turned around three times. Other players snatch and grab at him but leap away when he tries to catch a tormentor. When he succeeds, he must identify that person by touch. If he fails, he goes on being "it" for another turn; if he is correct, the other player becomes "it" and the game proceeds.

SARDINES

This Victorian version of Hide-and-Seek is best played in a large house with many rooms in the dark. One player goes off to hide while the others count to a hundred, then start looking for him. As each player in turn discovers the hidden one, he or she hides with him, squishing silently into whatever space is available until everybody is packed in like . . . well, like sardines. The loser is the last player to find the crowd.

TWENTY QUESTIONS

One player thinks of an object and tells the other players whether it is animal, vegetable, mineral, or a combination thereof. Players may ask up to 20 questions in an effort to guess what it is. All questions require a "yes" or "no" answer. If the group has not zeroed in on the object in 20 tries, the player who thought of the object is the winner.

MURDER

To begin, players draw slips of paper from a hat. Most are blank, but one bears a cross to designate the Murderer and another a circle, for the Detective. Naturally, the Murderer stays mum, but the Detective immediately identifies himself. The lights are turned out and the players disperse throughout the house. The Murderer draws up to his victim, whispers "You're dead," and the Victim at once screams horribly as the Murderer withdraws.

The Detective puts on the lights, calls everyone into the same room, and conducts an investigation to establish each person's whereabouts at the moment of the crime and their possible motivations for committing it. All except the Murderer must answer him truthfully. If the Detective confronts the Murderer with the direct question "Are you the Murderer?" the Murderer must answer and make a complete confession. The Detective has two chances to name his man; if he fails, the Murderer takes a bow.

Poinsettia Party
For the Holiday Season

By ELAINE, Entertainment Editor.

AFFORDING an opportunity for gay holiday coloring, easy to develop in both decorations and amusements, and suitable for a luncheon, tea, dinner party, or evening entertainment during any of the midwinter months, is the idea of a Poinsettia Party.

Invitations

With each note of invitation enclose part of a stemless poinsettia prepared in this way: Cut poinsettias from red crêpe paper in a convenient size for half of one flower to fit in each envelope. Paste the poinsettias on white notepaper and cut out around the petals, then cut each poinsettia half in two, in an uneven line. On the notepaper side of each piece of poinsettia write the following verse:

> This gay red flower cut in two
> Will bring your partner straight to you,
> If in your search you do not cease
> Until you find the other piece.

After all the guests arrive, explain that they are to match their pieces of poinsettia to find partners for the Poinsettia Contest.

Poinsettia Contest

Make a slip of paper for each couple with the following story written or typed, the words in parentheses to be left blank in the story, and to be filled in with floral names. Award a prize of a jar of poinsettias to the couple who succeeds in filling in the most blanks correctly in a given amount of time.

"It was Christmas day, and Miss Poinsettia and her fiancé (Sweet William) were not happy. Her mother was determined that she should not wed a poor man, but should (marigold), while his mother did not like Miss Poinsettia's flaming gown, preferred the color brown, and wanted him to wed (Brown-Eyed Susan). But he declared Poinsettia loved only him and (aster) to marry him in spite of all, because he would always sew on his own (bachelor's buttons) unless she would consent. Said he, 'I will never cease to im-(petunia), for no other girl is even worthy to tie on your little (lady's slipper).' At last when their parents found them under the (mistletoe) with their (tulips) together, they (rose) to the occasion and the nuptials were celebrated on Christmas afternoon, with the smart young curate called (Jack in the Pulpit) to perform the ceremony. The bride wore a veil of (queen's lace), and her gown was in the (pink) of perfection. The guests arrived in (phlox) and through the years the memory of that Christmas wedding was kept (evergreen) in their affections."

Miscellaneous Suggestions on Refreshments

Poinsettia Sandwiches: pimiento sandwiches cut in the shape of poinsettias.

Poinsettia Salad: lettuce leaves with poinsettia petals cut from pimientos laid on them, with an olive for the center.

Poinsettia Cakes: sponge cake or layer cake with white icing and on top a poinsettia made of red icing. Cookies cut in poinsettia shapes and covered with red icing.

Decorations

A large poinsettia of red crêpe paper may be laid flat in the center of the table, with a jar of poinsettias in the middle of it and a candlestick with a red candle at the point of each petal. This decoration may be used if the guests are seated at the table, or if the refreshments are served buffet fashion.

Poinsettia place-cards may be made in this way to stand by each guest's plate: cut small poinsettias from notepaper, paste over them red crêpe paper, attach to one end of a wire covered with black crêpe paper, bend the wire into a short spiral with a large circle at the end so the poinsettia will stand up beside the plate with the wire circle as a base. Write the guest's name on a card and attach it with a red ribbon.

Good Housekeeping
December, 1920

CHRISTMAS FEASTS

THE CHRISTMAS DINNER

"Christmas comes but once a year, And when it comes, it brings good cheer," says the rhyme I used to repeat when I was a child, looking forward eagerly to treats in store. Good cheer, indeed, is the hallmark of the season—and most especially, the Christmas dinner. This above all is the time when we recall our childhood by lovingly re-creating the dishes, the table settings, the "do you remembers" that in their turn will become the treasures of the next generation. Whether we conjure up the rich regalia of a Victorian feast or the simple unbeatable goodness of Grandma's cranberry sauce or Aunt Bessie's apple pie, for each of us the ethnic roots are different and the ceremony of Christmas brings together traditions that are uniquely precious.

My mother is English, my father was from Scotland, and my childhood was divided between the two countries. Though I have lived in America for decades now, our Christmas dinner is a re-creation of my earliest memories and my American family indulges me, letting me do it my way.

This year, as always, our long refectory table is covered by a heavy white cloth with two red tartan scarves running along the sides. Several years ago I bought a dozen pewter plates at an auction and I use them as "place plates"—they look good on the tartan. The napkins, too, are bright Christmas red. The centerpiece is long and low, with holly, pine-cones, red tapers, and tiny red and green Christmas balls arranged on a smoked-glass mirror just a little larger than the greenery, so that the reflection of the candlelight glows softly in the glass.

Each year, as I set out the foods I only serve at Christmas on that table specially dressed to receive them, I wonder again how it can be always the same, yet subtly different, traditional, but amazingly, ever-new. For each of us, Christmas comes but once a year—and it lasts for a lifetime.

Gifts piled at each place rather than under the tree are a feature of the 1870 Christmas dinner in Newburyport, Massachusetts. A "gothic" arch at the far end re-creates Dickens's sentiment for the season.

Christmas Dinner Menu

Walnuts and Sherry
Smoked Salmon with Thinly Sliced,
Buttered Brown Bread

Roast Goose with Sage and Onion Stuffing
Giblet Gravy
Brussels Sprouts with Bacon and Chestnuts
Braised Celery • Roast Potatoes

A Venerable Red Wine

Plum Pudding with Hard Sauce
Port and Stilton
Coffee and Chocolates

Roast Goose

A goose is not just the silly bird of nursery tales—it is deceptive in the kitchen, too. Buy an 8- to 9-pounder and you think you have enough to feed 40 people. You don't. You have to estimate about 1¼ to 1½ pounds for each person, because most of the weight is in the bones. One goose will serve six amply and eight comfortably.

(It may be difficult to find fresh geese, but a caring butcher will be able to supply tender ones, frozen. It is a good idea to buy the bird at least a day ahead, to give plenty of time for it to defrost gradually in a cool place.)

Geese are time-consuming to carve, so to avoid having to do this at the table, I always roast an extra one, purely for display, and put it on a beautifully decorated silver platter. Usually I carry the perfect bird over to the sideboard as though it were the head of John the Baptist. Back in the kitchen, I slice the other goose very thinly, at my leisure. Fortunately, goose is at its

best at room temperature and the display bird will make a fine salad later, with some watercress, cold boiled potatoes, sliced apples, and walnuts.

Serves 6–8

10-pound goose
Salt and pepper
Sage and Onion Stuffing (recipe follows)
1 cup boiling water
3 tablespoons cold water

Preheat the oven to 450 degrees.

Discard all the inside fat from the goose. Rinse the bird well inside and out; pat it dry with paper towels. Sprinkle the cavity with salt and pepper, then fill it loosely with the stuffing. Close the cavity and truss the goose, using poultry pins and kitchen string. Rub the skin with more salt and pepper and prick it all over with a carving fork.

Set the goose breast side down on a rack in a shallow roasting pan and pour in the boiling water. Roast in the preheated oven for 30 minutes. Take it out and prick the skin again all over, basting with some of the fat from the pan.

Lower the oven temperature to 350 degrees. Continue roasting the goose, turning it every half hour and ending breast side up. At each interval, repeat the pricking and basting process, and remove the excess fat. Roast until the internal temperature reaches 180 to 185 degrees, as measured by a meat thermometer inserted into the thigh. The total roasting time will be 2½ to 3 hours.

About 15 minutes before the total time has elapsed, sprinkle on the cold water. (If the breast becomes too brown at any point, cover it with foil.)

sandra caplan ciarocchi

Sage and Onion Stuffing

1 pound potatoes, peeled and halved, if
  large
2 tablespoons melted butter
2 medium-sized onions, peeled and finely
  chopped
2 tart apples, peeled, cored, and finely
  chopped
1 tablespoon crumbled dried sage
1 teaspoon chopped fresh parsley
Salt and pepper

Put the potatoes in a medium-sized saucepan, cover them with cold water, add salt, and
bring to a boil. Lower the heat and simmer for
15 to 20 minutes or until just tender; drain.
Dice the potatoes.

Heat the butter and cook the onions and apples for 8 minutes until they have softened. Stir
in the diced potatoes and the herbs. Season to
taste with salt and pepper. Fill the stuffing into
the cavity of the goose.

Giblet Gravy

Makes 2 cups

1 small onion, finely chopped
1 stalk celery, thinly sliced
3 sprigs parsley
Goose giblets (with the liver), cut into
  small pieces
3 cups chicken broth
2 tablespoons butter
3 tablespoons flour
Salt and pepper
⅓ cup heavy cream (optional)

Put the onion, celery, parsley, and giblets in
a heavy saucepan. Add the chicken broth and
simmer, uncovered, for 1½ hours, or until the
liquid has reduced to 1½ cups. Discard the parsley and bony neck. Strain off the broth. Put
the remaining solids in a food processor fitted

with a steel blade. Add ½ cup of the broth and
process until the giblets are finely chopped.

Heat the butter in a small saucepan. Stir in
the flour and cook for 2 minutes, until the flour
is lightly browned. Using a wire whisk, stir in
the remaining broth and the processed giblets. Season generously with salt and pepper.
Add the cream, if desired.

Braised Celery

Serves 6

12 stalks celery, cut into 2-inch lengths
2 tablespoons butter
1 onion, finely chopped
2 carrots, diced
1 bay leaf
½ cup chicken broth
2 teaspoons tomato paste
1 ripe tomato, peeled, seeded, and chopped
2 tablespoons finely chopped parsley

Preheat the oven to 325 degrees.

Simmer the celery in salted water for 5 minutes. Drain and place in a shallow baking dish.
Add all the remaining ingredients except the
chopped tomato and parsley. Cover and cook
in the preheated oven for 45 minutes. Add the
tomato and cook for 5 more minutes. Uncover
and garnish with parsley just before serving.

Roast Potatoes

Serves 6

18 small potatoes
3 tablespoons butter
1 tablespoon vegetable oil
Coarse salt
Freshly ground black pepper

Preheat the oven to 350 degrees.

Peel the potatoes and pat dry with paper towels.

Heat the butter and oil in a shallow roasting pan just large enough to hold the potatoes. Roll the potatoes in the hot butter and oil to coat their surfaces. Roast the potatoes in the preheated oven for 1 hour, until the insides are soft and the surfaces are crisp and nicely browned. Transfer to a hot serving dish and sprinkle with salt and pepper to taste.

Brussels Sprouts with Bacon and Chestnuts

Serves 6

1¾ pounds brussels sprouts
1½ pounds chestnuts
¾ pound bacon, diced
4 tablespoons butter

Trim the brussels sprouts, discarding any wilted outer leaves. Cut a cross in the base of each sprout so it will cook quickly.

Cut a cross in the base of each chestnut to prevent it from exploding. Simmer the chestnuts in boiling water for 1 hour, then peel.

Fry the bacon until crisp. Drain.

Simmer the brussels sprouts, covered, in boiling salted water for 15 minutes, or until just tender; drain. Heat the butter in a skillet and add the chestnuts and sprouts; toss until hot. Transfer to a dish and garnish with the bacon.

Plum Pudding

The plum pudding of Victorian England is heavily laden with symbolism, in addition to the visions of sugarplum fairies and Dickensian nostalgia. The rich, dark pudding is customarily round to represent the good, fertile earth. The sprig of holly with its red berries symbolizes the blood of Christ, and the brandy flames stand for the fires of the underworld that, happily, are extinguished as goodness triumphs over evil. The silver charms traditionally baked into the pudding are the talismans that promise good fortune and prosperity in the year to come.

This may seem like a lot of plum pudding, but it is hardly worth the trouble of preparing a smaller amount. The extra puddings make most acceptable gifts. Besides, the full recipe uses up the complete boxes of raisins and currants, which otherwise would remain in your kitchen cupboard for another year!

Makes 5 1-quart puddings

15-ounce box (2½ cups) golden raisins
15-ounce box (2½ cups) dark raisins
15-ounce box (2½ cups) currants
2 cups mixed fruit rinds
1½ cups chopped glacéed cherries
1½ cups slivered almonds
1 tart cooking apple, peeled, cored, and grated
Grated rind of 2 oranges
2 teaspoons allspice
2 teaspoons cinnamon
1 tablespoon ground nutmeg
1 teaspoon ground cloves
2 teaspoons baking soda
1 teaspoon salt
1 cup flour
5 cups freshly made bread crumbs
½ pound ground beef suet
2½ cups firmly packed light brown sugar
4 eggs, lightly beaten
3 tablespoons molasses
1 cup brandy or dark Jamaica rum

Put all the ingredients into a very large mixing bowl and mix them together with your hands. (This is the only practical way of doing it.) Butter the insides of 5 1-quart molds or bowls and divide the mixture among them. Cover with a double thickness of aluminum foil and tie the foil securely with string.

Put the molds in a fish poacher, metal roasting pan, or a similar container and add sufficient boiling water to come three-quarters of the way up the sides of the molds. Cover the container with more foil. Cook over low heat for 4 hours, refilling with water from time to time. Let the puddings cool in the water.

When they are completely cold, store the molds in a cool place for a month or more, force-feeding them a little more brandy from time to time.

Reheat the puddings by steaming them in the same "double boiler" arrangement for an hour, though you can cook them for 2 hours or longer without harming them.

When ready to serve, unmold the hot pudding carefully onto a plate with a rim. Heat 2 ounces of brandy in a small saucepan. Remove from the stove, light the brandy, and pour it, flaming, over the pudding. Carry the pudding to the table. Walk slowly—if you run, the flames will be extinguished by the rushing air.

Hard Sauce

Here is the essential accompaniment for the plum pudding.

Makes 1 cup

½ pound unsalted butter
1 cup confectioners' sugar
¼ cup brandy or rum

Beat the butter in an electric mixer or food processor until softened. Beat in the sugar and add the brandy or rum a little at a time. Mound the sauce in an attractive bowl and cover with transparent wrap (to prevent the alcohol from evaporating) until ready to serve. Serve the sauce at room temperature.

A HOLIDAY BUFFET

A buffet party gives enormous pleasure and there are many ways of planning such an evening without expending a great deal of effort. It is easy enough to make a huge mound of pasta, a sauce, and a tossed salad. Beef, lamb, or two or three chickens can be put into the oven an hour or so ahead and, with baked potatoes, will take care of themselves while you are dressing.

Nonetheless, there are many factors that must be considered in making arrangements for any party. Perhaps the most important thing is to be brutally honest, not only about your own culinary expertise but also about the time, money, and space you have available.

The Food

Invariably, we start with a simple menu and then keep adding to it and adding to it until there is far too much food and an almost infinite variety. Why is it, do you suppose, that in our anxiety to please everybody we offer a choice of fish, chicken, beef, pasta, vegetables, salads, and goodness knows what else and let those charming, polite guests attack everything like a swarm of locusts? They dump a bit of this and a bit of that on the plate, heaping it up indiscriminately, muddling together all the disparate flavors into an unattractive heap. It always happens. You can count on it.

So restrain yourself and set a good example. If you decide to serve ham, offer as an alternative a well-roasted plump chicken or two. At least if the ham and chicken arrive on the same plate they will taste good together. And keep in mind that you can always buy what you dare not attempt to make.

The ideal things to serve at a buffet are those that nature has already made divisible into single portions—an artichoke and a lobster, for example, or a stuffed egg followed by a chicken leg or two. Half an avocado, a small trout, or a salmon steak are quick to prepare, and, for dessert, individual pastries, molded or moussed creams, or frozen desserts served in separate dishes, are still easier to cope with than four-and-twenty blackbirds all baked in the same pie.

Timing

Consider carefully just how long it will take to arrange the room, clean, shop, chop, cook, and generally fuss about, and then double it. It is essential not only to commit all your arrangements and shopping lists to paper but also to make a realistic written timetable.

Serving the Food

Plan, if possible, to have two identical settings of food and china along either side of the table to speed the flow of traffic. Tuck the flatware inside a napkin so that it can all be picked up at one time. If any guests offer help, accept it gratefully and tell them *exactly* what you would like done. A warning: Though your children may be the apples of your eye, they can rarely offer help of any consequence until they grow above the height of the table. If you can engage professional or reasonably efficient and willing help, it is well worth the cost.

Cleaning Up

Have somebody else do it.

Menu

Chicken Terrine
Scallops and Crème Fraiche
An Assortment of Cheeses, Breads,
and Crackers
Boned Roast Leg of Lamb with Herbs
Madeira Sauce
Tabbouleh Salad
Steamed Buttered Zucchini
Tossed Salad
Frozen Orange Shells • Chocolate Mousse

Chicken Terrine

Do not be afraid to make this terrine, even if you have never attempted such a thing before. I have made it many times; it is always a success and nothing can go wrong with it. At a buffet party, it is a good idea to cut the first few slices yourself and arrange them on the serving plate. An untouched terrine can be quite intimidating to some people.

Serves 12

2 cups uncooked pork sausage
½ pound boiled ham, diced
2 cloves garlic, finely chopped
2 eggs, lightly beaten
1 teaspoon oregano
4 tablespoons chopped parsley
2 tablespoons brandy or Madeira
1½ teaspoons salt
Freshly ground black pepper
4 tablespoons butter, softened
½ pound thinly sliced bacon, or thin slices
    of fresh pork fat
3½ cups chopped roasted chicken
½ cup finely chopped parsley

Preheat the oven to 350 degrees.

Mix together the sausage, ham, garlic, eggs, oregano, parsley, brandy, salt, pepper, and butter.

Line a 2-quart casserole with three-quarters of the bacon slices. Layer a third of the sausage mixture over the bacon. Cover with a layer of half the chopped chicken. Repeat the layers, using another third of the sausage mixture, the remaining chicken, and finishing with the remaining third of the sausage. Cover with the remaining bacon slices and put a lid on the casserole. Set the casserole in a larger pan, filled to a depth of 3 inches with hot water, and bake in the preheated oven for 1¼ hours.

Remove the lid and cover the casserole with aluminum foil. Let the terrine cool to room temperature, then place a weight (2 cans of soup, for example) on top of the foil. (Weighting a terrine makes the mixture more compact, which facilitates cutting.) Chill for at least 48 hours.

To serve, unmold the terrine onto a serving platter or board and surround it with a border of finely chopped parsley. (You can serve it with or without the bacon.)

Scallops and Crème Fraîche

This exquisite dish takes less than five minutes to make and will provoke more admiring comments than anything else you serve. Heap the scallops in the center of a serving plate lined with Boston or Bibb lettuce leaves.

Serves 8

1½ pounds very fresh bay scallops
3 tablespoons fresh lime juice
1 cup crème fraîche (available at specialty
    food shops) or a mixture of ⅓ cup each
    sour cream, whipped heavy cream, and
    plain yogurt
Freshly ground black pepper
Grated rind of 1 lime

Marinate the scallops in the lime juice for 2 hours. Drain them thoroughly and fold in the crème fraîche or cream mixture. Season with black pepper and garnish with grated lime rind.

Boned Roast Leg of Lamb with Herbs

If you have the butcher bone the legs of lamb, this impressive and delicious dish is surprisingly straightforward to make. You may want to have someone help you with the slicing once the lamb is set on the table.

Serves 24

4 cups freshly made bread crumbs
½ cup finely chopped parsley
½ cup chopped chives
2 tablespoons rosemary
2 teaspoons thyme
9 cloves garlic
Salt and pepper
½ cup chopped pistachio nuts
3 legs of lamb, boned, each weighing 4–5
   pounds after the bones are removed
4 tablespoons butter, melted

Preheat the oven to 350 degrees.

Put 1 cup of bread crumbs in the food processor and add the herbs, garlic, and salt and pepper to taste. Process just until finely chopped. Put this mixture in a bowl and stir in another cup of crumbs and the pistachio nuts. Divide the stuffing into thirds.

Lay each boned leg on the counter skin side down and spread the stuffing over the cut surface of the meat. Roll up each leg and tie very tightly with string at 1-inch intervals. (If it is not tied tightly, the lamb will not slice neatly.) Put the stuffed lamb legs on roasting racks or wire cake-cooling racks set over baking dishes.

Roast the lamb, allowing 25 minutes to the pound, or until the meat reaches an internal temperature of 140 degrees. About 20 minutes before the total cooking time has elapsed, remove the lamb roasts from the oven. Cover them evenly with the remaining 2 cups bread crumbs, pressing the crumbs firmly over the surface of each roast. Drizzle with butter. Return them to the oven and continue roasting until the crumbs are lightly browned.

Let the lamb rest, covered with a tent of foil, for 15 minutes before slicing, so that the juice that has risen to the surface will redistribute itself all through the meat.

Madeira Sauce

Serves 24

6 tablespoons butter
1 onion, finely chopped
½ pound mushrooms, thinly sliced
6 tablespoons flour
2 teaspoons tomato paste
3 cups beef broth
3 cups chicken broth
½ cup Madeira
Salt and pepper

Heat the butter and cook the onion for about 3 minutes until softened but not brown. Add the mushrooms and cook for 2 minutes. Stir in the flour and cook for 2 more minutes, then stir in the tomato paste. Add the beef and chicken broths gradually, stirring until thickened. Simmer over very low heat for 15 minutes. Stir in the Madeira and simmer for a few minutes longer. Taste and season with salt and pepper if necessary.

Tabbouleh Salad

Serves 24

14 ounces (approximately 1¾ cups) cracked
wheat (available at health food stores or
Middle Eastern specialty shops)
Approximately 4 cups boiling water
12 scallions, finely chopped
½ cup finely chopped pimientos
4 carrots, peeled and grated

DRESSING:
3–4 teaspoons salt
Freshly ground black pepper
3 cloves garlic
2 teaspoons Dijon mustard
½ cup chopped fresh parsley
½ cup fresh lemon juice
1 cup vegetable oil

GARNISH:
1 tomato, cut into wedges
1 lemon, cut into wedges

Pour enough boiling water over the cracked
wheat to cover it completely. Let stand for 1½
hours, or until the wheat has absorbed all the
water. Fluff up the wheat by picking up a handful and letting it drift between your fingertips to
separate the grains. (It will seem a little starchy
at this stage, but the grains will separate more
completely when you add the dressing.) Mix in
the scallions, chopped pimientos, and grated
carrots.

Combine all the dressing ingredients in a
food processor or blender and process; toss
with the tabbouleh. Mound in a bowl and garnish with tomato and lemon wedges.

Steamed Buttered Zucchini

If you have a food processor with a blade designed for cutting french fries, use it for cutting
the zucchini. If you are not so blessed, slice the
zucchini into very thin rounds with a very sharp
knife. If you do not have a large vegetable
steamer, cook the zucchini in two batches.

Serves 24

4 pounds small zucchini
½ cup white vermouth or chicken broth
⅓ cup fresh lemon juice
Salt and pepper
4 tablespoons butter, cut into small pieces

Wash and slice the zucchini. Pour the vermouth or broth into a large wide pan. Put a
vegetable steamer in the pan and add the zucchini. Sprinkle with the lemon juice and season
to taste with salt and pepper. Dot with butter.
Cover and steam over low heat for 8 minutes.
(Do not cook too rapidly or the vermouth will
boil away.) Taste the zucchini and continue
cooking for another minute or two if necessary.

Splendid Salad Dressing

It is sad to make a splendid salad and not have
a splendid dressing to glorify it. Here is my favorite. Make it up several days in advance to let
it season and then thin it down with light cream
or oil and vinegar (one part vinegar to three
parts oil). This dressing is particularly good with
bold and beautiful greenery such as arugula,
spinach, romaine lettuce, and watercress.

Serves 24

2 eggs
½ cup shallots, scallions, or 1 small onion,
coarsely chopped
2 cloves garlic

½ cup tarragon vinegar
2 teaspoons mild prepared mustard
1½ cups vegetable oil or equal parts vegetable and olive oil
2 teaspoons dried sage
½ teaspoon dried thyme
½ cup heavy cream
1 cup grated Gruyère or Swiss cheese
Salt and pepper

Put the eggs, shallots, garlic, vinegar, and mustard in a blender or food processor. Turn it on and add the oil in a slow, steady stream, as though making mayonnaise. Add the remaining ingredients. Season to taste with salt and pepper and continue processing until the cheese is thoroughly incorporated.

Chocolate Mousse

There are many different types of chocolate mousse. This one is very rich, very smooth, and should be eaten in very small quantities, very slowly. I am suggesting this as an alternative dessert for some of the guests; double the quantity if you plan to serve it without the oranges.

Serves 12

½ pound semisweet chocolate
8 egg yolks
8 tablespoons butter, softened
6 tablespoons Grand Marnier
8 egg whites
Crystallized violets

Break the chocolate into small pieces and put these in a small bowl set over a saucepan of simmering water. Cover with a plate or another bowl and leave for 10 minutes until the chocolate has melted.

Beat the egg yolks in a mixer until they are very thick. Fold in the butter, Grand Marnier, and melted chocolate with a spatula. Beat the egg whites until they stand in soft peaks. Fold the chocolate mixture into the egg whites. Spoon the mousse into small dessert dishes, or serve guests from one large serving bowl. Chill for at least 4 hours before serving, decorated with crystallized violets.

Frozen Orange Shells

Serves 24

12 perfect navel oranges
1 quart orange sherbet, softened
1 cup whipped cream
24 orange or tangerine sections
Cinnamon or cocoa powder
3 tablespoons Grand Marnier (optional)

Cut the oranges in half, even the bottoms by cutting off a small slice, if needed, and scoop out the pulp with a grapefruit knife. Fill the shells with sherbet, mounding it attractively. Put the filled shells in the freezer until you are ready to serve.

Just before serving, spoon a tablespoon of whipped cream in the center of each shell. Top with an orange segment and sprinkle the edge of each shell with cinnamon or cocoa.

If you like, you can mix Grand Marnier into the softened sherbet before filling the shells for freezing.

A PROFESSIONAL PARTY

At most office parties, the ratio of available square feet of floor space to the number of feet that will be crowded onto the floor is not conducive to the service of fancy food. And because eating is usually less important than gossiping and scoring points, it is wise to serve food that can be eaten in one (non-bulging) mouthful.

A suave, professional office partygoer knows how to ask a question and immediately start chewing his food in order to be ready to respond to the answer. This enables each eater to keep the conversation going with the consummate skill of two singles tennis players—one serves and the other returns. Being fast on your feet and quick with your wits can be important at this kind of gathering. Two-bite foods put a person at a distinct disadvantage in establishing a dialogue.

So keep the food as straightforward as possible. The more complicated it is, the more toppings or trappings it has, the greater the likelihood of dropping it, causing possible embarrassment, potential hazard, and most important, distraction from the agenda at hand.

For a successful party, as for so much else in life, the rule is: Keep it simple. You can rely on the conversation to provide its own spice.

"It comes with beard, boots and padding. The reindeer, though, are extra."

Menu

Chicken Liver Pâté
Mushrooms Stuffed with Goat Cheese
Salami with Clementines or Tangerines
Mozzarella with Roasted Peppers
Chicken Wings with Plum Sauce
Steak Tartare
Mousse of Smoked Trout
Guacamole
Shrimp with Cocktail Sauce
Shiny Fresh Vegetables

Chicken Liver Pâté

The currants add texture and an interesting flavor to this delicately seasoned pâté.

Makes 2 cups

7 tablespoons butter
1 small onion, finely chopped
1 clove garlic, finely chopped
1 teaspoon dried sage
1 pound chicken livers
¼ cup dry white vermouth
Salt and pepper
¼ cup currants, soaked in hot water for 10
    minutes, then drained

Heat 3 tablespoons of the butter in a skillet and cook the onion, garlic, and sage slowly for 5 minutes. Add the chicken livers. Increase the heat and cook the livers for 5 minutes, or until lightly browned but still pink in the center. Add the vermouth and cook for a few minutes longer. Put all these ingredients in a food processor and process until very smooth.

Soften the remaining 4 tablespoons of butter, add to the liver mixture, and mix well. Season to taste with salt and pepper, then stir in the currants.

Pour the mixture into small earthenware crocks or a terrine and cover with transparent wrap. Chill for at least 4 hours before serving.

Mushrooms Stuffed with Goat Cheese

If you cannot find any goat cheese, substitute softened cream cheese and add some fresh chopped herbs, such as a combination of parsley, chives, and tarragon.

Makes 24 pieces

24 small fresh mushrooms of uniform size
5-ounce package goat cheese
3 tablespoons finely chopped parsley

"I am given to understand it's Christmas, Miss Decker. Whom do I love?"

Remove the stems from the mushrooms. Wipe the caps with damp paper towels to remove any trace of soil. Put 1 teaspoon of cheese in each mushroom cap. Garnish with chopped parsley.

Salami with Clementines or Tangerines

This is a simple idea that looks quite dramatic, with cornucopias of salami arranged around a bunch of watercress. Clementines are the small seedless oranges that come into the shops around Christmas and are even sweeter than tangerines.

Makes 16 pieces

16 thin slices good-quality hard salami
3 ounces cream cheese
16 clementine or tangerine sections
16 capers
Watercress

Spread each slice of salami with a thin layer of cream cheese. Enclose a clementine segment and form into a cornucopia. Press the edges together and place, seam down, around the edge of a serving plate. Put a caper in each cone. Fill the center of the plate with watercress.

Mozzarella with Roasted Peppers

Here is a pleasant combination of ingredients that can be ready in five minutes. If this were to be the only appetizer, it would serve eight. As part of an array of nibbles, it will make another attractive morsel to taste.

Serves 6–8

1 pound fresh mozzarella cheese, cut into
    bite-sized pieces
8 ounces canned roasted peppers, drained
    and cut into small pieces
2-ounce can anchovies, drained and
    chopped (optional)
2 tablespoons fresh lemon juice
⅓ cup light olive oil or vegetable oil
1 tablespoon fresh oregano or chopped
    fresh basil
Freshly ground black pepper

Toss all the ingredients together and serve in a glass bowl. Have some plates and forks handy.

Chicken Wings with Plum Sauce

We made this dish once, intending to serve it to guests at a buffet, but every one of the wings mysteriously disappeared in the kitchen. You might want to double the quantity, just in case.

Serves 6

⅓ cup soy sauce
2 tablespoons sugar
1 tablespoon dry sherry
2 thin slices fresh ginger, finely chopped
2 tablespoons plum jelly
⅓ cup water
2 pounds chicken wings

Put all the ingredients except the chicken wings in a medium-sized saucepan and mix well. Add the chicken wings and heat to boiling.

Lower the heat and simmer for 20 minutes, stirring occasionally. Uncover and cook for 15 minutes, basting constantly, until only ½ cup liquid remains. Serve the wings hot, in a chafing dish, enveloped in the sauce.

Steak Tartare

Lately it has been as unfashionable to admit to eating red meat as to acknowledge watching television; nevertheless, there are still a few who recognize a good thing when they see one. Serve steak tartare with squares of black bread or spooned into hollowed-out cherry tomatoes, and be sure it is all eaten up at once.

Serves 12

2 pounds finest quality lean ground beef
2 egg whites, lightly beaten
1 small onion, finely chopped
1 tablespoon capers
½ teaspoon salt
Freshly ground black pepper
1 teaspoon prepared mustard
2 teaspoons Worcestershire sauce
2 tablespoons vodka

Grind the beef in the food processor, using 1-second-on/1-second-off timing, for approximately 4 seconds until the correct consistency is reached. Take care not to overprocess or you will find yourself with a puree of beef.

Add the remaining ingredients and serve immediately, before the beef darkens.

Mousse of Smoked Trout

For a very grand presentation, put a whole smoked trout on a bed of green leaves in the center of a silver serving tray and arrange slices of cucumber topped with the smoked trout mousse around the edge of the tray. If you use

the long slim cucumbers that are grown hydro-
ponically, the slices will look good with some of
the skin left on.

Serves 10–12

2 smoked trout (about 6 ounces each)
3 ounces cream cheese
¼ cup chopped onion
1 tablespoon fresh lemon juice
Dash hot pepper sauce
Cucumber slices
Lemon wedges
Parsley

Set 1 whole trout in the center of your serving tray. Remove the skin and bones from the
second trout and put the fish in a food processor. Add the cream cheese, onion, lemon
juice, and hot pepper sauce and process into a
smooth puree. Mound teaspoons of mousse on
the cucumber slices and arrange around the
sides of the tray. Garnish with lemon wedges
and parsley.

Guacamole

If you like guacamole spicy, increase the
amount of hot pepper sauce—a dash at a time,
tasting as you go. You can always add a drop
more, but you can never call one too many
home again.

Makes 2 cups

2 medium-size ripe avocados, peeled, pitted
    and quartered
2 scallions, thinly sliced
½ cup chopped, seeded ripe tomato
2 tablespoons fresh lime juice
1 teaspoon salt
Freshly ground pepper
Dash of hot pepper sauce

Put all the ingredients in a food processor
and process until smooth. Serve with corn chips.

"Oh, all right, Wilkerson—but only this once!"

Shrimp with Cocktail Sauce

It is very easy and inexpensive to make your
own shrimp cocktail sauce, and it certainly
tastes more piquant than the bottled kind.
Whether you serve the shrimp arranged around
the edge of a glass bowl containing the sauce
or mounded on a platter alongside it, shrimp
always disappear first at a party. It's one of
the rules.

Makes 1⅓ cups

SAUCE:
1 cup tomato ketchup
1 teaspoon prepared horseradish
¼ teaspoon hot pepper sauce or ⅛ tea-
    spoon cayenne pepper
¾ teaspoon chili powder
2 cloves garlic, finely chopped
1 tablespoon fresh lemon juice
½ teaspoon salt

1½ pounds cold cooked shrimp

Combine all the sauce ingredients and serve
in a glass bowl, with the shrimp. Toothpicks
are a good idea, but most people just use their
fingers.

Shiny Fresh Vegetables

There are few foods more appetizing than a bowl of glistening, barely cooked, very fresh vegetables. Absolutely any combination of vegetables can be used. This is like arranging a bunch of flowers fresh from the garden; you cannot go wrong. Just take immense care not to overcook the vegetables. They must be bright and crisp.

Serves 10–12

3 small yellow onions, quartered
1 pound carrots, sliced on the diagonal
2 green peppers, with ribs and seeds removed, cut into small triangles or strips
2 red and 2 yellow peppers, cut into small triangles or strips
1 bunch of broccoli, cut into florets
½ pound snow peas, trimmed
⅓ cup olive oil

Fill a large saucepan with water, salt it, and bring to a boil. You will be cooking each vegetable just until tender but still crisp, so the order is important.

First, put in the onions (they will separate into strips in the water) and boil them for 2 minutes. Add the carrots to the onions and cook for 3 minutes, then add the peppers and the broccoli; cook for 2 to 3 more minutes. Finally, add the snow peas and cook for 1 minute.

Drain the vegetables in a colander, then plunge the colander into a bowl of very cold water to crisp the vegetables and brighten their color. Shake them free of all water and toss in just enough oil to moisten. Serve at room temperature in a beautiful glass bowl and let the guests help themselves. They make an attractive accompaniment to any of the other suggested appetizers.

OFFICE PARTY

This holy night in open forum
Miss McIntosh, who handles Files,
Has lost one shoe and her decorum.
Stately, the frozen chairman smiles

On Media, desperately vocal.
Credit, though they have lost their hopes
Of edging toward an early Local,
Finger their bonus envelopes.

The glassy boys, the bursting girls
Of Copy, start a Conga clatter
To a swung carol. Limply curls
The final sandwich on the platter

Till hark! a herald Messenger
(Room 414) lifts loudly up
His quavering tenor. Salesmen stir
Libation for his Lily cup.

"Noel," he pipes, "Noel, Noel."
Some wag beats tempo with a ruler.
And the plump blonde from Personnel
Collapses by the water cooler.

Phyllis McGinley

A PORTRAIT OF THE HOLIDAYS

A PORTRAIT
OF THE HOLIDAYS

Idyllic scenes of wintry Christmas fun have always fascinated artists as Americans from the 19th century onward have revelled in the great good times of this special season. Here are some evocations of Christmas past that are not so far from Christmas present, glimpses of a time when horse-drawn sleighs were the necessary means of transportation and city ladies tucked their tiny hands into warm muffs. This is the Christmas of our romantic fantasy, when the clean, white, soft flakes stop falling only when the earth is blanketed with a perfect coverlet that knows no coating of urban grime.

Some artists, like Louis Rhead, whose cover illustration for a Christmas *Scribner's* magazine of the 1890s shows a girl carrying mistletoe home from the snowy woods, offer decorative interpretations of a holiday theme; genre painters like William Sydney Mount offer us a first-hand look at rollicking celebrations in the days when country folk made their own music for dancing.

What would we know of Victorian America were it not for the artists who worked for Currier & Ives—among them Charles Parsons, whose famous skating scene appears here. Over a time span of some 50 years the firm produced close to 8,000 such lithographs, many of them hand-colored, which were sold for $1.50 to $3.00 apiece.

Some of the best-loved portrayers of everyday life in the 20th century are here, too. Grandma Moses' paintings offer delightful composites of Christmas inside and out in the farm country she knew so well: "I like to paint old-timey things," she once said, "something real pretty. Most of them are daydreams, as it were."

Closing this nostalgic portfolio are several of Norman Rockwell's insightful, inimitable glimpses of Christmas behind the scenes in small-town America. He created over 300 such scenes as covers for the *Saturday Evening Post* over a period of 40 years, and it is easy to see why he was the most popularly acclaimed illustrator America has ever had.

Here, then, in a capsule, is our imaginary paradise, where there are rhapsodies of remembrance, laughter without end, and snow on the ground—with just enough wind to float everyone's mufflers jauntily towards the cloudless blue sky.

Of such stuff dreams are made—when we wish upon the Christmas star!

Scribner's: For Xmas, c. 1895
Louis Rhead, American, 1857–1926. Colored zincograph, 128.3 × 89.7 centimeters. The
Art Institute of Chicago: Gift of George H. Porter.

Rustic Dance after a Sleigh Ride
William Sidney Mount, American, 1807–1868. Oil on
canvas, 22 × 37¼ inches. Courtesy, Museum of Fine
Arts, Boston: M. and M. Karolik Collection.

Musicians in the Snow (detail)
Anonymous, American, 1876. Oil on canvas,
76.2 × 101.6 centimeters. Courtesy, Museum of
Fine Arts, Boston: M. and M. Karolik Collection.

Through the Woods
Lowell Herrero, American, 1986. Oil on canvas, 20 × 24 inches.

Central-Park, Winter: The Skating Pond
Charles Parsons for Currier & Ives, American, 1862. Colored lithograph. Courtesy, The Museum of the City of New York: Harry T. Peters Collection.

Christmas at Home
Grandma Moses, American, 1945. Oil on pressed wood, 18 × 23 inches.

Joy Ride
Grandma Moses, American, 1953. Oil
on pressed wood, 18 × 24 inches.

It is snowing some, the Kidos had a nice tree, and wish you could see the mess this morning. I trust you are all well and geting along fine, The flowers are lovely and are growing more so. I have had a grand Chrismass, and now am in for a gay new years, won't they ever let me be, but it is all nice and they mean it for my good;

now here is Happ new year to you and all, may you have health and prosperity in all things, this coming year, Grand mar moses.

Christmas at Home (detail)

Letter from Grandma Moses to Mr. & Mrs. O.K. December 29, 1950.

Christmas Day
Jo Sickbert, American, 1982. Acrylic on board, 18¼ × 26½ inches.

Santa's Surprise
Norman Rockwell, American, 1894–1978. Watercolor on
posterboard, 13.375 × 11.125 inches. Collection of Hallmark
Cards, Inc.

Boy in Santa Suit
Norman Rockwell, American, 1894–1978. Oil on board,
12 × 6½ inches. Collection of Hallmark Cards, Inc.

Jolly Postman
Norman Rockwell, American, 1894–1978. Watercolor on posterboard, 12.25 × 10.25 inches. Collection of Hallmark Cards, Inc.

Trimming the Tree
Norman Rockwell, American, 1894–1978, Watercolor on posterboard. 13.375 × 11.4375 inches.
Collection of Hallmark Cards, Inc.

TOYLAND, TOYLAND

THE TOYS THAT WERE ONCE UNDER THE TREE

A little child has nothing but amazement to bring to the magical spectacle of abundance heaped before him on Christmas morning. Faced by such unimagined largesse, he has no idea of its extent and no one has prepared him with "appropriate" behavior for this, the first truly overwhelming experience of his young life.

So when the last present has been handed out and freed from its cocoon of wrappings and he asks "Is that all there is?" he means no offense; he is just curious, and genuinely wants to know how far this unprecedented extravaganza is going to go.

In gift-giving philosophies at the turn of the century, a toy was more than a plaything—it was a device for instruction and improvement. The toy bank taught children the practice and virtue of thrift; other toys were designed to teach them how they were to come by the money which, in ensuing years, they would save. These toys, always the ones most prized under the tree and all year round, were miniaturized replicas of the forms of the adult world, true to life in every detail. They were really guided fantasies; they taught children the joys of power, and how that power was apportioned in the adult world. And because they were so clearly gender-specific, a child knew perfectly well before the age of five which spheres of influence were open to him or her in the life to come.

The hand-carved blocks have the alphabet in front and a town's worth of buildings on their backs, a two-way gift for the preschool set.

The driver of a painted iron fire engine races his spirited team to the rescue.

Ready to move in, this doll has brought her own cradle and quilt and a small but tastefully chosen wardrobe.

This dollhouse version of Peter Goelet's New York City brownstone was made in 1845 for his nieces.

On Christmas morning back then, one of the best treats a boy could find in his stocking was a well-turned wooden top, a simple device he could play with from dawn to dusk. With a quick pull on the string wrapped under its broad head, he could make it spin on floors and tabletops, clattering noisily, until the time when his mother said, "*Will* you stop doing that! That's enough!"

Tops were marvelous toys for trying the patience of parents, and, over the first half of the century, they got better and better at it. By the late 1930s, a boy could find an enormous top under the tree, made of molded tin and shaped like a flying saucer (although the boy didn't know that, because flying saucers had not been invented yet). The top would be painted a bright red, and all around its outer edge would be lighted windows, and in the windows, painted faces. And when the boy pressed down repeatedly on the handle at the top of the top, he could make it spin faster and faster, and as the painted faces flew by, they would blur into

A Lionel train set and at least one loop of track made a lucky boy king of locomotive land.

abstract patterns, whizzing. Meanwhile the top would hum and, with acceleration, shriek and whine at a pitch so high that soon the entire household would be half distracted.

They just don't make tops like that anymore.

They do still make *some* things, though, the way they used to. You can go down into the Smoky Mountains in North Carolina and find

'Twas the night before Christmas, when all through
    the house
Not a creature was stirring, not even a mouse;
The stockings were hung by the chimney with care,
In hopes that St. Nicholas soon would be there;
The children were nestled all snug in their beds;
While visions of sugar-plums danced in their heads;
And mamma in her 'kerchief, and I in my cap,
Had just settled our brains for a long winter's nap;
When out on the lawn there arose such a clatter,
I sprang from the bed to see what what was the matter.
Away to the window I flew like a flash,
Tore open the shutters and threw up the sash.

In 1901, a granny looking for a good secret project could buy this doll family stamped out on cloth, needing only to be scissored free, sewn together, and firmly stuffed.

cornhusk dolls, made by old ladies there, that are every bit as good as any made a century ago. These dolls come down to us from the American Indians, who made them for their own children and taught the early settlers how to do it. Often they are lady dolls, with cornhusk skirts down to the ground. They have hair of the finest cornsilk, and some are holding cornhusk babies, cornhusk baskets for going to market, or both. Always they wear cornhusk hats or poke bonnets and their painted-on faces suggest the stolidity of country life. They are not dolls for cuddling; they are too fragile. They are dolls for looking at.

Used to be, though, that a girl could cuddle a rag doll. Back then, you didn't buy a rag doll from the store; your grandmother made you one from the fabric scraps in her basket. Rag dolls had floppy legs and arms, and plump little bodies stuffed with lots of torn silk and rayon stockings, all wadded up. Often, rag dolls were made to look like monkeys, though the specific identity depended on granny's skill with a nee-

The moon, on the breast of the new-fallen snow,
Gave the lustre of mid-day to objects below,
When, what to my wondering eyes should appear,
But a miniature sleigh, and eight tiny rein-deer,
With a little old driver, so lively and quick,
I knew in a moment it must be St. Nick.
More rapid than eagles his coursers they came,
And he whistled, and shouted, and called them by name;
"Now, Dasher! now, Dancer! now, Prancer and Vixen!
On, Comet! on, Cupid! on, Donder and Blitzen!
To the top of the porch! to the top of the wall!
Now dash away! dash away! dash away all!"

dle, so sometimes they turned out to be clowns, sailors, spiders, or Little Bopeeps.

Penny, nickel, and dime banks were lots of fun in those days. They were made of heavy stamped metal and were "mechanical," in that the toy figures on top could turn and twist and throw a coin with the pressing of a lever. But the child always knew that once he surrendered his penny to the toy Punch and Judy or Three Bears, who then popped it straight into the coin slot, that penny was gone forever.

The year 1906 was the inaugural year of the teddy bear, made to honor Teddy Roosevelt by some toymaker with an eye on the main chance. The toy became a craze, a national enthusiasm which has continued to the present day. Teddies were universally approachable, indiscriminately rewarding, and practically indestructible. For a child, there is nothing wrong with a teddy bear and everything right. With its fuzzy plumpness and cheerfully bland expression, it begs to be cuddled, dragged about, and stood on its head. However abandoned, its

mood is placid, content, and unblaming; a teddy does not know the meaning of indignity.

The china doll, on the other hand, was the soul of pretension and elitism. With her icy blue eyes and rosily pouting mouth, she let little girls know that they would never be as pretty as she, and that they better be extremely careful about how they treated her. Every china doll hated boys, it seems, and if a boy came anywhere near enough to touch one, that china doll would automatically crack or shatter to pieces, and the boy would be blamed for it.

For boys, the very best present in the world was a Lionel electric train set, with miles of track and mighty miniature locomotives to run along it, tugging passenger cars and freight cars and cabooses picture-perfect to the last detail. And with the set came a wealth of complementary pieces, including switches and signaling devices, over- and underpasses, way-stations and terminals, and even whole whistle-stop towns, all minute models of the great American transportation system upon which the modern na-

This cast-iron bank, from about 1890, performs when a coin is placed in the dog's mouth. Dog jumps through hoop, deposits coin in barrel—saved!

As dry leaves that before the wild hurricane fly,
When they meet with an obstacle, mount to the sky;
So up to the house-top the coursers they flew,
With the sleigh full of Toys, and St. Nicholas too.
And then, in a twinkling, I heard on the roof
The prancing and pawing of each little hoof —
As I drew in my head, and was turning around,
Down the chimney St. Nicholas came with a bound.
He was dressed all in fur, from his head to his foot,
And his clothes were all tarnished with ashes and soot;
A bundle of Toys he had flung on his back,
And he look'd like a pedlar just opening his pack.

tion was founded and upon which it depended for its continued prosperity.

It was easy for the boys in absolute control of these sets to imagine themselves directors of complex networks of supply and demand, and in running several trains at a time, a boy could go, in his imagination, from locomotive engineer to captain of industry in the flick of a switch.

But it was different for girls. Their Lilliputian worlds consisted of dollhouses, fitted out with furniture that was often perfect down to the last detail of cabinetry and joinery, and over this domestic empire a little girl could exercise her complete dominion.

(Dollhouses and doll furniture were originally the pleasure only of very rich little girls, in a time when builders and cabinetmakers were accustomed to presenting clients with detailed miniatures of commissioned houses or furniture. These models were passed on to daughters of the house, and so envied that a whole new business arose in domestic miniatures intended solely for play.)

A really fine dollhouse would be a mansion of many rooms, all open at one side like stacked stage sets for the invention and enactment of domestic dramas. The locomotives of girls' play were miniature people, not machines, and these little china (later plastic) doll-women or girls could be bought in boxed sets. Usually they wore antebellum dress with crinolines and pantalettes, and changes of costume were available to order. They had hinged arms and legs, and could be made to sit in their ornate rooms, to "walk" through them, with help, or be stood to gaze through glassine windows draped with flounced curtains. They could be made to give tea parties with tiny tea sets on tiny tea tables, and then made to wash up at tiny sinks in tiny kitchens.

Boys, it was understood, would rather die than play with dolls and dollhouses; girls loathed Lionel train sets. Yet it sometimes happened that boys and girls played together, and accommodated to one another's interests, and found furtive pleasure in toys that belonged to

His eyes — how they twinkled! his dimples how merry!
His cheeks were like roses, his nose like a cherry!
His droll little mouth was drawn up like a bow
And the beard of his chin was as white as the snow;
The stump of a pipe he held tight in his teeth,
And the smoke it encircled his head like a wreath;
He had a broad face and a little round belly
That shook, when he laughed, like a bowl full of jelly.
He was chubby and plump, a right jolly old elf,
And I laughed, when I saw him, in spite of myself;
A wink of his eye and a twist of his head,
Soon gave me to know I had nothing to dread;

the other sex, which they were not supposed to like. So naturally this practice was discouraged and had to be done, for the most part, in secret.

But there was one important plaything which boys and girls could *never* share 80 years ago, because there were no secret circumstances for it, and that was the era's great invention, for boys: the Flexible Flyer. This was such a sled as there had never been before, made of pine and trimmed in red and green, slick as a whistle and polished to perfection—but that was not the main point. Unlike earlier sleds, the Flyer had *controls*, which were what made it flexible. For the first time, the boy on board was not just a passenger; he could control the direction of the runners, left and right, and thus become, at least in the course of a run down a snowy hillside, the master of his own destiny. He could become, in short, a pilot.

Girls, of course, were not given Flexible Flyers. Eighty years on, however, women are pilots. Could it be that toys have the power to instruct even those to whom they are not given?

Indeed, it sometimes happens that the toy a child wants and doesn't get has more influence than every other thing he finds glittering under the tree.

Is that all there is? When a child asks that, he asks with a child's innocence and with a child's wisdom. Somehow we know, from infancy perhaps, that what is not under the tree is quite as important as what is, one way and another.

This mohair "Teddy" made by the Ideal Toy Corporation of New York in about 1910 was named for a bear cub spared by TR and forever famous.

In 1901 a child could make Christmas scenes from paper-covered cubes.

He spoke not a word, but went straight to his work,
And fill'd all the stockings; then turned with a jerk,
And laying his finger aside of his nose,
And giving a nod, up the chimney he rose;
He sprang to his sleigh, to his team gave a whistle,
And away they all flew like the down of a thistle.
But I heard him exclaim, ere he drove out of sight,
"Happy Christmas to all, and to all a good night."

Clement C. Moore,
1862, March 13th originally written many years ago.

At Toys 'R' Us, numbers mark special toys kept behind glass; most are stacked ceiling-high on open shelves.

For Tots, All Roads Lead to Toys 'R' Us

Whether we like it or not, our habits in toy-buying have altered vastly in the past 25 years, owing to market evolutions that have nothing to do with us or with our personal inclinations. The powerful new influences on the toy market —which is now a multi-billion-dollar industry —are plastics, television, and a ubiquitous retail organization called Toys 'R' Us. Here's how it works.

Plastics. This infinitely malleable material has changed everything about the making of toys: their look, their durability, or lack of it, and their cost. Toy designers have been able to go wild, creating fun, colorful plastic playthings for kids.

Lego, one of the most successful toys made possible by plastic, was created by a Danish company called Interlego A/S. The family-run business has produced the Lego System of Play since 1955. Parents in 125 countries are glad it does.

Television. As children's cartoon programs became more popular, advertisers recognized the huge potential for selling toys, games, and, incidentally, breakfast cereals and snacks, through this medium.

And now that the teen market is growing thin, beverage companies such as Coca-Cola and Pepsi are directing their messages to the pre-teen market; and for that effort, Saturday morning is prime time. Expect cries for Pepsi to join demands for plastic versions of cartoon stars. Whichever came first, the commercial or the cartoon, the fact is that kids are bombarded with come-ons for all sorts of toys. Children persuade Mom or Dad or Grandma. . . .

Toys 'R' Us. Charles Lazarus is the person responsible for Toys 'R' Us, the place where kids take Mom or Dad or Grandma after watching TV.

Supermarket toy stores were unheard of before Lazarus transformed his Washington-based children's furniture store into one called Children's Supermarket in the mid-1950s. He soon changed the name to its current catchy one and, as retailing in general became more diverse, he also changed the way toys were sold. Specifically, Lazarus stocked toys in large quantities and took advantage of that fact to sell them at discount prices.

In 1966, he sold his flagship store and three outlets to Interstate Stores for $7.5 million. Lazarus continued to manage the stores and by 1974 had opened 43 more branches. In 1978 the company reorganized to become, officially, Toys 'R' Us, and to brace itself for rapid growth. By 1975 the revenues from Toys 'R' Us were roughly $200 million annually; compare that with their 1985 gross of more than $2 *billion*.

What does Charles Lazarus do that the friendly toyshop owner on Main Street USA does not? For starters, he buys entire lines of toys, and never lets his stock run low. He has a no-questions-asked returns policy and standardized inventory in all outlets. Today, all Toys 'R' Us stores are hooked up by computer to the central office in New Rochelle Park, New Jersey. If a store sells the last of a certain item, additional stock is automatically reordered and shipped to the branch. Store managers never order inventory.

Toys 'R' Us (and its imitators, such as Child World, Lionel Leisure, and others) is so successful that toy manufacturers often check with Lazarus before putting a new toy into production. They design boxes so that they can be stacked (to the ceiling in these mammoth toy stores), and often equip them with transparent fronts so that customers can see what they are getting.

Today, Christmas sales account for about 50 percent of the year's toy sales nationwide. Clearly, the industry depends on our Christmas spending. And we depend on their abundant supply.

Tiptoeing into Toyland

Except for the spindly high heels no Christmas shopper would wear, and the lack of a black mink coat, Gale Jarvis could be any of the frantic young upscale parents nervously pondering the goods of F.A.O. Schwarz. But instead of just reading the price tags, Gale Jarvis is changing them. She's repositioning the Talking Big Bird, shuffling the Captain Power sets, counting the customers at the cash register to see if it's time for the doormen, dressed as Nutcracker soldiers, to let in more eager toy buyers. Ms. Jarvis is the executive vice president of F.A.O., in charge of merchandising for the city's most prestigous toy store.

For Mrs. Jarvis and her staff, the 1987 Christmas buying season started the preceding January, when they flew to Tokyo for a toy fair. In February, there were shows in Germany, England, France, Italy and New York. And throughout the year, they made the rounds of the downtown toy showrooms.

No effort is too great in the hunt for something unusual. Ms. Jarvis tells with glee of a recent long, bumpy ride up an Italian mountainside to visit a man who makes giant stuffed animals by hand. After much bargaining, she bagged several 8-foot-tall camels ($5,000 each). But the toy turned out to be impossible to photograph for the Schwarz catalogue because it was too big to fit in the cab that was going to the photography studio. One camel ended up guarding the Schwarz escalator, waiting for a child with a high-ceiling prewar apartment.

"We're very conscious of the quality. That goes with price," says Ms. Jarvis. "If a cheap toy breaks, you throw it away. If an expensive toy breaks, our customer brings it back. The other thing we look for is play value. Breadth—how many things does the toy do? Longevity—how long will the child play with it? And then, does it have *meaning*? Those are the things that make a toy F.A.O."

Louise Lague
The New York Times
November 15, 1987

The Bear Market

If teddy bears alone are able to gross toy manufacturers $100 million, it should come as no surprise that the bear-hunting consumer can find bears of every shape, size, color, and texture. There are bears that talk, bears that tell stories, bears that growl (gently), and bears that only want to be hugged. There are traditional mohair-furred Steiff bears, squeezable, plush-filled Gund bears, purple Zummi Gummi bears from Fisher-Price, and pastel Care Bears with suns, rainbows, and hearts emblazoned on their chests.

Teddy bears have long been familiar members of the nursery. Christopher Robin was enthralled with his Pooh, and Paddington Bear captured the fancy of an entire London family. Today's kids crowd into movie theaters to view the latest antics of the Care Bears and buy books about an adorable bear wearing overalls named, appropriately enough, Corduroy.

Worlds of Wonder, a hitherto little-known company, introduced Teddy Ruxpin in 1985, a bear outfitted with a microchip-operated cassette that enables him to talk, tell stories, sing songs, and wiggle his nose. Even with a price tag of about $70, Teddy Ruxpin was snapped up by nearly 950,000 shoppers during the 1985 Christmas season.

In 1986, Ruxpin's competition entered the market. The shelves of toy stores were crowded with Gabby Bear from Select Merchandise, Smarty Bear from Galoob, Hasbro's Amazing Bingo Bear, and Axlon Games's A.G. Bear—who differs from the others in that he only growls softly and murmurs. These bears all retail for about the same price as Teddy Ruxpin, except for A.G. Bear, whose attributes allow him to be a little less expensive.

Some of these bears are computer-driven rather than cassette-driven, which means they are voice- or touch-activated and thereby are suppose to encourage "interaction" with the child.

NON-VIOLENT SUPERHEROES

Since 1983, a small, Houston-based toy company called Wee Win Toys has been quietly gaining a share of the superhero market with its Heroes of the Kingdom line of Biblical action figures. The dolls, with movable parts and molded biceps, represent Jesus Christ, Samson, David, Goliath, and more—men who share a collective history not untouched by violence. Yet Wee Win, and other Christian toy manufacturers, feel that these toys offer parents a good alternative to He-Man, GI Joe, and the vast multitude of The Masters of the Universe.

Other Christian toys include Wee Win's Prince of Peace Pets, Rainfall Toys' Kingdom Critters, and Praise Unlimited's Judah the Christian Soldier and Grace the Pro-Life Doll. These toys are sold through Christian bookstores and home parties.

Prehistoric Creatures All the Rage

The Cabbage Patch Kids have had their day, and toys of choice in the late '80s are now led by anything ending in "saurus," as in *Tyrannosaurus Rex* and any number of long-extinct dinosaurs. Godzilla also appears in the inner circle, though he isn't an ancient creature at all, but rather a monster invented for a crazed Japanese horror movie. Godzilla comes six feet tall this year, and could well be the undoing of some visiting aunt on a night prowl.

Other specimens are less life-threatening; 70-million-year-old dinosaurs, for example, can be had in placid profile as a chalkboard, or imprinted on ties or bedsheets. Harper & Row's Perennial Library offers a paperback book which can be disassembled and cut up to create "a perfect, three-dimensional dinosaur skeleton," and the Smithsonian Institution will encourage your child to snap together its plastic replica of a *Quetzalcoatlus northropi* skeleton (Q.n., for short)—a disgusting, carnivorous, nasty, creepy-looking, horrible prehistoric bird which will probably give your child years of pleasure.

Attraction and awe are reflected in the eyes of a two-year-old viewing model dinosaurs from the safe side of a gift shop display window in New York's Museum of Natural History.

Buying Christmas Presents for *Your* Children

As parents, you want to do the right thing by your kids at Christmastime. You want them to have lots of fun with the toys and games you get for them, and you also want to select *some* gifts that aren't entirely daffy and indulgent; after all, you are parents and you want to help your kids grow and learn, even in play.

To do your gift-giving well, you need to make a reasonable plan. But no matter how organized you become, don't forget that the whole process is supposed to be fun—fun for the kids and fun for *you.*

Here are some hints that may be helpful.

• Encourage your children to write Christmas lists, whether in the form of a wish-list for Santa or an actual list an older child knows *you* will fulfill. Go over the lists with them (the

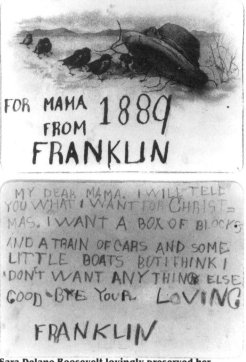

Sara Delano Roosevelt lovingly preserved her seven-year-old son's Christmas list.

---

time-honored method of getting Santa's list to him is to burn it, so some parents snatch a quick copy before sending it up the chimney) and never say absolutely yes or no to anything.

Listen carefully to the child's tone of voice when he talks about a toy or game. Enthusiastic? Whiney? Lukewarm? (The toy may be one all his friends want but he is not totally sold.) Shy? (He may be asking for something he is not sure you would approve of, or something that you think he isn't old enough for.)

• When selecting a toy, look for one that offers a variety of play experiences. One expert describes the best toy as being 90 percent "kid" and 10 percent "toy." You may be intrigued by a remote-control kitten or puppy that scurries across the floor, and so will your child— for about five minutes.

Toys such as Lego, Erector sets, blocks, well-conceived video games (the kind that come with boards for audience participation), puzzles, Etch-A-Sketch (the new model is computer-driven so that the child can create simple animation), dolls, doll furniture and clothes, and doctor kits are all good choices. They encourage the child to play, to imagine, and to solve problems. One more thing: don't forget the batteries!

• As you shop, give in to a few of your own impulses. While it is not a good idea to enter a toy store without having made some firm decisions about what to buy and how much you can spend, if some silly or fluffy toy catches your fancy, chances are it will appeal to your child as well.

• Buy toys that are age-appropriate. You may think your daughter is going to be an astrophysicist, but she may not be ready for a computer when she is four or five. Play is a means for a child to gain confidence and feel in control of her environment. She needs the kind of toys that will enhance her play, not overwhelm it.

• If you feel you have bought a few too many gifts, put some away. Save them for the dreary days of January and February, when you and your child may be housebound with the flu or the weather. This strategy helps alleviate the stress of Christmas-morning overload, when too many presents—and too much excitement—can push any child over an emotional edge.

The Right Gift for *Their* Children

Whatever revolutions may have occurred in the toy industry, nobody has yet solved the problem of toy-buying for somebody else's child. If anything, the job is harder than it ever was; the sheer abundance of kinds of toys now available can be bewildering to the well-meaning uncle, cousin, or family friend.

Children are ready for different toys at different ages, and not everyone, clerks in toy stores included, knows precisely what is best for every child. Obviously, a two-year-old is not going to know what to do with a bicycle or a baseball bat, but will the little tyke appreciate a Cabbage Patch Kid? (Yes.) Would a ten-year-old feel slighted if you bought her a jigsaw puzzle? (Probably not.) During the holidays, aunts, cousins, godparents, and assorted adult friends scurry about selecting gifts they hope will be appreciated and, most importantly, played with.

There are a couple of simple guidelines that will appreciably improve your odds of making a good selection. First of all, do not depend on the age range printed on the box. This is determined by the toy manufacturer according to safety requirements and not necessarily according to the capability of a child of a specific age. If the box says "3 and under," the toy is (probably) safe for a very young child—no small parts to choke on—but may not be appropriate for a six-month-old baby, or, conversely, a two-year-old. If the box says "10 to adult," this means the toy may include some small parts or sharp edges; it does not always mean that a ten-year-old will love it. The toy might be geared toward an even older child who can assemble a complicated toy—and follow the instructions (frequently a master feat in itself!).

Second, when in doubt, buy a classic toy. There are reasons why Lego, Yo-Yos, skateboards, board games such as Monopoly and Candyland, wooden building blocks, Slinkys, and Mr. Potato Head have been around all these years. They are good, reliable toys that kids like. Think back to when you played with the same toys and use your own memory as a guide.

UGLY TOYS—WHY DO KIDS LIKE THEM?

Remember *Beauty and the Beast?* What about goblins and witches and nasty old trolls? Kids love to be scared and they revel in the grotesque. The toy manufacturers of the '80s are simply cashing in on these enthusiams. From Alf (above), the weird but wonderful alien from the TV series bearing his name, through D. Compose and Slime Pit to the Inhumanoids and Garbage Pail Kids, children are being bombarded with ugliness. They love it.

Psychologists from coast to coast insist that this preoccupation with the darker side of life is perfectly natural. It's a way for children to deal with some innate fears, to exhibit a bit of healthy rebelliousness, and (not the least important) to "gross out" the grown-ups in the crowd.

Toys for Your Tots

When children are tiny—which means from infancy through the fifth year and later—the safety of their toys is of supreme importance. When buying for small children, *insist* on these standards:

• Smooth, rounded edges that won't cut fingers
• Toys labeled "non-toxic"
• Materials that resist shattering and splintering
• Fire-resistant materials, where applicable
• Construction that won't come apart on the first tug
• The Underwriters Laboratories (UL) seal on electrical toys

By the time children are one year old, they are very nearly as discriminating as Cole Porter ever was, but not so wise about what pretty thing is nice in the hand but not in the mouth. Follow these guidelines, suggested by the National Safety Council, to delight their fancies while safeguarding their bodies:

First Year—Age of Awareness

TOYS TO CHOOSE:
• Brightly colored objects
• Toys that squeak
• Sturdy rattles
• Washable stuffed dolls with embroidered or well-fastened eyes

Mattel Color Spin

• Colorful mobiles to hang out of reach
• Smooth, unbreakable large objects to chew on

TOYS TO AVOID:

• Heavy toys
• Those with sharp edges that might cut or scratch
• Toys with small parts that can be pulled off and put into ears, nose, and mouth
• Objects that break easily

Fisher-Price Puffalumps

Second Year—Investigative Age

TOYS TO CHOOSE:

• Rubber or washable squeak toys
• Soft stuffed dolls or animals
• Push-pull toys with strings or rounded handles
• Blocks with rounded corners

TOYS TO AVOID:

• Small toys which can be swallowed
• Toys with small, removable parts
• Stuffed animals with glass or button eyes
• Toys with sharp edges

Third Year—Explorative Age

TOYS TO CHOOSE:

- Stable kiddie cars and tricycles
- Stable rocking horses
- Big, fat crayons
- A sandbox with bucket and shovel
- Cars or wagons to push around
- Wooden animals
- Simple musical instruments

TOYS TO AVOID:

- Objects with sharp or rough edges that can cut or scratch
  Objects with small removable parts
  Small objects, such as beads, marbles, and coins

Mattel Pull Wagon

- Toy telephones
- Clothes for dressing up
- Playground equipment, to be used *only* with parental supervision

TOYS TO AVOID:

- Cutting toys
- Toys that operate on electricity
- Flammable costumes
- Toys too heavy for child's strength

Fisher-Price Little People Airport

Fourth Year—Imitative Age

TOYS TO CHOOSE:

- Dolls with simple clothing
- Doll buggies and furniture
- Trucks and tractors
- Non-electrical trains
- Drums
- Building blocks
- Small brooms and carpet sweepers

Fifth and Sixth Years— Creative Age

TOYS TO CHOOSE:

- Modeling clay
- Simple construction sets
- Blackboards and dustless chalk
- Paints and coloring books
- Dollhouses and furniture
- Paper cutouts (with blunt scissors)
- Simple sports equipment
- Jump ropes

TOYS TO AVOID:

- Shooting and target toys without soft tips
- Vehicles that tip over easily
- Toys with pinching or cutting points

Mattel Barbie Doll

Seventh Year—Age of Activity

TOYS TO CHOOSE:

• Workbenches with sturdy but lightweight tools
• Construction sets for models
• Sleds
• Roller skates
• Kites
• Equipment for playing store, bank, filling station, etc.
• UL-approved electrical toys
• Puzzles and games
• Sewing materials
• Dolls and doll equipment

TOYS TO AVOID:

• Complicated electrical toys

• Toys too large or complicated for child's strength and ability
• Skateboards
• Sharp-edged tools
• Toys that shoot projectiles

Eighth Through Twelfth Years— Age of Specializing Skills and Tastes

TOYS TO CHOOSE:

• Hobby materials (for activities such as arts and crafts, photography, coin and stamp collecting, and puppet shows)
• Musical instruments
• Gym and sports equipment
• Construction sets
• Electric trains
• Bicycles

TOYS TO AVOID:

• Air rifles, chemistry sets, skateboards, and dart or arrow games, *unless* used under parental supervision

Fisher-Price Micro Explorer Set

Story-Time Tapes

Weave Christmas magic with the sound of your voice and a fairy tale—story-time tapes for children make perfect Christmas gifts and stocking stuffers. Blank cassettes are inexpensive and the finished products are easy and fun to produce. A good story never wears out; long after the latest Saturday morning cartoon has lost its appeal, *Rumpelstiltskin* and other classics will be mesmerizing young folk of all ages.

Selecting a Story

Look for the following characteristics:

1. A clear plot with lots of action
2. Natural, succinct dialogue
3. Simple, straightforward characters
4. An energetic, varied style
5. Plenty of humor.

Children (especially those under eight) are direct creatures who take things literally. True, they love fantasies such as James Barrie's *Peter Pan* or nonsense like Dr. Seuss's *The 500 Hats of Bartholomew Cubbins*, but symbolism usually bores them.

If you plan to record a story that your youngster can follow with the text, pay attention to the illustrations, too. (Children under five can listen longer to a story that they can *see* as well as hear.)

Tactics for Taping

Pick a story you enjoy. If it gives you pleasure, you'll infuse your reading of it with immediacy and energy that will be transmitted to your children when they hear it.

Never tape alone (if you can help it). You need other folks around (preferably two) to provide different voices and add pizzazz—plus sound effects—to your tape. So grab some family members (older siblings may be gung-ho for

the project) or a couple of friends or neighbors to join in your taping sessions.

Know your material. Study the text well, and determine how the story is put together. Where are its high and low points? Where is the climax? What are the relationships of the characters to one another? Where does each thought begin and end? And where do you want to slow your reading down to give emphasis to a crucial point or speed it up to keep the action moving?

Be prepared. Assemble everything you need ahead of time, such as tapes (I suggest you buy only those with 15 to 30 minutes per side, as longer recordings won't hold most youngsters' attention), sound effects gear (a piece of sheet metal for thunder, bells for Santa's sleigh, and so forth), and any musical instruments or records you need. And be sure to pick a time and place for recording that's free from distractions.

Choose a page-turning cue. If you want your child to follow the story in a book, you'll need to have a uniform signal (for each story) to let him or her know when to turn the page. After you sound the signal, wait a moment before you continue reading . . . so that the child has a chance to flip the page.

Speak clearly and with energy. Read slowly yet naturally, giving emphasis to consonants for clarity—without, of course, slipping into a stilted pattern of over-enunciating your words. You'll probably find it worthwhile to make a practice tape to help you figure out recording levels and different voices for various characters. Play around with the text as you work to see what effects you can produce.

As you read, *see* the scenes, images, and people of the story in your mind's eye. This technique—if you can perfect it— will add a touch of enchantment to your interpretation.

Maggie O'Conner
Mother Earth News
December, 1983

RECORDABLE CLASSICS

PICTURE BOOKS

The Giving Tree by Shel Silverstein

The Tale of Peter Rabbit by Beatrix Potter

Make Way for Ducklings and *Blueberries for Sal* by Robert McClosky

Frederick by Leon Lionni

The Story of Ferdinand by Munro Leaf

All of the *Curious George* books by H.A. Rey

Horton Hatches the Egg and *The 500 Hats of Bartholomew Cubbins* by Dr. Seuss

Millions of Cats by Wanda Gag

The Velveteen Rabbit by Margery Williams

Stone Soup by Marcia Brown

Mike Mulligan and His Steam Shovel by Virginia Burton

The Red Balloon by Albert Lamorisse

The *Tin Tin* books by Hergé

COLLECTIONS OF STORIES

Grimm's Fairy Tales (including "The Bremen Town Musicians," "Rumpelstiltskin," "The Three Spinning Fairies," "Goldilocks," "Little Red Riding Hood," "The Golden Goose," and "Clever Gretel")

Just-So Stories and *The Jungle Book* by Rudyard Kipling

Jack Tales and *Grandfather Tales* by Richard Chase

Uncle Remus Stories by Joel Chandler Harris (be certain to find an easy-to-read translation of the original dialect)

NOVELS

Charlotte's Web by E.B. White

Alice in Wonderland by Lewis Carroll

Peter Pan by James Barrie

The Wind in the Willows by Kenneth Grahame

Rabbit Hill by Robert Lawson

Bambi by Felix Salten

Winnie the Pooh and *The House at Pooh Corner* by A.A. Milne

Mary Poppins by P.L. Travers

POEMS

"A Visit from St. Nicholas" ("'Twas the Night Before Christmas") by Clement C. Moore

"The Pied Piper of Hamelin" by Robert Browning

"Hiawatha's Childhood" by Henry Wadsworth Longfellow

"The Creation" by James Weldon Johnson

"Jabberwocky" by Lewis Carroll

"Raggedy Man" by James Whitcomb Riley

"Ballad of Johnny Appleseed" by Helmer O. Oleson

POETRY COLLECTIONS

Mother Goose

A Child's Garden of Verses by Robert Louis Stevenson

When We Were Very Young and *Now We Are Six* by A.A. Milne

Old Possum's Book of Practical Cats by T.S. Eliot

A Letter from Santa Claus

Palace of St. Nicholas
in the Moon
Christmas Morning

My Dear Susie Clemens:

I have received and read all the letters which you and your little sister have written me. . . . I can read your and your baby sister's jagged and fantastic marks without any trouble at all. But I had trouble with those letters which you dictated through your mother and the nurses, for I am a foreigner and cannot read English writing well. You will find that I made no mistakes about the things which you and the baby ordered in your own letters—I went down your chimney at midnight when you were asleep and delivered them all myself—and kissed both of you, too. . . . But . . . there were . . . one or two small orders which I could not fill because we ran out of stock. . . .

There was a word or two in your mama's letter which . . . I took to be "a trunk full of doll's clothes." Is that it? I will call at your kitchen door about nine o'clock this morning to inquire. But I must not see anybody and I must not speak to anybody but you. When the kitchen doorbell rings, George must be blindfolded and sent to open the door. You must tell George he must walk on tiptoe and not speak—otherwise he will die someday. Then you must go up to the nursery and stand on a chair or the nurse's bed and put your ear to the speaking tube that leads down to the kitchen and when I whistle through it you must speak in the tube and say, "Welcome, Santa Claus!" Then I will ask whether it was a trunk you ordered or not. If you say it was, I shall ask you what *color* you want the trunk to be . . . and then you must tell me every single thing in detail which you want

the trunk to contain. Then when I say "Good-by and a merry Christmas to my little Susie Clemens," you must say "Good-by, good old Santa Claus, I thank you very much." . . . Then you must go down into the library and make George close all the doors that open into the main hall, and everybody must keep still for a little while. I will go to the moon and get those things and in a few minutes I will come down the chimney that belongs to the fireplace that is in the hall—if it is a trunk you want—because I couldn't get such a thing as a trunk down the nursery chimney, you know. . . . If I should leave any snow in the hall, you must tell George to sweep it into the fireplace, for I haven't time to do such things. George must not use a broom, but a rag—else he will die someday. . . . If my boot should leave a stain on the marble, George must not holystone it away. Leave it there always in memory of my visit; and whenever you look at it or show it to anybody you must let it remind you to be a good little girl. Whenever you are naughty and somebody points to that mark which your good old Santa Claus's boot made on the marble, what will you say, little sweetheart?

Good-by for a few minutes, till I come down to the world and ring the kitchen doorbell.

Your loving Santa Claus
Whom people sometimes call
"The Man in the Moon"

Mark Twain to his daughter, Susie

ANTICIPATING THE DAY

ANTICIPATING THE DAY

As the year comes full circle, it comes time to make ready, once again, for Christmas. In a sense, the preparations have gone on for months and, for suppliers, the planning may have started years in advance. Christmas catalogs close up tight in the spring; the Christmas rush to order merchandise shows up in July, and promotionally we are hotfooting it toward Christmas even before the Thanksgiving turkey grows cold on the table.

Emotionally, however, the spirit of Christmas moves at a more deliberate pace, in a gathering torrent of delightful anticipation. The memories come flooding in.

The warmth of the kitchen with the summer harvest of jellies and relishes bubbling on top of the stove, with gleaming gift jars ranged to receive them. The "may I lick the spoon?" tastes of the spicy, fruit-stuffed batters of fall, mounded into loaf pans or onto cookie sheets to be baked as presents. The oven itself, the kitchen's heart, with the special once-a-year foods taking shape within it, adding their unique scents to an atmosphere already electric with excitement.

The thrill of opening the tiny door to December 1st on the Advent calendar and seeing the first of a succession of surprise pictures, gradually increasing in size and splendor to the wonders of the 25th.

The stifled giggles and whispers behind closed doors and the rushing of mysterious parcels in plain brown wrappers up the stairs to the secret hiding place (which, it turned out years later, everyone knew about).

In the days of our blissful belief, when we were very young, our adrenalin would be in overdrive by the time we had to go to bed on Christmas Eve—leaving cookies and milk, or perhaps an orange, near the fireplace for Santa Claus with a *last* written reminder of what we wanted most to find in the stockings hanging limply from the mantel.

Once in bed, we would toss and turn, then sit up to listen for the tiny hoofbeats of Santa's reindeer landing on the roof. Sleep seemed as if it would never come . . . and the

---

The Germans originated Advent calendars to honor the month prior to Christ's birth by opening a new door each day—a custom that has spread to the New World, too.

• 308 •

WELCOME TO
CHRISTMASVILLE!

BAKERY

Two of the calendars shown closed on the previous page display the secrets that lay behind their numbered doors. Hallmark's resident poets made Christmasville into a positive avalanche of evocative couplets, while the snow-mantled cottage that seemed shut tight for the winter turns out to be harboring a host of cordial folk enjoying every aspect of the holiday season.

sound of talk and laughter would float up from downstairs. Why did the grown-ups take so long to go to bed? Santa couldn't possibly come while anyone was still awake.

Eventually, of course, sleep *would* come and we wouldn't even know it . . . until that magic moment when our eyes suddenly blinked open and it was, it truly was, Christmas Day.

So Christmas comes again—and despite all the changes we have made in it, and the commercial advantages we have found in it, we cannot remove the loving spirit from this dearest of holidays, nor abate our sense of awe that this splendid celebration had its beginnings so simply and humbly in a stable with a tiny baby lying on a bed of hay.

ACKNOWLEDGMENTS AND CREDITS

Acknowledgments

The editors wish to extend special thanks to the following: Hallmark Cards, Inc. and the Hallmark Historical Collection and Corporate Archive.

The New York Public Library—General Research Division, Microforms Division, U.S. History Division, Rare Books and Manuscripts Division, and Periodicals Room; Mid-Manhattan Branch of the New York Public Library and the New York Public Library Picture Collection; Reynaldo Alejandro, Curator of the Culinary Collection, New York Public Library; Jay Hildreth, Library of the Performing Arts at Lincoln Center; Frank Walker, Fales Library, New York University; Brooklyn Public Library; and Lothian Lynas, New York Botanical Garden.

Janey Fire and Karla Friedlich, Museum of American Folk Art; Jane Kallir, St. Etienne Gallery; Sally W. Barnes, The Colonial Williamsburg Foundation; Martha Moses, Staten Island Academy; Phillip V. Snyder, collector; John Springer, collector.

Tina Houston, Supervisory Archivist, Lyndon Baines Johnson Library; Liz Safly, Harry S. Truman Library; Michael Desmond, Research Assistant, John Fitzgerald Kennedy Library; John E. Wickman, Director, and Martin M. Teasly, Assistant Director, Dwight D. Eisenhower Library; Annemarie Huste, former White House chef.

Kit Mahon, Campbell Soup Company; Paul Costello, Director of Public Affairs, and Bridget M. O'Hara, Public Relations, Marshall Field's; Dorothy Desir, Corporate Gift Services, Bloomingdale's; Susan Olden, Corporate Director, Saks Fifth Avenue; Jacqueline Roberge, Director of Personal Shopping, Anita Gallo, Vice President, Fashion Merchandising, and Michael Del Viscio, B. Altman's; Gail Kittenplan, Personal Fashion Advisor, Lord & Taylor; Jan Roberts, Director, Publicity and Special Events, Neiman-Marcus; Susan Hastings, Marketing Director, Georgetown Park.

Donald McNeil, Managing Editor and Publisher, and Philip H. Jones, Associate Editor/Northeast, *American Christmas Tree Journal*; Ida Deans, *Toy and Hobby World*; Christine Smith, Public Relations, National Safety Council; Jeanne O'Neill, Department of Public and Employee Communications, U.S. Post Office.

Valuable assistance was also provided by the following state and local agencies and associations: Business Council of Alabama; Alaska State Chamber of Commerce; Arizona Department of State Tourism and Valley of the Sun Visitors Bureau; Arkansas State Chamber of Commerce; California Department of State Tourism and Chambers of Commerce of Amador, Hollywood, Monterey, and Oxnard; Colorado Association of Commerce and Industry and Colorado Tourism Board; Connecticut Department of State Tourism; Delaware State Office of Development; Washington DC Convention Bureau; Florida Department of Tourism; Office of the Governor, State of Georgia, and Georgia Department of Industry and Trade; Chamber of Commerce of Hawaii and Hawaii Visitors Bureau; Idaho Travel Council, Idaho Convention and Visitors Bureau, and Sun Valley Chamber of Commerce; Illinois State Tourist Information Center; Indiana Department of Tourism; Iowa Department of Visitors and Tourism; Kansas Chamber of Commerce and Industry; Kentucky Department of Tourism; Office of the Governor, State of Louisiana, Louisiana Office of Tourism, and Greater Baton Rouge Chamber of Commerce; State of Maine Publicity Bureau; Maryland Chamber of Commerce and Maryland Office of Tourism Development; Massachusetts Department of Commerce and Development; Michigan State Chamber of Commerce and Michigan Travel Bureau; Minnesota Office of Tourism; Mississippi Tourism Bureau; Missouri Tourism Commission and Missouri Chamber of Commerce; Montana Office of Travel Promotion; Nebraska Association of Commerce and Industry and Nebraska Department of Economic Development, Travel, and Tourism; Greater Reno-Sparks, Nevada, Chamber of Commerce; New Hampshire Office of Vacation Travel and New Hampshire Department of Resources and Economic Development; New Jersey State Chamber of Commerce and New Jersey Office of Tourism; Greater Albuquerque, New Mexico, Chamber of Commerce and Santa Fe, New Mexico, Chamber of Commerce; New York Department of Tourism; North Carolina Department of Travel and Tourism and Greater Raleigh Chamber of Commerce/Information Center; Greater North Dakota Association—North Dakota State Chamber of Commerce; Ohio Office of Travel and Tourism; Oklahoma Department of Tourism; Oregon Department of Tourism and Salem Chamber of Commerce; Pennsylvania Chamber of Commerce and Pennsylvania Department of Commerce/Bureau of Travel and Tourism; Rhode Island Department of Economic Development/Office of Tourism; South Carolina Chamber of Commerce; Chamber of Commerce, Pierre, South Dakota; Donelson-Hermitage, Tennessee, Chamber of Commerce; Texas State Chamber of Commerce and Texas Department of Highways/Travel Division; Utah State Chamber of Commerce and Utah Convention and Visitors Bureau; Vermont State Chamber of Commerce; Virginia Chamber of Commerce; Washington State Office of Tourism and Seattle/King County Convention and Visitors Bureau; Office of the Governor, State of West Virginia, West Virginia Department of Culture and History, and West Virginia Department of Commerce/Office of Travel and Tourism; Wisconsin Department of Development; Office of the Governor, State of Wyoming, Jackson Chamber of Commerce, and Lander Chamber of Commerce.

Picture Credits

pp. 8, 10, 11 Santa Fabio—Collection of Mr. and Mrs. James O. Keene   12–14 Illustrations by Dana Burns   16 The Bettmann Archive   17 Top: Mort Gerberg—reproduced by special permission of *Playboy* magazine: (Copyright © 1963 by *Playboy*); bottom: American Heritage Picture Collection   18 Courtesy Smithsonian Institution, American Heritage Picture Collection   19 Courtesy The Henry Francis du Pont Winterthur Museum, American Heritage Picture Collection   20 H. Armstrong Roberts, Inc. 21 Courtesy South Dakota State Historical Society 22 Courtesy The Henry Francis du Pont Winterthur Museum, Joseph Downs Manuscript Collection   23 Gerald K. Smith, NBC Burbank Photo—courtesy Hope Enterprises   26 New York Public Library Picture Collection 27–30 Wide World Photos, Inc.   33 Courtesy Convention and Visitors Bureau of Greater Kansas City   34 Top: Wide World Photos, Inc.; bottom: F.B. Grunzweig—F-Stop Pictures   35 Top left: courtesy Lil Junas—Bethlehem Area Chamber of Commerce, PA; top right: courtesy Yosemite Park and Curry Co., CA; bottom: © 1988 The Walt Disney Company   36 T. McNee—FPG International   37 Top: S.L. Craig, Jr.—Bruce Coleman, Inc.; bottom: courtesy Maui Intercontinental, Wailea, HI   38 Top: courtesy Chester County Tourist Bureau, PA; bottom: Martha Swope   39 Left: Bo Parker—courtesy Rockefeller Center Management Co.; top right: Wade H. McKoy—Jackson Hole Area Chamber of Commerce, WY; bottom right: FPG International   40 Top: courtesy Winterfest and Boat Parade, Ft. Lauderdale, FL; bottom: Bob Woodall—courtesy Jackson Hole Area Chamber of Commerce, WY   41 Timothy Eagan—Woodfin Camp and Associates   42–43 Steve Solum—Bruce Coleman, Inc.   44 Top: B.A. Cohen—courtesy Natchitoches Chamber of Commerce, LA; bottom: courtesy Salt Lake Convention and Visitors Bureau, UT;   45 Top: Joel Greenberg—Seaport Marketplace, NY; bottom: Cary Hazlegrove—Nantucket Filmworks, MA; 46 T. McNee—FPG International   47 Top: R. Krubner—H. Armstrong Roberts, Inc.; bottom: FPG International 48 Ron Goor—Bruce Coleman, Inc.   49 Sara Krulwich—*The New York Times*   57 FPG International   61 F-Stop Pictures   65 Mort Gerberg—reproduced by special permission of *Playboy* magazine: (Copyright © 1963 by *Playboy*) 67, 69 Courtesy Marshall Field's, Chicago, IL   71 Copyright © 1987, Chicago Tribune Company (all rights reserved, used with permission)   72 Anthony Accardi   73 Courtesy Home Shopping Network, Clearwater, FL   74–75 Courtesy Neiman-Marcus, Dallas, TX   76–80 Mort Gerberg

81 Illustration by Helene Berinsky   82 Anthony Accardi 83 Mort Gerberg   85 Illustrations by Juan Suarez-Botas 86 Illustration by Helene Berinsky   88 Courtesy Hallmark Cards, Inc., Kansas City, MO   90 Illustrations by Helene Berinsky   91 FPG International   92 H. Armstrong Roberts, Inc.   93 Illustration by Dana Burns   94 Bill Aller—*The New York Times*   96 Mort Gerberg   97 Anthony Accardi   98 New York Public Library Picture Collection   101–109 Illustrations by Tony Kramer   110 Illustration by Dana Burns   114 Bottom left: © 1985 "Holly" LHW 05 Stop Press Ltd.; bottom right: © 1985 "Crown of Star" LHW 1 Stop Press Ltd.   115 © 1985 *The New Yorker* magazine   118 © The Hearst Corporation 119 Top: Published by Roger la Borde ©; bottom: © Mary Engelbreit, Inc.   120 Bottom right: Gordon Fraser Gallery, Newtown, CT © 1984   124, 127, 128 Illustrations by Marc Rosenthal   130 The Bettmann Archive   131 Top left and bottom left: The Bettmann Archive; bottom right: New York Public Library Picture Collection   132 Top: David Willardson; bottom: courtesy Hallmark Cards, Inc. 133 Top: David Willardson; bottom left: courtesy Hallmark Cards, Inc.; bottom right: David Willardson   134–135 Mark Romanelli   136–137 Mort Gerberg   138–139 Artwork by students of Staten Island Academy, NY, grades 1, 2, 3 139 Top left: Larry C. Morris—*The New York Times*; center left: Richard Sandler—*The New York Times*; bottom left: Tony Jerome—*The New York Times*   140 American Heritage Picture Collection   141 Rollin A. Riggs—New York Times News Service   142 Courtesy Hallmark Cards, Inc. 143 Top: Renand Thomas—FPG International; center: R. Crachiola—FPG International; bottom: Mort Gerberg 144–145 Bernard Gotfryd—Woodfin Camp and Associates 146–147 Jose R. Lopez—*The New York Times*   148 Culver Pictures, Inc.   149 Top left: Dale Swanson—*The Oregonian*; bottom: Richard Wells 150 Mort Gerberg 152–153 Roy Coggin—Collection of Phillip V. Snyder 154 Top: Courtesy Library of Congress—American Heritage Picture Collection; center: Courtesy American Museum of Natural History—American Heritage Picture Collection; bottom: American Heritage Picture Collection 155–157 Courtesy Northeastern Forest Experimental Station, Broomall, PA   158 Courtesy Sequoia and Kings Canyon National Park, CA   160 Courtesy American Tree Company, Pittsburgh, PA   162 Vince Compagnone —*Los Angeles Times*   164 Courtesy National Christmas Tree Growers Association, Inc., Milwaukee, WI   166 Drawing by Geo. Price © 1938, 1966 The New Yorker Maga-

zine, Inc.   169 Top: Roy Coggin—Collection of Phillip V. Snyder; bottom: Courtesy the Smithsonian Institution—Collection of Phillip V. Snyder   170 Roy Coggin—Collection of Phillip V. Snyder   171 Top left: Roy Coggin—Collection of Phillip V. Snyder; bottom left: 1910 Sears Catalog; right: Anthony Accardi—Collection of Phillip V. Snyder   172 Roy Coggin—Collection of Phillip V. Snyder   174 Top: Edison National Historic Site, West Orange, NJ; bottom: Roy Coggin—Collection of Phillip V. Snyder   175 Roy Coggin—Collection of Phillip V. Snyder   176 Illustration by Tony Kramer   178 Camera Graphics—*Better Homes and Gardens* (December 1940) 179 Top left: Camera Graphics—*Better Homes and Gardens* (December 1940); top right: Dennison's *Book of Christmas*, 1923; bottom: Camera Graphics—*Better Homes and Gardens* (December 1940)   180 Bottom: Camera Graphics—*Better Homes and Gardens* (December 1940) 181 Roy Coggin—Collection of Phillip V. Snyder   183–190 Illustrations by Ann Shirazi   193 Photograph by Jean Vallier   205 American Heritage Picture Collection 206–207 American Heritage Picture Collection   208–215 Courtesy Hallmark Cards, Inc.   216 Mort Gerber 218 Courtesy Hallmark Cards, Inc.   219 Left: courtesy Hallmark Cards, Inc.; right: A.M. Rosario—New York Metropolitan Committee for UNICEF 220–221 Courtesy Hallmark Cards, Inc.   222 Top: courtesy Franklin D. Roosevelt Library; bottom left: UPI/Bettmann Newsphotos; bottom right: courtesy Hallmark Cards, Inc.   223 Top: courtesy Hallmark Cards, Inc.; bottom: courtesy Lyndon Baines Johnson Library   224–225 Courtesy Hallmark Cards, Inc.   226–227 Cambridge-Essex Stamp Co., Inc.   228 Illustration by Helene Berinsky   231 New York Public Library   232 Illustration by Dana Burns   233 Gregory Thorp—courtesy the Rev. John Andrew, Rector, St. Thomas Church, and Gordon Clem, Headmaster, St. Thomas Choir School, New York City   235 Anthony Accardi   236 Courtesy Hallmark Cards, Inc.   238 Dith Pran—*The New York Times*   240 Anthony Accardi   241 Reprinted by permission, V. Gene Meyers and New Woman © 1984   242–245 The Bettmann Archive   246 FPG International   247 Mort Gerber   249 Courtesy Bitcards, Inc.   251 Culver Pictures, Inc.   252 Copyright © 1920, The Hearst Corporation, reprinted courtesy of *Good Housekeeping*   255 Courtesy The Historical Society of Old Newbury, MA   256–259 Illustrations by Sandra Caplan Ciarrochi   260–265 Illustrations by Isadore Seltzer   266–267 Mort Gerber 269 Mort Gerber   270 Illustration by Isadore Seltzer 273 Copyright © 1988, The Art Institute of Chicago 278 Copyright © 1984, Grandma Moses Properties Co., NY   279 Letter copyright © 1952 (renewed 1980), Grandma Moses Properties Co., NY; "Joyride" copyright © 1984, Grandma Moses Properties Co., NY   280–281 Courtesy Jack O'Grady Graphics, Chicago, IL   286 American Heritage Picture Collection   287 Top: American Heritage Picture Collection; bottom: Courtesy The Museum of the City of New York   288 Courtesy The Museum of the City of New York   289 Top: Lawrence Scripps Wilkinson Collection—Courtesy The New-York Historical Society, New York City; bottom: Courtesy The New-York Historical Society, New York City   290–293 Lawrence Scripps Wilkinson Collection—Courtesy The New-York Historical Society, New York City   294 Courtesy Toys 'R' Us   296 Courtesy Bloomingdale's, NY   297 Marilynn K. Yee—*The New York Times*   298 Courtesy Franklin D. Roosevelt Library   299 Carl Rose—Reprinted from the *Saturday Evening Post* © 1947, The Curtis Publishing Co.   300 Courtesy Coleco Industries, Inc., West Hartford, CT   301 Left: Courtesy Mattel Toys, Hawthorne, CA; right: Courtesy Fisher-Price, East Aurora, NY   302 Top: Courtesy Mattel Toys; bottom: Courtesy Fisher-Price 303: Top: Courtesy Mattel Toys; bottom: Courtesy Fisher-Price   305 Anthony Accardi   306 Top left: The Bettmann Archive   309–311 Courtesy Hallmark Cards, Inc.

Text Credits

9 "The Gospel According to St. Luke," Chapter II, Verses 1–15, *Holy Bible*, King James Version, 1611   10 "The Gospel According to St. Matthew," Chapter II, Verses 1–12, *Holy Bible*, King James Version, 1611   19 Shaker Collection, Rare Books and Manuscripts Division, The New York Public Library, Astor, Lenox and Tilden Foundations, quotations from Ms. 21 and Ms. 74   23 "Home for Christmas," from *The Family Christmas Book* by Elizabeth Bowen (Englewood Cliffs, NJ, Prentice–Hall, Inc., 1957, 1958) Reprinted by permission   27 "Bess and Harry Truman's Christmas Dinner," December 25, 1952. Courtesy the Harry S. Truman Library; "Franklin Delano Roosevelt's Roast Duck with Potato Dressing," from *A Treasury of White House Cooking*, copyright © 1972 by Francois Rysavy and Frances Spatz Leighton, by permission of Collier Associates   28 "Dwight and Mamie Eisenhower's Stone Crab Bisque," from *White House Chef*, copyright © 1957 by Francois Rysavy and Frances Spatz Leighton, by permission of Collier Associates; "Martha Washington's Great Cake," from *The Presidents' Cookbook* by Poppy Cannon and Patricia Brooks. Copyright © 1968 by Poppy Cannon and Patricia Brooks. Reprinted by permission of Harper & Row, Publishers, Inc.; "Jacqueline and John Kennedy's Christmas Eve Dinner," courtesy Annemarie Huste   29 "Lyndon and Lady Bird Johnson's Deer Meat Sausage," from *A Treasury of White House Cooking*, copyright © 1972 by Francois Rysavy and Frances Spatz Leighton, by permission of Collier Associates; "Pat Nixon's Christmas Tree Cookies," from *A Treasury of White House Cooking*, copyright © 1972 by Francois Rysavy and Frances Spatz Leighton, by permission of Collier Associates; "Pat Nixon's Christmas Tree Cookies," from *A Treasury of White House Cooking*, copyright © 1972 by Francois Rysavy and Frances Spatz Leighton, by permission of Collier Associates; "George Washington's Eggnog," from *Christmas in the White House* by Albert J. Menendez.

Copyright © 1983 Albert J. Menendez. Reprinted and used by permission of The Westminster Press   30 "Rosalynn Carter's Cranberry Ring Mold," from *Christmas in the White House* by Albert J. Menendez. Copyright © 1983 Albert J. Menendez. Reprinted and used by permission of The Westminster Press; "Benjamin Harrison's Christmas Turkey," from *The Presidents' Cookbook* by Poppy Cannon and Patricia Brooks. Copyright © 1968 by Poppy Cannon and Patricia Brooks. Reprinted by permission of Harper & Row Publishers, Inc.; "Nancy Reagan's Monkey Bread," courtesy Nancy Reagan's Press Office, The White House   64 "The Gift Behind the Gift," by Greg Easterbrook, *The New York Times*, December 24, 1983. Copyright © 1983 by The New York Times Company. Reprinted by permission   79 "A Road Map For Your Christmas Shopping," from *Good Housekeeping*, December 1940. Courtesy *Good Housekeeping*, a publication of Hearst Magazines, a division of The Hearst Corporation   80 "The Golden Age of Little Black Books," from *Harper's Bazaar*, December 14, 1895. Copyright © 1895, The Hearst Corporation. Courtesy *Harper's Bazaar*   81 "Notorious Novelty," from *Harper's Bazaar*, December 7, 1895. Copyright © 1895, The Hearst Corporation. Courtesy *Harper's Bazaar*   82 "Suiting A Man," by Frederick Eberstadt from *Vogue*, December 1986. Copyright © 1986 by Frederick Eberstadt. Reprinted by permission of International Creative Management, Inc. and courtesy *Vogue*. Copyright 1986 by The Conde Nast Publications, Inc.; "Button Palace," from *Harper's Bazaar*, December 7, 1895. Copyright © 1895, The Hearst Corporation. Courtesy *Harper's Bazaar*   83 "Gifts Which Embarrass: A Protest from Men," from *Good Housekeeping*, December 1910. Courtesy *Good Housekeeping*, a publication of Hearst Magazines, a division of The Hearst Corporation   84 "Timeless Stories with Timely Morals," from *Esquire*, December 1987. Copyright © 1987 by Esquire Associates. Reprinted with permission from *Esquire*   85 "Christmas Books," by John Harris from *The Atlantic*, December 1985. Copyright © 1985 by John Harris. Reprinted by permission   89 "The Tip of All Time," by Phillip Snyder from *December 25th: The Joys of Christmas Past*. Copyright © 1985 by Phillip V. Snyder. Reprinted by permission of Dodd Mead & Company, Inc.; Tipping chart, from *Money*, December, 1986 Copyright © 1986, Time, Inc. All rights reserved. Reprinted by special permission   99 "Poor Richard's Almanack" by Benjamin Franklin, Doubleday, Doran & Co., Inc., 1928. Copyright © 1928 by Rimington & Hooper. Permission granted by Doubleday, a division of Bantam, Doubleday, Dell Publishing Group, Inc.   110 "Fruitcake Is Forever," by Russell Baker, *The New York Times Magazine*, December 25, 1983. Copyright © 1983 by The New York Times Company. Reprinted by permission   134 "Santa Seminars," adapted from "Graduation Day At Santa U," by Bob Spitz, *Life*, December 1985. Copyright © 1985 by Bob Spitz. Reprinted by permission of Wallace & Sheil Agency, Inc.   139 "Two Believers, One Skeptic," taken from article "Two Believers . . . The Skeptics," *The New York Times*, December 24, 1985. Copyright © 1985 by The New York Times Company. Reprinted by permission   172 "A Collector's Advice to Collectors," by Phillip V. Snyder from *The Encyclopedia of Collectibles*, Time-Life Books. Reprinted by permission of Time-Life Books, Inc.   214 "The Complete Christmas Card," by Brock Bower, *Harper's*, December 1985. Copyright © 1985 by Brock Bower. Reprinted by permission of Candida Donadio & Associates   217 "This Computer Can Rhyme . . . For Three Bucks Each Time," from "For The Fun of It," *Changing Times*, January 1986. Copyright © 1986 Kiplinger Washington Editors, Inc. Reprinted with permission from *Changing Times Magazine*   221 From "Epstein, Spare That Yule Log!" from *Verses from 1929 On* by Ogden Nash. Copyright © 1933 by Ogden Nash. First appeared in *The New York American*. Reprinted by permission of Little, Brown and Company   230 "Collecting Christmas Books," by Patrick McGuire, November/December 1985, *American Book Collector*. Copyright © 1985 The Morethus Press, Inc. Reprinted by permission   232 "Heavenly Music: Bach to Bop," by Jon Pareles from *Harper's Bazaar*, December 1985. Copyright © Jon Pareles. All rights reserved. Reprinted by permission   234 "Do You Hear What I Hear?" by John T. Bills, quoted by Kenneth Nichols from December 1958 *Reader's Digest*. Originally appeared in *Akron Beacon Journal*, January 8, 1952. Reprinted with permission from *Reader's Digest* and *The Akron Beacon Journal*   240 Excerpt from lyrics of "White Christmas" by Irving Berlin. Copyright © 1940, 1942 Irving Berlin. Copyright © renewed 1968, 1969 Irving Berlin. Reprinted by permission of Irving Berlin Music Corporation   241 Excerpt from lyrics of "Rudolph the Red-Nosed Reindeer" by Johnny Marks. Reprinted by permission of St. Nicholas Music Inc.   242 "Christmas On Film," originally "Master James Is Home For Christmas," by John Springer, *American Heritage*, December 1983. Copyright © *American Heritage*, a subsidiary of Forbes, Inc. Reprinted with permission   248 "Christmas Videos: A Selection," from *The Video Sourcebook*, published by National Video Clearinghouse, Inc., Syosset, NY. Reprinted by permission   252 "Poinsettia Party For the Holiday Season," by Elaine, Entertainment Editor, from *Good Housekeeping*, December 1920. Copyright © 1920, The Hearst Corporation. Courtesy of *Good Housekeeping*, a publication of Hearst Magazine, a division of The Hearst Corporation   270 "Office Party," *Times Three* by Phyllis McGinley. Copyright © 1957 by Phyllis McGinley, renewed © 1985 by Phyllis Hayden Blake. All rights reserved. Reprinted by permission of Viking Penguin Inc.   295 "Tiptoeing Into Toyland," adapted from *The World of New York* magazine, November 15, 1987 article "F. A. O. Schwartz: The Twelve Weeks of Christmas" by Louise Lague. Copyright © 1987 by The New York Times Company. Reprinted by permission   304 "Story-Time Tapes," excerpted and adapted from "Homemade Story-Time Tapes," by Maggie O'Conner. Adapted with permission from *The Mother Earth News*. Copyright © 1983. All rights reserved

INDEX

Recipe Index

Subject Index

DATE DUE
